# WIIDHAA
## AN INTRODUCTION TO GAMILARAAY

# WIIDHAA
## AN INTRODUCTION TO GAMILARAAY

JOHN GIACON

Published by ANU Press
The Australian National University
Acton ACT 2601, Australia
Email: anupress@anu.edu.au

Available to download for free at press.anu.edu.au

ISBN (print): 9781760463267
ISBN (online): 9781760463274

WorldCat (print): 1137804507
WorldCat (online): 1137804708

DOI: 10.22459/W.2019

This title is published under a Creative Commons Attribution-NonCommercial-NoDerivatives 4.0 International (CC BY-NC-ND 4.0).

The full licence terms are available at
creativecommons.org/licenses/by-nc-nd/4.0/legalcode

Cover design and layout by ANU Press.

The title, *Wiidhaa*, is the Gamilaraay Yuwaalaraay name of the Spotted Bowerbird, a bird who imitates the voices of many other birds and animals. In the traditional story his many voices attracted people whom he then killed and cooked *wii-dha* (on the fires), and then used their bones to decorate his bower. Today Wiidhaa also uses other objects for this, such as clothes pegs and bottle tops. Maliyan (Wedge-tailed Eagle) found out that Wiidhaa was killing the people. Maliyan overpowered Wiidhaa and then threw him onto the fire, where his brains heated and exploded out the back of his head. The photograph is actually of a Western Bowerbird, which is very similar to Wiidhaa.

Cover photo: © Mike Gillam.

This edition © 2020 ANU Press

# Contents

| | |
|---|---|
| Abbreviations | vii |
| Acknowledgements | ix |
| Gamilaraay Yuwaalaraay | xi |
| Language revival | xiii |
| Using *Wiidhaa* | xvii |

| | |
|---|---|
| Lesson 1. Hello, Goodbye, Questions | 1 |
| Lesson 2. 'This, That' Demonstratives; more questions | 15 |
| Lesson 3. Contrast / Take it! | 31 |
| Lesson 4. Who are you? Are you good? | 45 |
| Lesson 5. Verbs: *Y* class/ 'going to' (Allative) suffix | 63 |
| Lesson 6. Verbs: *Y* class 'future' and 'past' | 73 |
| Lesson 7. Where is it? The place (Locative) suffix | 81 |
| Lesson 8. Possession | 93 |
| Lesson 9. To, From and At | 103 |
| Lesson 10. Adjectives – *Gayrrda* | 119 |
| Lesson 11. *L* class verbs; transitivity; doer.to/Ergative suffix | 127 |
| Lesson 12. Doer.to/Actor and instrument | 143 |
| Lesson 13. Verbs: *NG* class, *RR* class | 155 |
| Lesson 14. What for/Whose/Who for? | 165 |
| Lesson 15. More Pronouns: Singular | 175 |
| Lesson 16. Verbs: Continuous – non-moving | 189 |
| Lesson 17. Verbs: Continuous – moving | 199 |
| Lesson 18. Further Suffixes | 207 |

| | |
|---|---:|
| Lesson 19. More Pronouns: Dual and Plural | 219 |
| Lesson 20. Pronouns: Locative/Allative and Ablative | 229 |
| Lesson 21. Other Third Person Pronouns | 237 |

| | |
|---|---:|
| Appendix 1. Resources | 245 |
| Appendix 2. Pronunciation Guide | 247 |
| Appendix 3. Case Summary | 255 |
| Appendix 4. Verb Summary | 261 |
| Appendix 5. Pronoun Summary | 271 |
| Appendix 6. Wordlist | 281 |

| | |
|---|---:|
| References | 289 |

# Abbreviations

GR    Gamilaraay
GY    Gamilaraay Yuwaalaraay
YR    Yuwaalaraay

Throughout the book GY is used when a statement refers to both languages. When a comment refers to only one language, for instance when contrasting the languages, GR and YR are used. In some other publications YG is used instead of GY, since more of the historical information comes from Yuwaalaraay.

**int**    intransitive
**tr**    transitive
\*    indicates that there is futher information later
>    'greater than'. This is used with pronouns. For instance *ngiyani* we(>2) means that *ngiyani* means we, more than 2 people.
#    This has a number of uses, including to indicate forms for which there is no direct historical evidence, but which we would expect, given what is found elsewhere in the languages.

# Acknowledgements

This book has been developed from the course notes for Gamilaraay 1, which has been taught at the University of Sydney since 2006 and at The Australian National University more recently. These notes were titled *Garay Guwaala 1*.

The move to a published book is largely due to Grazia Scotellaro's vision of an online Gamilaraay course, to her encouragement and technical and administrative assistance. The staff at ANU Press and at the College of Arts and Social Sciences, ANU, have done much of the design and technical work for the book. ANU Press also provided a grant to cover the cost of production, particularly the recording of Gamilaraay.

There are many speakers on sound files in the text. More recent recordings are of Peter Swanton, Priscilla Strasek, Suellen Tighe, Tracey Cameron and Rhonda Smith. Earlier speakers include John Brown, Auntie Maureen Sulter, Nathan Blacklock and Rhonda Ashby. A few are of John Giacon.

John Hobson has had a major role in the development of *Garay Guwaala 1*. He and Giacon wrote the first version in 2004, for the Gamilaraay 1 course at the University of Sydney. He also strongly advocated for the course. Jane Simpson has been instrumental in Gamilaraay 1 being introduced and maintained at ANU.

Many suggestions made by students over the years have been incorporated in this edition. Geoff Hunt has carefully reviewed the text and also made many suggestions and corrections. James Grieve made incisive and helpful comments. Emily Hazlewood and Teresa Prowse, at ANU Press, skilfully, patiently and carefully produced the final version of the book.

The passion of Gamilaraay Yuwaalaraay students, in particular, provides the motivation to continue working on the languages. A special thanks to those whose passion for the language has kept them involved and learning for many years, including Priscilla Strasek, who recently completed the ANU Gamilaraay 3 course, Tracey Cameron, who from 2020 will teach Gamilaraay 1 at the University of Sydney, and Suellyn Tighe.

# Gamilaraay Yuwaalaraay

The map (Figure 1) shows the approximate Gamilaraay Yuwaalaraay area, but it is likely they extended some way into Queensland. The name of both languages consists of the word for 'no' (*gamil, yuwaal*) and a suffix meaning 'with' or 'having'. In YR the word for 'no' has changed to *waal*. There are other no-with languages that are fairly similar to GY: Wiradjuri (*wiraay-dhuraay*), Wayilwan (*wayil-wan*) and Wangaaybuwan (*wangaay-buwan*). For more information about these languages see Giacon (2017).

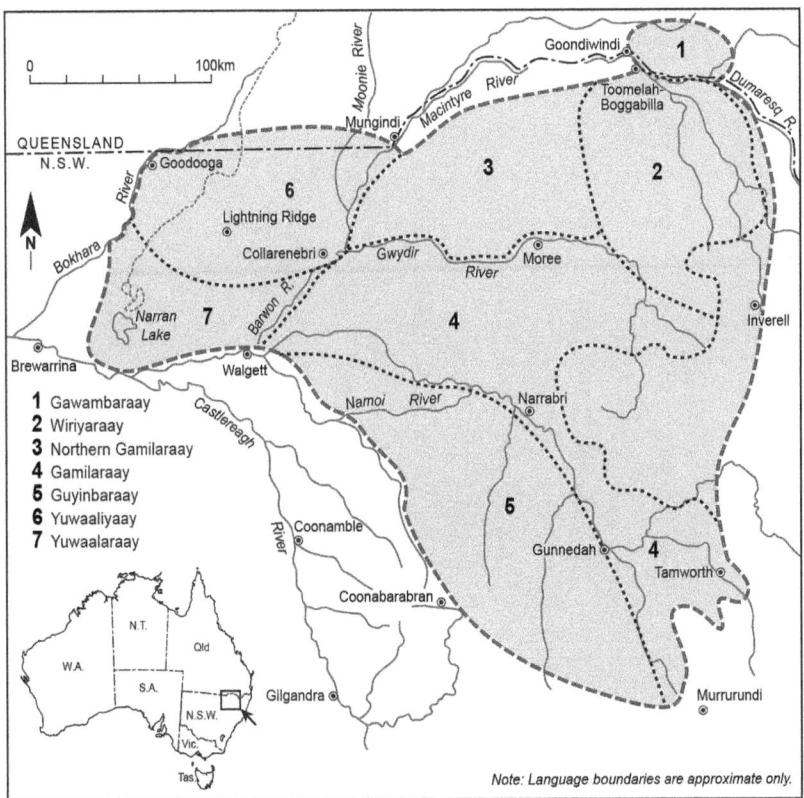

Figure 1: Map showing area of Gamilaraay Yuwaalaraay language use.
Source: Adapted from Austin, Williams & Wurm, 1980, p. 167.

The impact of colonisation was dramatic. Gamilaraay country, being better for agriculture than Yuwaalaraay, had a greater proportion of colonists, so Gamilaraay population and language declined rapidly. Change was slower in Yuwaalaraay country, so language knowledge persisted for much longer.

Recent years have seen many more GY people working on relearning and reusing their languages, and courses in schools, community, TAFE and university.

# Language revival

This is a very brief introduction to the important and challenging project often called language revival.

For many years Gamilaraay and Yuwaalaraay declined in use, so that by the 1990s most people were using only a few words. A few had a little more knowledge, but had few opportunities to use their language.

Then a dramatic reversal began. GY people began to reclaim and reuse their languages. In this they were marching with Indigenous people around the world who were asserting their rights and relearning and reusing their languages. In Australia, Kaurna and Gumbaynggirr were already on the way. GY people also went to the United States of America and Aotearoa/New Zealand to look at language revival there.

It is wonderful to see how quickly and widely reviving languages are being used – by individuals and families, in schools and even in parliaments. This is a major change. However, most of the language used is simple, for instance greeting, songs such as 'heads, shoulders, knees and toes' and welcomes to and acknowledgements of country.

A common revival pattern is for a small group to begin the process. The group often consists of local Indigenous people and one or more linguists. They work with the historical materials to find words and patterns of the language, then begin using and teaching what they have learnt. Others, including other Indigenous people, governments and education bodies often become involved. An important part of this process is adopting a spelling system. Fortunately the system already used by other Aboriginal languages is suitable for newly written languages, sometimes with minor adaptations.

The following sections look at some of the many challenges that arise in moving beyond simple language use. One of them is that learning any language is a challenging task, generally taking many thousands of hours, including trying the language with fluent speakers, who can refine the learner's use of language. The task of learning is greater in reviving languages because there are no fluent speakers, generally very few courses, and few resources such as texts, literature and videos.

A related challenge is finding or creating the opportunities to practise the language. The need for ongoing practise, ongoing language use, is clear when Gamilaraay 1 students do their course-final conversation assessment. They have learnt many features of the language, but it is a great challenge to use them in conversation. The students can, when focusing on one thing, use it; for instance, word-initial *ng*, correct word-order or the right case forms. However, they rarely develop the instinctual knowledge that enables them to focus on meaning rather than on details.

Another challenge is to describe the language so that, when courses are available, people can learn it. The following examples illustrate the difficulty of describing the language, the tendency to lose traditional features and to adopt English patterns in the revived language.

One feature of the language that has been recently described, but is rarely learnt, is the more complex use of pronouns. Looking at just one pronoun, the *Gamilaraay, Yuwaalaraay & Yuwaalayaay Dictionary* (referred to in this textbook as the *Dictionary* (Ash, Lissarrague & Giacon, 2003)), has *ngali* 'we(2)'. The more complete recent description (Giacon, 2017) points out that this is the inclusive form ('we' is the speaker and listener). If 'we' refers to the speaker and someone other than the listener GY does not use *ngali*, but *ngalinya* or *ngalilu*, depending on the type of verb. Currently only those doing more advanced GY courses are likely to learn this important traditional feature. They then need to keep using it so that it becomes instinctual.

While we have learnt more about *ngali*, other features of the language await a fuller description. For example, the dictionary has *manuma-li* 'steal', and an example sentence involving a dog stealing bones. The assumption was that there was one GY word that was in all circumstances the equivalent of English 'steal'. We now know that the *ma-li* in the verb implies 'action done with hand', and a dog stealing a bone would *manudha-li* (*dha-li* 'do with mouth'). It seems logical that there would be other words to translate 'steal'. For instance, Wangaaybuwan, a very closely related language, has *manuma-li*, *manundha-li*, as GY has, but also has *manungga-li* and *manumbi-li*. We do not know the detailed meaning of the last two. Wangaaybuwan also has *-dhi-li* 'do with foot', so presumably a soccer player taking the ball from the opposition would *manudhi-li* it. Since GY and Wangaaybuwan are quite similar it is quite likely GY also had five or more words for 'steal'. If there were a fluent speaker they would be able to tell us all the traditional GY for 'steal'.

In an ideal world there would be a GY committee overseeing language research, a linguist or linguists doing the research, a process for making a decision and then a process for communicating that decision to GY speakers. Until those structures are created, most people will use the existing dictionary, and will wrongly assume there is a GY word that has the same meaning as English 'steal'. This will be changing traditional GY.

In the case of pronouns and 'steal', ongoing research has found some traditional patterns that can now be learnt. There will be other areas where traditional knowledge has not been recovered, and so the simplified language will be used, language which has often adopted English patterns.

In summary, the challenges facing GY, and other reviving languages, include understanding as much as possible of the traditional language, deciding what to do when there are gaps in knowledge, communicating new language knowledge, and making it possible for people to study the language in depth.

# Using *Wiidhaa*

Learning another language is, as I said above, challenging – more so if this is the first time you have attempted to do this. *Wiidhaa* has 21 lessons. Each lesson has a vocabulary section, a grammar section that details some patterns or rules of the language, often some pronunciation guidance, example sentences and then suggested practice exercises.

You need to develop your own strategies for learning. Some learners like to use flash cards for vocabulary, or use online learning tools such as Quizlet and Memrise. A number of these have been developed for Gamilaraay 1. Pronunciation is difficult to learn without feedback – you often will not be aware of how you are saying words and sentences. It will help to listen to the sound files a number of times. These are incorporated in the electronic versions of this book, and are also available for download as mp3s – go to yuwaalaraay.com/advanced-learners.

As well as reading the grammar sections – the rules and examples – you can test your understanding with quizzes at gamilaraay.moodlecloud.com.

Perhaps the biggest challenge is developing conversational Gamilaraay – hearing and speaking it in real time. This needs practise. It helps if you can regularly meet with others to read Gamilaraay and to develop your own conversations.

As well as *Garay Guwaala 1* you will need other materials. The *Dictionary* (Ash, Lissarrague & Giacon, 2003) can be purchased at fivesenseseducation.com.au (search for Gamilaraay). It, and most of the other resources discussed, can be downloaded at yuwaalaraay.com. Often it is more convenient to use the finder list than the full dictionary. Since the dictionary was published (2003) some new words have been developed. These are found in the dictionary supplement, at the same site. It is planned to have an online dictionary. When this is finalised a link will be put on yuwaalaraay.com.

*Gayarragi, Winangali* is a wonderful resource. It is a computer program that has dictionary information, extensive sound, most of it from traditional speakers, songs, games and more. Download it from yuwaalaraay.com/online-resources.

Some materials, such as the picture dictionary, are available at tinyurl.com/gymoodle. Sign in as a guest.

## Extension

Some lessons have extension material. This is for background only, and most of it is not something you will need to know for this course. It is more for interest and later courses. Ignore it if you wish.

## Appendices

Appendices 2 to 5 are generally helpful when you have already worked through a topic and need to check some detail. They summarise material covered in *Garay Guwaala 1*, but also have more detailed and advanced information on the topic.

The appendices are:

- Appendix 1: Resources
- Appendix 2: Pronunciation Guide
- Appendix 3: Case Summary
- Appendix 4: Verb Summary
- Appendix 5: Pronoun Summary with Pronoun Chart from *Gaay Garay Dhadhin*
- Appendix 6: Wordlist

# LESSON 1
# Hello, Goodbye, Questions

Lesson 1, like most lessons, has vocabulary, a grammar section, practice exercises and conversations/extra examples. Early lessons also have pronunciation information. The grammar section in this lesson covers greetings and simple questions and answers.

## Vocabulary

Each lesson has a vocabulary section – Gamilaraay words that are used in that lesson. The vocabulary is mostly presented as one Gamilaraay word corresponding to one English word. This is a simplified presentation, to gently introduce you to the language. Very rarely does one word in Gamilaraay correspond in meaning to one word in English. Sometimes there are notes following the wordlist. You will get a better idea of the meaning and use of the Gamilaraay word if you also check the information in the dictionary, but even that is not generally a complete description of the use of the word.

Text such as 'GGU 1.1' below indicate that there is a sound file of the following Gamilaraay text. The sound files are available online. See Appendix 1: Resources.

In early lessons the vocabulary has verbs in command form, since that is the form that is being used. In later lessons verbs are given in future form, the usual citation form.

 **Audio:** GGU 1.1.mp3 is available in the electronic edition

| *Garay**                          | Words            |
|-----------------------------------|------------------|
| *winangala!, winangaldaya!*       | listen!          |
| *garay guwaala!**                 | speak!           |
| *garay guwaaldaya!*               |                  |
| *ngamila!, ngamildaya!**          | look!            |
| *yaama*                           | hello            |
| *yaama*                           | question word    |
| *yaluu**                          | goodbye, see ya  |
| *baayandhu**                      | goodbye, see ya  |
| *maliyaa*                         | friend           |
| *dhagaan**                        | brother          |
| *baawaa**                         | sister           |
| *yawu*                            | yes              |
| *gamil**                          | no/not           |
| *gaba**                           | good             |
| *biiba**                          | paper            |
| *baadhal*                         | bottle           |
| *nguu**                           | book             |
| *bina*                            | ear              |
| *mil*                             | eye              |
| *mara*                            | hand             |
| *dhina*                           | foot             |

See the pronunciation guide (Appendix 2) at the end of the book for an explanation of how the writing system works.

When you see * in the wordlists, look for extra information below.

 **Audio:** GGU 1.2.mp3 is available in the electronic edition

The first three entries in the wordlist are mainly 'teacher talk' – for use by the teacher. Two forms of each verb are given here: the first form suggests the action requested is brief and quickly completed. The second form is a continuous verb, which mean the action is ongoing. *Winangaldaya*, for example, means 'keep listening' or 'start listening and keep listening'.

\**Garay* is most commonly translated as 'word' but is also used to translate some related concepts such as 'statement', 'sentence' and 'language'.

\**Guwaala* by itself means something like: 'tell', 'say'. The use of *guwaala* will be covered in more detail later.

\*'!' after a verb means it is the command form, telling someone to do something. When you look up a verb in the *Dictionary* you will find the **future** form. The future form of the verbs/phrase in the list above are: *ngami-li, winanga-li* and *garay guwaa-li*.

\**Yaluu* actually means 'again, more'. As a greeting, it is used as an abbreviation of phrases such as: *Yaluu ngali ngamilay*, 'We(2) will see each other again'. *Baayandhu* 'soon' has a similar farewell use.

\**Baawaa* traditionally meant 'older sister', and your mother's sister's children and father's brother's children were also 'sister' and 'brother'. *Baawaa* is now used like English/European 'sister'. *Dhagaan* also had a different meaning from the current use of 'brother'. Many Aboriginal people use 'brother', 'sister' and abbreviations such as 'bruv', 'sis', 'cuz' when greeting each other.

\**Gamil* is the same as the English word 'no' **in some circumstances**. At other times, it is the same as the English 'not':

*gamil* = 'no' as a one word statement:
e.g. 'Are you well?' '**No**.'

*gamil* = 'not' in longer statements:
e.g. 'I did **not** go.'

It is not the equivalent of 'no' in 'no + noun' phrases:
e.g. 'no money, no water'.

That will be covered in later lessons.

\**Gaba* translates many English words such as 'good', 'sweet', 'right', 'beautiful' and more.

\**Biiba* is from English 'paper', and *baadhal* from …

\**Biibabiiba* was a word developed in the 1990s for 'book' from *biiba* 'paper'. It was decided for two reasons to generally translate 'book' with *nguu*, originally 'paperbark tree': first, a move away from English borrowings, and second because *biibabiiba* implies that reduplication (doubling) indicates plurality: 'many of', 'many of'. Generally, GY reduplication is like English '-ish', so traditionally *biibabiiba* would mean 'paperish' rather than 'lots of paper'.

> Word development: Active languages constantly develop new words – sometimes for new things, sometimes replacing existing words. These new words fit into the existing patterns of the language because the speakers instinctively know the patterns of their language, and make sure the words fit them. In language revival no one is an instinctive speaker of the language so new words will only fit into the traditional patterns of the language to the extent that those developing them know the patterns of the traditional language.

Each lesson has a grammar section that introduces Gamilaraay language rules. Language learners can easily assume that the rules of their main language applies to other languages. Traditional Gamilaraay is very different from English and traditional features will only be retained if speakers learn and adopt them.

## Grammar: Greetings

In traditional Aboriginal societies, where people mostly lived in small groups, the sorts of greetings and farewells used today were not common. However, as people have moved into different social settings, greetings and farewells have been developed. Below are some current simple examples. No doubt, in time people will develop more greetings, perhaps based more on traditional patterns.

 **Audio:** GGU 1.3.mp3 is available in the electronic edition

When meeting people:

| | |
|---|---|
| *Yaama maliyaa.* | Hello friend/mate. |
| *Yaama baawaa.* | Hello sister. |
| *Yaama dhagaan.* | Hello brother. |

When leaving:

| | |
|---|---|
| *Yaluu maliyaa.* | Goodbye friend/mate. |
| *Yaluu baawaa.* | Goodbye sister. |
| *Yaluu dhagaan.* | Goodbye brother. |

*Yaluu* is 'again' and when used as a greeting is short for 'see you again', 'talk again', etc. Use *baayandhu* 'soon' in the same way:

| | |
|---|---|
| *Baayandhu maliyaa.* | Goodbye friend/mate. |
| *Baayandhu baawaa.* | Goodbye sister. |
| *Baayandhu dhagaan.* | Goodbye brother. |

Try to use them. It is good if you can find people who will reply to you. It may be easier to use the greetings with babies or your pets – they won't be struggling to understand or answer you.

## Yugal 'Song'

*'Bina Mil' winangala*! 'Listen to "Bina, Mil"', and then sing along.

*Garay ngadaa*. 'The text is below' (and sound, in the electronic edition), with all three verses. The *yugal*/song is also on the CD *Yugal* (Giacon, 2002) and in *Gayarragi, Winangali* (which also has Yuwaalaraay versions). There is a more recent GR version by Loren Ryan (tinyurl.com/gyresources). *Winangala* 'listen' and then *bawildaya* 'sing along'.

### Bina mil – 'Ears, eyes (hands and feet)'

 **Audio:** GGU 1.4.mp3 is available in the electronic edition

| ***Bina Mil*** | |
|---|---|
| *Bina, mil, mara, dhina* | Ear, eye, hand, foot |
| *Mara, dhina,* | Hand, foot |
| *Mara, dhina,* | Hand, foot |
| *Bina, mil, mara, dhina* | Ear, eye, hand, foot |
| *Yulunga, yulunga, yulunga* | Dance, dance, dance |

## Bina Mil

| | |
|---|---|
| *Ngulu, biri, mubal, buyu* | Face, chest, stomach, leg |
| *Mubal, buyu* | Stomach, leg |
| *Mubal, buyu* | Stomach, leg |
| *Ngulu, biri, mubal, buyu* | Face, chest, stomach, leg |
| *Baraya, baraya, baraya* | Hop, hop, hop |
| *Wara, dhuruyaal, dhalay, dhaal* | Left hand, right hand, tongue, cheek |
| *Dhalay, dhaal* | Tongue, cheek |
| *Dhalay, dhaal* | Tongue, cheek |
| *Wara, dhuruyaal, dhalay, dhaal* | Left hand, right hand, tongue, cheek |
| *Burrumbaya, burrumbaya, burrumbaya* | Skip, skip, skip |

## Grammar: Questions and answers

We now learn how to ask some yes/no questions using intonation, and some answers to these. Other questions are covered in later lessons.

An intonation question has the same words as a statement, but with a rising tone, a rising pitch at the end of the sentence.

Say these English sentences as statements and questions.

You eat fish
This is the best you can do
You went to the festival
Water

Use the same intonation pattern to ask questions in Gamilaraay.

| A: | (pointing to book) | *?Nguu?* |
|---|---|---|
| B: | | *Yawu, nguu.* |
| A: | (pointing to book) | *?Mil?* |
| B: | | *Gamil, nguu.* |

LESSON 1. HELLO, GOODBYE, QUESTIONS

There has been no study of the actual question intonation pattern used on the Yuwaalaraay tapes, so for the present we assume the pattern is the same as English.

My impression is that intonation questions are more common in spoken language than they are in written. They are certainly very common in the Yuwaalaraay tapes.

Gamilaraay generally uses English punctuation – a very convenient practice. GY people could decide to do some things differently, for example by using a ? at the start of questions, or at the start of intonation questions. This practice has been adopted above.

## Practice

Repetition is essential in learning language. You need to develop ways of doing this that work for you. For this section go around the class saying *Yaama* and *Yaluu/baayandhu* to others. Then expand the greetings, adding *baawaa, dhagaan* or *maliyaa*.

Look for ways to keep the practice interesting, for instance A calls M '*baawaa*' (M = Male), or say *Baayandhu* when *Yaama* is needed.

| | |
|---|---|
| A: | *Yaama baawaa* |
| M: | *Gamil, dhagaan.* |
| A: | *Yawu, Yaama dhagaan.* |
| M: | *Yaluu A.* |
| A: | *Yaluu Bill.* |

If you are by yourself have pictures of people and take both sides of conversations like that above.

## Questions

One person indicates something and then says a word with question intonation, a rising tone. Another person answers.

 **Audio:** GGU 1.5.mp3 is available in the electronic edition

WIIDHAA

For example, point to your ear and with rising inflection say:

| *?Bina?* | An ear? |

The answer will be:

| *Yawu.* | Yes. | |
| Or *Yawu, bina.* | Yes, an ear. | (be sure to pause after *Yawu*) |

Or point to an eye and say:

| *?Bina?* | An ear? |

The answer will be:

| *Gamil.* | No. |
| Or *Gamil, mil.* | No, it's an eye. (be sure to pause after *Gamil*) |

Repeat this with other body parts and with the words *Dhagaan* and *Baawaa*.

Then, move around, greet the new person, ask and answer questions, farewell each other and move on. Below is a sample conversation between A and B:

| A: | *Yaama maliyaa.* | Hi friend. | |
| B: | *Yaama Baawaa.* | Hi sister. | |
| A: | *?Mara?* | (Is this a) hand? | (holding our or pointing to a hand) |
| B: | *Yawu, mara.* | Yes, it's a hand. | |
| B: | *?Mil?* | (Is this an) eye? | (pointing to an ear) |
| A: | *Gamil. Bina.* | No. It's an ear. | |
| B: | *Gaba.* | Good. | |
| B: | *?Mary?* | (Are you) Mary? | (indicating A) |
| A: | *Yawu, Mary.* | Yes, I am Mary. | |
| A: | *Yaluu Dhagaan.* | See ya brother. | |
| B: | *Yaluu Baawaa.* | Bye sister. | |

Remember: you need to keep speaking and hearing Gamilaraay.

LESSON 1. HELLO, GOODBYE, QUESTIONS

# Pronunciation

It is always a challenge to learn the sound system of a new language, and Gamilaraay is no exception. It has sounds you are not used to making, some differences that matter in English do not matter in Gamilaraay and some differences that matter in Gamilaraay will not be noticed by an English speaker.

One help to good Gamilaraay pronunciation is listening to the sound files. Sound is incorporated in the electronic edition and is also available at yuwaalaraay.com and tinyurl.com/gymoodle. Some of the sound files may not be updated to the current version of the text. You can also hear relatively fluent speakers on *Gayarragi, Winangali*, but they are often speaking fairly casually, so with some different pronunciation. Think of the difference between formal English 'I'm going to' and more casual, more common 'I'm gunna/guwana'.

It takes a while to learn how to interpret the letters – if you are only used to reading English you will need to give letters new meaning. You will do better if you are used to reading languages like Italian or Japanese where there is generally a 'one letter' = 'one sound' system (or a pair of letters = one sound).

For this lesson we will focus on vowels, the GY use of 'h' and stress.

## Vowels

In Gamilaraay, as in many Aboriginal languages, there are three vowels, written '*a, i, u*'. Each is found as short: '*a, i, u*' and long: written '*aa, ii, uu*'.

> Vowels are sounds that are made with relatively free airflow through the mouth; e.g. the middle sounds in 'pit, pet, pat, put, pot, putt'.
>
> Most other sounds used in words are consonants, where the airflow is not free. Sometimes airflow is restricted: 'f, v, s'; sometimes air comes out of the nose: 'n, m, ng'; sometimes airflow is stopped: 'd, p, g, t', etc.
>
> Wikipedia is a good source for more comprehensive information about vowels and consonants.

### Short vowels

| | |
|---|---|
| *a* | is mostly like the sound in 'putt' |
| *i* | is mostly like the sound in 'pit' |
| *u* | is mostly like the sound in 'put' |

### Long vowels

| | |
|---|---|
| *aa* | is mostly like the sound in 'Karl' |
| *ii* | is mostly like the sound in 'keel' |
| *uu* | is mostly like the sound in 'cool' |

### Don't neutralise vowels

In English speech many vowels are 'neutralised', i.e. you can't tell which vowel it is. The highlighted sections in the following words can sound the same, especially in relaxed speech: Har**old**, barr**el**, Nation**al**, cheerf**ul** and in bott**le** (linguists would write **əl** to indicate the sound, ə is called schwa).

Neutralised vowels are rare in Gamilaraay, so English speakers need to be careful to pronounce vowels correctly. It is common for them to pronounce the *il* in *gamil* and the *al* in *mubal* as **əl**. Be careful to maintain the vowel sound, *i* and *a*.

**Beware:** The letter 'u' in English can indicate two main sounds: in 'but' and 'put'. In GR it **only** represents the sound in 'put'.

***h:*** In Gamilaraay 'h' occurs only in ***dh*** and ***nh***. The ***h*** indicates that the tongue tip is on the bottom teeth or between the teeth, and the tongue is pressed up, so that the top of the tongue is on the top teeth. In ***dh***, as in ***d***, the airflow stops and then is released. In ***nh***, as in ***n***, the air comes out your nose.

Try the sounds *dha, nha, dhi, nhi, dhu, nhu*, then alternate with *da/na*, etc.: e.g. *dha, da, nha, na* …

It is generally easy to distinguish ***dh*** and ***d***, but harder to distinguish ***nh*** from ***n***.

## Stress

It is common to emphasise parts of a word – some English examples, with the stressed part **bolded** are:

**Eng**lish, I**tal**ian, in**form**, in**vest**, **pho**to, Sa**ha**ra **des**ert, ice cream des**sert**.

 **Audio:** GGU 1.6.mp3 is available in the electronic edition

A simple introduction to Gamilaraay stress rules is:

If there are only **short vowels**, the first syllable is stressed and then put minor stress on every second syllable after that. In the examples below, the **underlined-bold** syllables have the main stress, plain **bold** secondary stress.

| | |
|---|---|
| *<u>**bi**</u>na* | *<u>**bi**</u>-na* |
| *<u>**ma**</u>ra* | *<u>**ma**</u>-ra* |
| *<u>**ga**</u>mil* | *<u>**ga**</u>-mil* |
| *<u>**wi**</u>nan**ga**la* | *<u>**wi**</u>-na-**nga**-la* |

If there are **long vowels**, they are all stressed:

| | |
|---|---|
| *<u>**yaa**</u>ma* | *<u>**yaa**</u>-ma* |
| *<u>**baawaa**</u>* | *<u>**baa-waa**</u>* |
| *dha<u>**gaan**</u>* | *dha-<u>**gaan**</u>* |
| *ya<u>**luu**</u>* | *ya-<u>**luu**</u>* |

*Mali**yaa*** has the main stress on the long vowel, which is last, and secondary stress on the syllable two away from the main stress.

Be especially careful of words that end with a long vowel, e.g. *yaluu, maliyaa*. It is common for learners to shorten the final long vowel.

Practise the difference between **long** and **short vowels** (*a* and *aa*, *i* and *ii*, *u* and *uu*) by listening to and saying the words below and notice the difference (only some of them are real words).

 **Audio:** GGU 1.7.mp3 is available in the electronic edition

WIIDHAA

| yaama | yama | yamaa |
| yaluu | yalu | yaaluu |
| gaba | gabaa | gaaba |
| maliyaa | maaliya | maliya |
| bina | binaa | biina |

### Being creative

It is great if you can use Gamilaraay in new situations. However, be aware that the patterns of Gamilaraay are often very different from the patterns of English, and since what most learners know is English, they often put English patterns into their Gamilaraay. This can happen with pronunciation: it is easy to say '*n*' instead of '*nh*'; it is very easy to shorten the second part of *yaluu* and say *yalu*, with the stress on the '*ya*'.

## *Winangala, garay guwaala, yawala.*
## Listen, say and read.

This section of the lesson has extra text and sound that you can listen to, read and repeat. When sound files have been made you can download them from the website and use them on your phone, in the car and elsewhere. Repetition, including repeated listening, is essential in language learning.

 **Audio:** GGU 1.8.mp3 is available in the electronic edition

### More greetings, family words

This contains more kin terms that may make it easier for you to practise Gamilaraay.

| *Yaama gunii.* | Hello mum. |
| *Yaluu gunii.* | Goodbye mum. |
| *Yaama bubaa.* | Hello dad. |
| *Baayandhu bubaa.* | Goodbye dad. |
| *Yaama walgan.* | Hello aunt. |
| *Yaluu walgan.* | Goodbye aunt. |
| *Yaama garruu.* | Hello uncle. |

# LESSON 1. HELLO, GOODBYE, QUESTIONS

| | |
|---|---|
| *Baayandhu garruu.* | Goodbye uncle. |
| *Yaama dhaadhaa.* | Hello pop. |
| *Yaluu dhaadhaa.* | Goodbye pop. |
| *Yaama badhii.* | Hello gran. |
| *Baayandhu badhii.* | Goodbye gran. |
| *Yaama birraliidhuul.* | Hello baby. |
| *Baayandhu birraliidhuul.* | Goodbye baby. |
| *Yaama buruma.* | Hello dog. |
| *Yaluu buruma.* | Goodbye dog. |

 **Audio:** GGU 1.9.mp3 is available in the electronic edition

Listen to the text below on the sound file.

*Winangala!*
*Biiba?*
Listen!
(Is that) paper?
*Yawu, biiba.*
Yep, paper.

*Winangala!*
*Mara?*
Listen!
(Is that) hands?
*Yawu, mara.*
Yep, hands.

*Winangala!*
*Baadhal?*
Listen!
(Is that) a bottle?
*Yawu, baadhal.*
Yep, a bottle.

# LESSON 2
# 'This, That' Demonstratives; more questions

This lesson introduces Gamilaraay demonstratives – words like 'this' and 'that', and 'What?' questions.

## Vocabulary

 **Audio:** GGU 2.1.mp3 is available in the electronic edition

As well as the words below, more words will be introduced in the song and conversations. Develop strategies for learning words, starting with the ones you use more frequently. There may be resources such as Quizlet, but they may not include recent revisions to the text. Be careful with pronunciation.

| *Garay* | **Words** |
|---|---|
| *gaabu!* | hush! |
| *wanagidjay!** | leave it! |
| *yulunga!* | dance! |
| *bawila!** | sing! |
| | |
| *wiyayl* | pen |
| *nguu/biibabiiba* | book |
| *gaala* | mug |
| *bundi* | club |
| *gali* | water |
| *buruma* | dog |
| *dhigaraa* | bird |
| *dhuru* | snake |

WIIDHAA

| *Garay* | **Words** |
|---|---|
| *minya?* | what? |
| | |
| *nhama* | that, this, the, there |
| *nhalay* | this, here, that |
| *nhamalay* | that |

\*The word *wanagidjay* is almost always used as a one-word expression, something like the English 'Stop it', 'Leave it' or 'Quit it'.

\*The *a* in *bawila* is a bit like 'o' in 'pot'.

## Pronunciation

This lesson focuses on **ny** and **dj**, has some further information on stress when there is a vowel+*y* or a long vowel+*y* combination and has comments on variation.

 **Audio:** GGU 2.2.mp3 is available in the electronic edition

**ny, dj:** The tongue position for *ny* and *dj* is the tongue tip on the bottom teeth. Similar to the *nh* and *dh* sounds, but with the top of the tongue not touching the teeth. There are similar sounds in English, but they are made with the tongue tip on the top of the mouth. Practise *minya, wanagidjay*.

For now treat **short vowel+*y*** and **long vowel+*y*** like a long vowel – that is, it is stressed.

*Nha<u>lay</u>* has the stress on the second syllable, *nhama<u>lay</u>* has the main stress on the last syllable, with some stress on the first.

Later you will meet works with *iy, aay, uy* and *uuy*. Remember to stress these parts of the word.

*Wanagidjay* does not follow the usual rules. The stress is on the first and last syllable: ***wanagidjay***. This is likely because it is influenced by the stress in *wanagi* 'will throw'.

The word Gamilaraay consists of **ga**_mil_ 'no' and the suffix -a**raay** 'with, having' (see Lesson 18). Traditional speakers tend to keep those stresses, saying **Ga**mila**raay**, with the _a_ like 'o', or, since g and k are equivalent and _aay_ is occasionally said 'oy', **Ko**mila**roi**. You can hear Arthur Dodd and Fred Reece say the word in sentence 958 in _Gayarragi, Winangali_.

## Variation

Sounds are influenced by the other sounds around them. For instance, in English 'illegal' is often said something like 'allegəl', and 'a' in 'watch' and 'yatch' sounds like 'o'. In Gamilaraay there is similar variation:

_a_ in _gamil_ 'no' and _bawili_ 'will sing' can sound like 'o' in 'pot'.

_a_ in _yanay_ 'will go' can sound like 'e' in 'bed'.

There is also variation depending on how carefully people are speaking.

# Grammar: Demonstratives

Demonstratives are words like 'this, that, then, there'. A simple definition is that they draw the listener's attention to what is being spoken about. They are a complex area of language, often with a range of options that carry subtle differences in meaning. Here we will be using a simplified version of Gamilaraay demonstratives – partly because this is an introductory course, and partly because we have not been able to clearly describe the actual use of the complex Gamilaraay demonstrative system.

We begin with demonstratives _nhama, nhalay_ and _nhamalay_.

**Nhama** has many translations in English, including most commonly 'that/those' and 'the', less commonly 'there', as well as other translations. A demonstrative that ends in -_ma_ indicates that the speaker assumes that the hearer knows what is being referred to. For example, '_Bina nhama?_' 'That is an ear.' _Nhama_ is much more frequently used (around 3,000 occurrences on the Yuwaalaraay tapes) than _nhalay_ and _nhamalay_. It is often used to refer to something that is already part of the conversation or that needs no introduction.

In the following, two people are looking at an object:

 **Audio:** GGU 2.3.mp3 is available in the electronic edition

A: *Minya nhama?*
 What that?
 What's that?
B: *Gaala nhama.*
 Cup that.
 That's a cup.

> The second line above gives English that indicates the meaning of the Gamilaraay above it. Linguists call this a 'gloss' and the line an 'interlinear gloss'. The gloss is an indication of the meaning of a word, and does not show the detailed meaning or other information. The third line is an actual translation.

*Nhalay* also has many translations, but is most commonly 'this, these, here'. It is generally used to introduce something new. Use *nhalay* when something **new** is being **emphatically pointed out** or **focused on**. When referring to objects, *nhalay* is only used for things that are **close**. It usually occurs before the noun in statements like '**This** is a knife'. In storytelling or narratives *nhalay* is often used to introduce a new character. Later reference to the character can be with *nhama* or other demonstratives. It is much less common than *nhama* (around 200 occurrences on the Yuwaalaraay tapes – see Appendix 1).

The *-lay* part of the word indicates that the speaker is drawing attention to the object, pointing it out physically or saying 'notice this' about some new topic in the conversation.

Once you have pointed out something using *nhalay* you can then refer to it using *nhama*.

A: *Nhalay buruma ngay.*
 This dog mine.
 This is my dog.
B: *?Gaba nhama buruma?*
 Good that dog?
 Is that a good dog.

A: *Yawu, gaba.* // *Yawu, gaba nhama.*
Yes, good.
Yes, it is good.

**Nhamalay** is used to introduce and draw attention to something that is not close to the speaker:

*Wiyayl nhamalay.* (pointing to the pen that is not near you)
pen that
That is a pen.

Once you have pointed out something using *nhamalay* you can then refer to it using *nhama*.

A: *Nhamalay buruma ngay.*
That (distant, pointed to) dog mine.
That is my dog.
B: *Gaba nhama buruma?*
Good that dog?
Is that a good dog?
A: *Yawu, gaba.*
Yes, good.
Yes, it is good.

> The description of demonstratives in this version of *Garay Guwaala 1* has been substantially changed from earlier versions, following further investigation of the sources, the most important of which are the Yuwaalaraay tapes. In previous versions, *nhalay* was defined as 'close to the speaker' and *nhama* as 'not close', and *nhamalay* was not discussed.
>
> It is to be expected that as we learn more about them and work out better how to teach about them that the sections on demonstratives will change – more than most other sections of the grammar.

## Word order

 **Audio:** GGU 2.4.mp3 is available in the electronic edition

Notice that demonstratives most commonly occur in second position in a sentence or clause:

*Gaba nhama nguu.*
Good that book.
That's a good book.

*Gagil nhalay nguu.*
Bad this book.
This book is no good.

(However, pronouns also mostly occur in second position, and they take precedence over demonstratives, which then move to third position – see later lessons.)

The exception is when the demonstrative is being emphasised. The demonstrative then goes first. (In general what is being emphasised in a statement goes first.) *Nhalay* is relatively common in first position, as are other demonstratives that end in *-lay*, since they are often pointing out something new.

*Nhalay bigibila.*
**This** is an echidna.
**Here's** an echidna.

A different word order changes the emphasis:

*Bigibila nhalay.*
This is an echidna.

If you point to an eye – your own or someone else's – you can say:

*Nhalay mil.*
This is an eye.

(This can also be translated 'Here is an eye'.)

If you are talking about any eye(s), but without strongly drawing attention to it, you can say:

*Nhama mil.*
That is an eye. (Those are eyes.)

(This can also be translated 'There is an eye'.)

You would use this for instance if you are naming a series of body parts – *Nhama mil, nhama ngaay, nhama muru.* 'That's an eye, that's a mouth, that's a nose'.

Often there is no singular/plural distinction in Gamilaraay – in other words:

| | |
|---|---|
| *nhalay* | this, these |
| *nhama* | that, those |
| *dhinawan* | emu, emus, etc. |

Below are some more sentences including demonstratives.

 **Audio:** GGU 2.5.mp3 is available in the electronic edition

*Nhalay dhinawan.*
**This** is an emu. **These** are emus.

*Nhalay mil.*
**This** is an eye. **These** are eyes.

*Nhamalay biiba.*
**That** is paper. **Those** are papers.

*Ngamila! Bigibila nhama.*
Look. That is a porcupine/echidna. // There's an echidna there.

*Winangala! Dhinawan nhama.*
Listen. That is an emu. Those are emus.

To practise your Gamilaraay you might like to combine English words in the Gamilaraay structures you know, e.g. Car *nhama*, *Nhalay* Mary, etc. As you learn more Gamilaraay you can use less English.

WIIDHAA

# Grammar: *Yaama* Questions

In Lesson 1 we used intonation to ask yes/no questions. You can also use *yaama* for this. (This is the older use of *yaama*. It seems the use of *yaama* as a greeting began after colonisation.)

*Yaama* is the first word of a question. You may need to reorganise the rest of the sentence to keep demonstratives (and pronouns) second.

| | | |
|---|---|---|
| Q. | *Yaama nhama dhinawan?* | Is that an emu? |
| A. | *Yawu, dhinawan nhama.* | Yes, that is an emu. |
| Q. | *Yaama nhama mil?* | Is this an eye? |
| A. | *Gamil nhama mil.* | That is not an eye. |

## Yes/no answers

The answer to a yes/no can be a simple *yawu* 'yes' or *gamil* 'no'. (We will not do 'maybe/don't know' answers now.)

🔊 **Audio:** GGU 2.6.mp3 is available in the electronic edition

| | | |
|---|---|---|
| Q. | *Yaama nhama wiyayl?* | Is that a pen? |
| A. | *Yawu.* | Yes. |
| A. | *Gamil.* | No. |

After *yawu* 'yes' you can pause, and add confirmation by repeating part of the question:

| | | |
|---|---|---|
| Q. | *Yaama nhama wiyayl?* | Is that a pen? |
| A. | *Yawu, wiyayl nhama.* | Yes, that is a pen. |

There are more possibilities if the answer is *gamil* 'no'.

| | | | |
|---|---|---|---|
| Q. | *Yaama nhama gali?* | Is that water? | |
| A. | *Gamil.* | No. | |
| A. | *Gamil nhama gali.* | That is not water. | (**no pause** after *gamil*) |
| A. | *Gamil, gamil nhama gali.* | No, that is not water. | (**pause** after first *gamil*) |

The presence or absence of pauses in the speech makes a big difference to the meaning. The pause is shown by a comma when writing. In the next lesson, you will learn another way to answer this type of question.

| | | |
|---|---|---|
| Q. | *Yaama nhama mil?* | Is this an eye? |
| A. | *Gamil nhama mil.* | That is not an eye. |
| Q. | *Yaama nhalay mil?* | Is **this** an eye? |
| A. | *Gamil.* | No. |
| Q. | *Yaama nhalay mil?* | Is **this** an eye? |
| A. | *Gamil, gamil nhama mil.* | No, that is not an eye. |

 **Audio:** GGU 2.7.mp3 is available in the electronic edition

Learning to use ***yaama*** and ***gamil***.

You might find it easy to use the following process:

- first write a Gamilaraay statement,
- then put ***yaama*** or ***gamil*** at the front,
- then make sure the word order is correct – demonstrative second.

| | | |
|---|---|---|
| *Mil nhama.* | That/this is an eye. | Statement |
| *Yaama nhama mil?* | Is that/this an eye? | Question |

In the 'interlinear writing' below, the second line shows words corresponding to the first line, but not in Gamilaraay word order.

So, to translate 'This is not paper' or 'Is this paper?' first translate 'This is paper'.

This is paper.
*Biiba nhalay.*

Then add *yaama* or *gamil*, and change the word order if needed.

*Yaama nhalay biiba?*
Is this paper?

*Gamil nhalay biiba.*
This is not paper.

WIIDHAA

## Grammar: *Minya?* 'What?' questions

In Lesson 1 we considered yes/no questions. They expect the answers 'yes', 'no' or 'don't know'.

'What?' questions look for a descriptive answer, often a name.

'What's that?' 'A car.' 'A tree.'

This is an example of a 'content' or 'information' question. The 'information' questions in this lesson all begin with *minya?* 'what?'. In later lessons, you will learn to ask other information questions: Who? Where? etc.

Remember the tongue position for the *ny* – tongue tip on the bottom teeth.

 **Audio:** GGU 2.8.mp3 is available in the electronic edition

*Minya nhama?* is much more common than *minya nhalay?*

*Minya nhama?*
What is that? / What are those?

The answers can vary.

| | |
|---|---|
| *Biiba.* | Paper. |
| *Biiba nhama.* | It's paper. |
| *Nhama biiba.* | That is paper. |

## Practice

 **Audio:** GGU 2.9.mp3 is available in the electronic edition

By now you know many nouns, and perhaps the names of people in the class. Introduce people and objects using *nhalay* and *nhamalay*, then talk about them using *nhama*.

A: *Nhalay bina, nhamalay girrinil.*
   This is an ear, and that is a door.
B: *Yawu, bina nhama, girrinil nhama.*
   Yes, that is an ear and that is a door.

A: *Mary nhamalay?*
B: *Yawu, Mary nhama.* or
   *Gamil, Dhagaan nhama, Harry nhama.*

In pairs or groups (or by yourself, taking both roles), ask and answer questions. Ask about body parts, the objects in the Lesson 2 vocabulary, and people's names.

## *Yaama*

A: *Yaama nhama bina?*
   Is this is an ear?
B: *Yawu, bina nhama.*
   Yes, that is an ear.

or

B: *Gamil, milbala nhama.*
   No, that is an eye.
A: *Yaama nhalay Harry?*
   Is this is Harry?
B: *Yawu, Harry nhama.*
   Yes, that is Harry.

or

B: *Gamil, Kim nhama.*
   No, that is Kim.

Use your practice pattern with *Minya?*. This is easy for the questioner since they don't need to know the name of the object asked about. Often in class it is more productive to ask when you can't remember a name, so use *Minya nhalay* and *Minya nhamalay?* frequently.

Kim: *Yaama Kath, minya nhama?*
Kath: *Nguu nhama, Kim.*
Kim: *Yaama Kath, minya nhamalay?*
   Hi Kath, what's that (over there)?
Kath: *Girrinil nhama, Kim.*
   That's a door, Kim.

## Translation

In the early stages, it is often a good idea to do translations in these two steps – word by word and then into sentence structure. Below are some more examples.

*Garay guwaala, baawaa!*
word tell sister!
Talk, sister!

*Minya nhalay?*
what this
What is **this**? or What's **this**?

*Nhama bigibila.*
that porcupine.
There is a porcupine.

*Yaama nhalay bigibila?*
question this porcupine
Is this a porcupine? (porcupine is close and pointed out)

*Yawu, bigibila nhama.*
yes, porcupine that
Yes, that is an echidna.

## *Winangala, garay guwaala, yawala.*
## Listen, say and read.

Use the text and sound to build your familiarity with Gamilaraay, to develop fluency.

 **Audio:** GGU 2.10.mp3 is available in the electronic edition

A: *Yaama dhagaan.* Hello brother.
B: *Yaama baawaa.* Hello sister.

## LESSON 2. 'THIS, THAT' DEMONSTRATIVES; MORE QUESTIONS

| | | |
|---|---|---|
| A: | *Minya nhama, Bobby?* | What is that, Bobby? |
| B: | *Nguu. Nhama nguu.* | A book. That is a book. |
| A: | *Yawu. Yaluu Bobby.* | Yep. Bye Bobby. |
| B: | *Yaluu Liz.* | Bye Liz. |

🔊 **Audio:** GGU 2.11.mp3 is available in the electronic edition

| | | |
|---|---|---|
| Q. | *Minya nhalay?* | What is this? |
| A. | *Wiyayl nhama.* | That is a pen. |
| Q. | *Minya nhama?* | What is this? |
| A. | *Nhama biibabiiba.* | That is a book. |
| Q. | *Minya nhalay?* | |
| A. | *Gali nhama.* | That is water. |
| Q. | *Minya nhamalay?* | What is that? (distant) |
| A. | *Buruma nhama.* | That is a dog. |
| Q. | *Minya nhamalay?* | |
| A. | *Nhama dhuru.* | That is a snake. |
| Q. | *Minya nhama?* | |
| A. | *Gaala nhama.* | That is a mug. |
| Q. | *Minya nhama?* | |
| A. | *Bundi nhama.* | That is a hitting stick. |

🔊 **Audio:** GGU 2.12.mp3 is available in the electronic edition

| | | |
|---|---|---|
| Q. | *Nhama nguu?*<br>Is that a book? | or *Yaama nhama nguu?* |
| A. | *Yawu, nguu nhama.*<br>Yes, that is a book. | |
| Q. | *Dhigaraa nhama?*<br>Is that a bird? | or *Yaama nhama dhigaraa?* |
| A. | *Yawu, dhigaraa nhama.*<br>Yes, that is a bird. | |
| Q. | *Nhamalay gali?*<br>Is **that** water? | or *Yaama nhamalay gali?* |
| A. | *Yawu, gali nhama.*<br>Yes, that is water. | |

WIIDHAA

Q. *Buruma nhama?*     or *Yaama nhama buruma?*
Is this a dog?
A. *Yawu, buruma nhama.*
Yes, that is a dog.
Q. *Biiba nhamalay?*     or *Yaama nhama biiba?*
Is that paper?
A. *Yawu, biiba nhama.*
Yes, that is paper.
Q. *Wiyayl nhama?*     or *Yaama nhama wiyayl?*
Is that a pen?
A. *Yawu, wiyayl nhama!*
Yes, that is a pen.
Q. *Dhuru nhama?*     or *Yaama nhama dhuru?*
Is that a snake?
A. *Yawu, dhuru nhama.*
(Yes,) that is a snake.

🔊 **Audio:** GGU 2.13.mp3 is available in the electronic edition

Q. *Winangala maliyaa, nhama biiba?*
Listen friend, is that paper?
Q. *Winangala maliyaa, yaama nhama biiba?*
Listen friend, is that paper?
A. *Yawu, biiba nhama maliyaa.*
Yes, that is paper friend/mate.
Q. *Winangala maliyaa, nhalay gali?*
Listen friend, is this water?
Q. *Winangala maliyaa, yaama nhalay gali?*
Listen friend, is this water?
A. *Yawu, gali nhama maliyaa.*
Yes, that is water friend/mate.
Q. *Winangala baawaa, biibabiiba nhama?*
Listen sister, is that a book?
Q. *Winangala baawaa, yaama nhama biibabiiba?*
Listen sister, is that a book?
A. *Yawu dhagaan, biibabiiba nhama.*
Yes brother, that is a book.

LESSON 2. 'THIS, THAT' DEMONSTRATIVES; MORE QUESTIONS

🔊 **Audio:** GGU 2.14.mp3 is available in the electronic edition

Q. *Winangala gunii, nhamalay dhaadhaa?*
Listen mum, is that granddad?
Q. *Winangala gunii, yaama nhama dhaadhaa?*
Listen mum, is that granddad?
A. *Yawu baawaa, dhaadhaa nhama.*
Yes sister, that is granddad.

# LESSON 3
# Contrast / Take it!

This lesson introduces some more words, including verbs; shows how to use the 'contrast' suffix, including in some answers to yes/no questions.

## Vocabulary

 **Audio:** GGU 3.1.mp3 is available in the electronic edition

| *Garay* | Words |
|---|---|
| *dhiyamala!* | pick up! |
| *wiimala!* | put down! |
| *garriya!* | don't! |
| | |
| *badjigal** | bicycle |
| *giidjaa* | ant (small, black) |
| *bandaarr* | kangaroo (grey) |
| *barran* | boomerang |
| *girrinil* | door |
| *murru* | bum |
| *muru* | nose |
| *yarral* | stone/coin |
| *budjigarr** | cat |
| *=bala** | contrast clitic |

*There is further information on *=bala* later in this lesson.

**Badjigal* an adaptation of 'bicycle' into the GY sound system. GY, like most Australian Indigenous languages, does not have fricatives, sounds made by forcing the air through a narrow opening in the mouth: 's, v, f, z, sh', etc. Often these become *dh* or *dj* in GY.

*Budjigarr* is from English pussycat. *b* in GY can be pronounced 'p' or 'b', but is more often 'b'. GY *d* can be pronounced 'd' or 't', so you might expect 'd' at the end of the word, but *d* is never found at the end of a GY word, but *rr* is, and it can sound like *d*.

## Pronunciation

*r* and *rr*

In GY the letter *r* represents a similar sound to English 'r'. *rr* in GY is a different sound. When speaking carefully it is trilled like Italian or Scottish 'r'. You may need practise to get this sound. Until you do, use *r*. The words *murru* and *muru* show it is important to distinguish between *r* and *rr*.

*rr* is a 'digraph', two adjacent letters representing one sound. Other examples are *dh*, *nh*, *ny* in Gamilaraay, 'sh', 'ch' in English.

There is some variation in the pronunciation of *rr* at the end of a word. It can be 'trilled', or in more casual speech it can sound like the English 'd' or 't' at the end of a word. Listen to Fred Reece's different pronunciations of *yinarr* 'woman' on *Gayarragi, Winangali*, sentence 927. Some variation in pronunciation is normal in any language, but generally people are not aware of it – they are focusing on the content of the message, not the sound. If you listen carefully you will hear many different pronunciations of words and phrases – differences that you otherwise do not notice. When I pay attention, I hear many variations in the pronunciation of 'Australia' and 'am going to', for instance. And we are more aware of differences in pronunciation in languages we are learning than in languages we use every day.

## Grammar

Remember, grammar is the patterns of a language. It is very easy for new learners to use the patterns of the language they are familiar with, such as English, when using a new language. To speak Gamilaraay relaxedly you need to learn the patterns and practise them until you can use them without thinking about them.

In 'fully alive' languages such as Māori or Italian you can start from what people say. You can ask people 'does this work?' or 'How do I say this in your language?' That option does not exist in Gamilaraay. We can look at the historical GY materials we have, but often they do not give an answer, so for Gamilaraay to become fully functional other ways will need to be found to answer those questions.

## Word order

 **Audio:** GGU 3.2.mp3 is available in the electronic edition

The word order in Gamilaraay, and in Aboriginal languages in general, is very variable (see *Dictionary*, p. 322; Giacon, 2017, p. 347 and elsewhere). In many instances what is to be emphasised, or what is new information, goes first. Below are two translations of 'Pick up the boomerang!', the first emphasising the object, the second emphasising the action:

*Barran dhiyamala!*
*Dhiyamala barran!*

The most common word order in simpler sentences is verb last. Other rules such as 'question words first, pronouns second' are covered later in this course. There are also more complex patterns in sentences not discussed here (see Giacon, 2017, p. 350).

### =bala

You can look at the examples that include *=bala* first, or you might like to read this explanation first.

Gamilaraay uses lots of suffixes.

(It will be simpler in the long run if you can get used to some technical words about language, like 'suffix', but if that puts you off pass over this section, for now at least.)

**Suffix:** A suffix is a bit attached to the end of a word. The bit<u>s</u> underline<u>d</u> are suffix<u>es</u>.

---

| walk<u>ed</u> | runn<u>ing</u> | happ<u>iness</u> | inspect<u>ion</u> | |

=*bala* is a special type of suffix that attaches to the first word in a phrase (mostly). This sort of suffix is called a clitic. The = sign is used to signal a clitic. Suffixes that are not clitics have a dash '-' at the start. For more about clitics look up Wikipedia, linguistic books, or www.sil.org/linguistics/GlossaryOfLinguisticTerms/. These articles are quite technical.

A simple description, sufficient for now, is that =*bala* is used when the focus of attention changes, when there is a change in what is being talked about. The next sentences show an English example, then 'yes' and 'no' answers to questions, with =*bala* used when the answer is a negative.

'Is that ant?' 'No, it=*bala* is a cat.' or 'No=*bala*, it is a cat.'

(Both patterns are found and, so far, we don't know the difference in meaning.)

*Giidjaa nhama?*
ant that?
Is that an ant?

*Yawu, giidjaa nhama.*
yes, ant that
Yes, that is an ant.

*Gamil, budjigarr=bala=nha.* (See Lesson 4 for =*nha*)
no, cat=bala=it.
No, it's a cat.

*Gamil=bala, budjigarr nhama.*
no=bala, cat it.
No, it's a cat.

*Yaama nhama nguu?*
question book that
Is that a book?

*Yawu, nguu nhama.*
yes, book that
Yes, that is a book.

*Yaama nhama nguu?*
question book that
Is that a book?

*Gamil, baadhal=bala nhama.*
no, bottle-but that
No, that is a bottle.

*Gamil=bala, baadhal nhama.*
no, bottle-but that
No, that is a bottle.

*Biiba nhama?*
paper that
Is that paper?

*Yawu, biiba nhama.*
yes, paper that
Yes, that is paper.

*Biiba nhama?*
paper that
Is that paper?

*Gamil=bala, girrinil nhama.*
no, door that
No, that is the door.

*Gamil, girrinil=bala nhama.*
no, door that
No, that is the door.

Some traditional examples have =*bala* twice:

*Gamil=bala, girrinil=bala nhama.*
no, door that
No, that is the door.

The = has been used to help you see the separate parts of the word. Generally, it will be left out (*girrinilbala* instead of *girrinil=bala*).

=*bala* is also used in other contrast situations, where it is quite common on *nhalay*.

The following examples are based on ones in the Yuwaalaraay tapes of Arthur Dodd and Fred Reece (see Appendix 1), so use new vocabulary.

WIIDHAA

*Ngaarrima burrul, nhalaybala gaay.*
that(distant) big, this=bala small
That one is bigger than this one.

*Nhama=bala nginu bilaarr, nhalay=bala ngay.*
that=bala your spear, this=bala mine
That is your spear and this is mine.

*Nhalay=bala ngay dhinggaa, ngaarrima=bala nginu dhinggaa.*
this=bala my meat, that(distant)=bala your meat
This is my meat and that is yours.

*Gilaa* (Galah) and *Wuulaa* (Frilled Lizard) had a boomerang-throwing contest in which *Gilaa* was hit on the head by a boomerang, the blood then flowing down his/her chest. After talking about *Wuulaa* becoming covered in prickles, the story continues:

*Nhalay=bala=nga Gilaa, guway-baraay=bala biri yanaylanha.*
This=bala=then Galah, blood-with=bala chest walks/is. (has a bloody chest)
And so the Galah now has a bloody, a red, chest.

*=bala* is also relatively common on *Minya*. Below an adapted section from tape 3219B. Here *=bala* is used because people are comparing their 'meat'. ('Meat' here is used of a person's totem. In GY it can also be used for other social divisions, which are called a person's 'skin' in much of Australia.)

A: *Dhulii=bala ngaya dhinggaa.*
   Sand.goanna=bala I meat
   My meat is Sand Goanna.
   *Minya=bala nginda?*
   What=bala you.
   What is yours?
B: *Bigibila=bala ngaya. Bigibila mari.*
   Porcupine=bala I. Porcupine murri.
   I am a porcupine blackfellow.

In tape 3994A *=bala* is used in circumstances where any contrast is not obvious.

*Minya=bala nginda guwaay?*
What=bala you said?
What did you say?

## Commands

 **Audio:** GGU 3.3.mp3 is available in the electronic edition

In previous lessons you learnt the commands:

| | |
|---|---|
| *ngamila!* | look! |
| *winangala!* | listen! |
| *garay guwaala!* | speak! |
| *bawila!* | sing! |
| *yulunga!* | dance! |
| *dhiyamala!* | pick up! |
| *wiimala!* | put down! |

Below are some longer sentences including command words, aka imperatives.

*Dhiyamala barran! Wiimala barran!*
Pick up the boomerang. Put down the boomerang.

*Barran dhiyamala. Wiimala barran.*
Pick up the boomerang. Put down the boomerang.

Remember an important rule about word order. If there is a more important bit of information, it generally comes first. For example, if there are a number of objects on the table (*barran* 'boomerang', *biiba* 'paper' and *wiyayl* 'pen'), you can emphasise it is the pen you want picked up by putting *wiyayl* first.

*Wiyayl dhiyamala.*
Pick up the pen.

If the person is holding a pen, then the only thing they can put down is the pen, so the main information in 'Put down the pen' is 'put down', so that will come first.

*Wiimala wiyayl.*
Put the pen down.

WIIDHAA

## Negative commands: Don't!

You can make a negative command by putting *garriya* as the first word.

> The earliest version of these lessons used *gamil* for this, to simplify things. While *gamil* is rarely found in negative commands, *garriya* is much more common.

*Garriya dhiyamala barran!*
*Garriya barran dhiyamala!*
Don't pick up the boomerang.

*Garriya dhiyamala barran!* with *dhiyamala* first after the *garriya*, emphasises that you don't want the other person to do the action, to pick up (but maybe they can do something else).

*Garriya barran dhiyamala!* with *barran* first after the *garriya* emphasises that you don't want the other person to pick up the boomerang (but maybe they can pick up something else).

 **Audio:** GGU 3.4.mp3 is available in the electronic edition

| | |
|---|---|
| *Winangala, garriya=bala garay guwaala.* | Listen, don't talk. |
| *Winangala, garriyabala bawila.* | Listen, don't sing. |
| *Bawila, garriya=bala garay guwaala.* | Sing, don't talk. |
| *Biibabiiba ngamila, garriyabala bawila.* | Look at the book, don't sing. |

# Practice

 **Audio:** GGU 3.5.mp3 is available in the electronic edition

## =bala

In pairs, greet one another, then point to an object and ask a question: e.g. point to your eye and say:

| | | |
|---|---|---|
| A: | *Yaama Billy.* | Hi Billy. |
| M: | *Gamil=bala, Mary.* | No, it's Mary. |

| | | |
|---|---|---|
| A: | *Madja Mary.* | Apologies Mary. |
| A: | *Bina?* | Is this an ear? |
| M: | *Gamil, Mil=bala.* | No, it's an eye. |
| A: | *aa, Mil nhama. Yaluu Mary.* | Oh, it's an eye. See you Mary. |
| M: | *Baayandhu Alan.* | See you Alan. |

Or tell a person to do something, they do the wrong thing, and you correct them.

| | | |
|---|---|---|
| X: | *Y, barran dhiyamala.* | Y, pick up the boomerang. Y picks up the pen. |
| X: | *Gamil wiyayl, barranbala.* | Not the pen, the boomerang. |
| X: | *Gaba.* | Good. |

It is good if you can come up with other ways of practising. It is good to check with the teacher since when you try something new you may not be aware of the GY rules that apply to that situation.

## Commands

 **Audio:** GGU 3.6.mp3 is available in the electronic edition

Move around the room, greet people and tell them what to do. (The greetings are not included in the following text.)

| | | |
|---|---|---|
| Abdul: | *Kim, wiyayl dhiyamala.* | Kim, pick up the pen. (Kim does it) |
| Abdul: | *Gaba, nguu dhiyamala.* | Good, pick up the book. (Kim looks at it) |
| Abdul: | *Garriya ngamila nguu, dhiyamala=bala=nha.* | Don't look at the book, pick it up. (Kim picks up book) |
| Kim: | *Abdul, Mary winangala.* | Listen to Mary. (Abdul does) |
| Kim: | *Gaba Abdul. Gamilaraay guwaala.* | Good Abdul, speak Gamilaraay. (Abdul sings) |
| Kim: | *Gamil Abdul. Garriyabala bawila, Gamilaraay guwaala.* | No Abdul. Don't sing, talk Gamilaraay. |

(Notice the different uses of *gamil* and *garriya* in the last line.)

WIIDHAA

One person at a time does an action, the rest of the class tells them to stop it.

| Class: | *Abdul, garriya bawila.* | Abdul, don't sing. |

## *Winangala, garay guwaala, yawala.*
## Listen, say and read.

### Answers with 'no'

 **Audio:** GGU 3.7.mp3 is available in the electronic edition

The different possible answers take a while to get used to, so here are more examples, and there are more in the extra text for this lesson.

| Q. *Yaama nhama giidjaa?* | Is that an ant? |

Here are four different answers:

| A. *Gamilbala.* | No. |
| A. *Gamil nhama giidjaa.* | That is not an ant. |
| A. *Gamil, gamil nhama giidjaa.* | No, that is not an ant. |
| A. *Gamil, yarralbala=nha.* | No, that is a coin. |

| Q. *Yaama nhama dhaadhaa?* | Is that grandfather? |

Here are seven different answers:

| A1. *Yawu.* | Yes. |
| A2. *Dhaadhaa nhama.* | That's grandfather. |
| A3. *Yawu, dhaadhaa nhama.* | Yes, that's grandfather. |
| A4. *Gamil.* | No. |
| A5. *Gamilbala nhama dhaadhaa.* | That is not grandfather. |
| A6. *Gamilbala, gamil=nha dhaadhaa.* | No, that is not grandfather. |
| A7. *Gamil, badhiibala nhama.* | No, it's grandmother. |

(Note: Previous versions often had *nhama* as the third word in the sentence or clause. This does not seem to happen in the limited number of such sentences in the sources.)

Here are commands with Lesson 3 words.

 **Audio:** GGU 3.8.mp3 is available in the electronic edition

| | |
|---|---|
| *Dhiyamala yarral!* | Pick up the coin/stone! |
| *Yarral dhiyamala!* | Pick up the coin/stone! |
| *Badjigal dhiyamala!* | Pick up the bike. |
| *Yarral wiimala!* | Put down the coin/stone! |
| *Wiimala yarral!* | Put down the coin/stone! |
| *Badjigal wiimala!* | Put down the bike. |
| *Giidjaa ngamila!* | Look at the ant. |
| *Ngamila bandaarr!* | Look at the kangaroo. |
| *Girrinil winangala!* | Listen to the door. |

Next, some negative commands:

 **Audio:** GGU 3.9.mp3 is available in the electronic edition

| | |
|---|---|
| *Garriya dhiyamala yarral!* | Don't pick up the coin/stone! |
| *Garriya yarral dhiyamala!* | Don't pick up the coin/stone! |
| *Garriya badjigal dhiyamala!* | Don't pick up the bike. |
| *Garriya yarral wiimala!* | Don't put the coin/stone down! |
| *Garriya wiimala yarral!* | Don't put down the coin/stone! |
| *Garriya badjigal wiimala!* | Don't put down the bike. |
| *Garriya giidjaa ngamila!* | Don't look at the ant. |
| *Garriya ngamila bandaarr!* | Don't look at the kangaroo. |
| *Garriya girrinil winangala!* | Don't listen to the door. |

Some more sentences:

 **Audio:** GGU 3.10.mp3 is available in the electronic edition

| | |
|---|---|
| *?Biiba nhama?* | Is that paper? |
| *Yawu, biiba nhama.* | Yes, that is paper. |
| *?Biiba nhama?* | Is that paper? |
| *Gamil, nhalaybala baadhal.* | No, this is a bottle. |
| *Yaama nhama gali?* | Is that water? |
| *Yawu, gali nhama.* | Yes, that is water. |

WIIDHAA

| | |
|---|---|
| *Yaama nhama gali?* | Is that water? |
| *Gamil, burumabala nhama.* | No, that is a dog. |
| | |
| *Winangala, biibabiiba nhama.* | Listen, that is a book. |
| | |
| *Dhigaraa nhama?* | Is that a bird? |
| *Yawu, dhigaraa nhama.* | Yes, that is a bird. |
| *Dhigaraa nhama?* | Is that a bird? |
| *Gamil, nguubala nhama.* | No, that is a book. |
| *Minyabala nhamalay?* | What is that? |
| *Wilbaarr nhama ngay.* | That is my car. |

 **Audio:** GGU 3.11.mp3 is available in the electronic edition

| | |
|---|---|
| *Badjigal dhiyamala!* | |
| *Dhiyamala badjigal!* | Pick up the bike! |
| *Giidjaa dhiyamala!* | |
| *Dhiyamala giidjaa!* | Pick up the ant! |
| *Bandaarr dhiyamala!* | |
| *Dhiyamala bandaarr!* | Pick up the kangaroo! |
| *Barran dhiyamala!* | |
| *Dhiyamala barran!* | Pick up the boomerang! |
| *Girrinil dhiyamala!* | |
| *Dhiyamala girrinil!* | Pick up the door! |
| *Yarral dhiyamala!* | |
| *Dhiyamala yarral!* | Pick up the stones/coins! |
| *Badjigal wiimala!* | |
| *Wiimala badjigal!* | Put the bike down! |
| *Giidjaa wiimala!* | |
| *Wiimala giidjaa!* | Put the ant down! |
| *Bandaarr wiimala!* | |
| *Wiimala bandaarr!* | Put the kangaroo down! |
| *Barran wiimala!* | |
| *Wiimala barran!* | Put the boomerang down! |
| *Girrinil wiimala!* | |
| *Wiimala girrinil!* | Put the door down! |
| *Yarral wiimala!* | |
| *Wiimala yarral!* | Put the stones/coins down! |

LESSON 3. CONTRAST / TAKE IT!

🔊 **Audio:** GGU 3.12.mp3 is available in the electronic edition

*Garriya barran dhiyamala!*
*Garriya dhiyamala barran!*
Don't pick up the boomerang!

*Garriya yarral dhiyamala!*
*Garriya dhiyamala yarral!*
Don't pick up the money/coins!

*Garriya badjigal wiimala!*
*Garriya wiimala badjigal!*
Don't put the bike down!

*Garriya yarral wiimala!*
*Garriya wiimala yarral!*
Don't put the money/coins down!

🔊 **Audio:** GGU 3.13.mp3 is available in the electronic edition

*Garriya barran dhiyamala!*
*Dhiyamalabala giidjaa!*
Don't pick up the boomerang!
Pick up the ant!

*Garriya yarral dhiyamala!*
*Barranbala dhiyamala!*
Don't pick up the money/coins!
Pick up the boomerang!

*Garriya wiyayl dhiyamala!*
*Dhiyamalabala biiba!*
Don't pick up the pen!
Pick up the paper!

*Garriya dhuru dhiyamala!*
*Burumabala dhiyamala!*
Don't pick up the snake!
Pick up the dog!

43

# LESSON 4
# Who are you? Are you good?

In this lesson, we introduce two more types of words, and introductory descriptions of them. **Pronouns** in English are words like 'I, my, me, you, they, her, it'. **Question pronouns (interrogative pronouns)** like *ngaandi* 'who?' are a subsection of pronouns. English **adjectives** include 'good, bad, tired, hungry, happy, red, old, little' and so on. They are generally describing words associated with people or objects. Gamilaraay (and Yuwaalaraay) has pronouns and adjectives, and they behave like English pronouns and adjectives in some ways, but not in others.

## Vocabulary

 **Audio:** GGU 4.1.mp3 is available in the electronic edition

| *Garay* | Words |
|---|---|
| *ngaandi?* * | who? |
| | |
| *ngaya* | I |
| *nginda* * | you (1 person) |
| =*nha, Ø, nhama,* + (Nominative)* | she/he*, it |
| *nguru*+ (Ergative) | s/he*, it (for later lessons) |
| | |
| *gagil* * | bad |
| *yinggil* | tired, lazy |
| *yuulngin* | hungry |
| *burrul* * | big |
| *gaay* | small |
| *dhinggaa* | meat |
| *garrangay* | duck |
| *man.ga* | table |

| *Garay* | **Words** |
|---|---|
| *man.garr* | bag |
| *giirr*\* | truly (personal evidence) |
| *miyay* | girl |
| *birray* | boy |

\**Ngaandi* is a question word – but it is not used in all circumstances where English uses 'who'. Like other question words/interrogatives, it is usually the first word in the sentence. (See the *Dictionary*, pp. 322ff for more information about question words. There are pronoun charts in the dictionary and picture dictionary, but some information on third person singular and dual pronouns has been modified.)

\**Nginda* 'you' refers to one person only, and 'doing the action' – hitting, etc. – not having the action 'done.to' them. The English 'you' translates into many Gamilaraay words.

\*She/he/it – see grammar section below.

\*Also, use *gagil* for 'no good/sick' 'wrong'. In fact, many of the GY adjectives have multiple English translations: *gaba* 'good', 'correct', 'right', 'sweet', etc.

\*There is also a suffix, *-bidi*, which means 'big'.

\**Giirr* 'truly' is most commonly used to start a sentence, when you want to make the point that this is true, a fact, and often indicates that you have personal evidence for what is being stated or have control over it. That is, it is not something you have been told. *Giirr* is most commonly found in sentences that involve 'I' and 'past tense': e.g. 'I saw the car'. It is found in other circumstances, for instance where the speaker has witnessed something or asserts that they will do it: e.g. 'I will wash the dishes'.

## Grammar

 **Audio:** GGU 4.2.mp3 is available in the electronic edition

### Pronouns: *Ngaya, nginda, =nha/nhama*

Remember, pronouns are mostly in second position, and suffixed pronouns on the first word.

*John ngaya. Mary nginda, Kim nhama.*
I am John, you(1) are Mary, and that is Kim.

The question pronoun *ngaandi*, like other question words, is first:

*Ngaandi ngaya? Ngaandi nginda? Ngaandi nhamalay?*
Who am I? Who are you(1)? Who is that (I am pointing out)?

It may take practise to get the *ng* sound at the start of a word. It is particularly easy to say *nyinda* instead of *nginda*.

### Nouns and adjectives together

This section first covers translation of **phrases** like 'good girl', 'hungry duck', 'big bag', where in English there is an adjective followed by a noun. Then it looks at sentences like: 'The duck is hungry'.

In English phrases, adjectives precede the noun ('big tree', not 'tree big'), and in English you can pile up lots of adjectives before the noun ('three big old green trees'). There are many languages, such as Māori, where adjectives **follow** the noun, and others such as Italian where some adjectives follow the noun and others precede it, or the position of the adjective affects its meaning. In many Aboriginal languages there is some variation, but in Aboriginal languages adjectives more often **follow** the noun.

Some early sources say that in GY adjectives follow the noun, but later sources have adjectives both before and after nouns. It is unclear what these languages did pre-invasion. Recent sources may well have been influenced by English.

The pattern we will follow here is:

GY adjectives follow the noun (**unless** you really want to stress the adjective).

| | |
|---|---|
| *miyay gaba* | good girl |
| *garrangay yuulngin* | hungry duck |
| *man.garr burrul* | big bag |
| *birray yinggil* | tired boy |
| *yinggil birray* | **tired** boy |

There are a number of patterns in sentences and questions that address the qualities of an object ('It is a good phone?' 'Is the phone good?'). Some examples are given below, but we do not have a full understanding of the differences in meaning between these slightly different options. This happens relatively frequently when there are not fluent speakers to learn from.

The most common pattern for a statement like 'the meat is good' is:

Adjective (demonstrative) noun.

 **Audio:** GGU 4.3.mp3 is available in the electronic edition

*Gaba nhama dhinggaa. Gaba nhalay dhinggaa.*
The/that meat good. This meat is good.

*Gagil nhama dhinggaa.*
That meat is no good.

*Burrul nhamalay girrinil.*
That's a big door (over there).

Similar patterns are found in questions, but note that when a demonstrative is used it comes second in the phrase.

*?Gaba dhinggaa?*
Is the meat good? It is good meat?

*Yaama gaba dhinggaa?*
Is the meat good?

*?Gaba nhama dhinggaa?*
Is that meat good?

*Yaama nhama gaba, dhinggaa?*
Is that meat good?

*Yaama gaba, nhama dhinggaa?*
Is that meat good?

In GY the adjective is more commonly next to the noun; it can be separated from it, often to allow a pronoun or demonstrative to be in second position.

🔊 **Audio:** GGU 4.4.mp3 is available in the electronic edition

*Man.garr ngaya burrul dhiyamay.*
I picked up the big bag.

*Man.garr dhiyamala burrul.*
Bag pick.up big.
Pick up the big bag.

However, it would be common for a sentence like that to have a pause:

*Man.garr dhiyamala, burrul.*

So it could also be translated as:

Pick up the bag, the big one.

The GY sources rarely have two adjectives together. That may be traditional, but other Aboriginal languages do have a sequence of adjectives. In Pitjantjatjara, the order is the reverse of English, as in 'cars red big three'.

## She/he/it; Who?

For now use *=nha*, Ø or *nhama* for 'she/he/it'. In Lesson 11 you will learn when to also use *nguru* 'she/he/it' in other situations. The choice of *=nha*, Ø or *nhama* for 'she/he/it' seems to depend on how much 'she/he/it' is being emphasised. The most common translations of 'she/he/it' is *=nha*. It can also be written *=NHa*, to show that the first part, the consonant, can change. Sounds are influenced by what comes before and after them, so the suffix is easily said *=nya* after *y* or *i*, and *=na* after word final *n*, *l* and *rr*. In fact, the pronunciation of *nhama* can change in the same way.

If it is obvious who is being talked about, then 'she/he/it' can be 'Ø', particularly with verbs. Using *nhama* seems to indicate more attention, more emphasis on the person spoken about.

> There has been, and continues to be, revised analysis of this area of GY. So, older pronoun charts will have different information about singular and dual third person pronouns.

| | |
|---|---|
| *Ngamila!* | Look! Look at him! |
| *Winangala!* | Listen. Listen to her! |
| *Dhiyamala!* | Pick it up! |

'She/he/it' can, in fact, be translated by a range of demonstratives. While *nhama* is the most common, other demonstratives including *nhalay* and *nhamalay* are found, but not frequently.

For the present, use *ngaandi* for 'Who?' Later lessons expand on this.

*Ngaandi nginda?*
Who are you? (one person)

*Ngaandi ngaya?*
Who am I?

*Ngaandi=nha* is not found, probably because when the question is being asked you are drawing considerable attention to the person being asked about, and so a more emphatic demonstrative such as *nhama* or *nhalay* is used.

*Ngaandi nhama?*
Who is she/he?

(When referring to someone already the focus of attention, e.g. if both hear a voice, or are looking at someone.)

*Ngaandi nhalay?*
Who is she/he?

(When the questioner is drawing the hearer's attention to someone close.)

*Ngaandi nhamalay?*
Who is she/he?

(When the questioner is drawing the hearer's attention to someone not close.)

## Position of pronouns

(This language rule has been modified, after re-examining the sources.)

Pronouns predominantly occur in second place in the clause or sentence. (This pattern applies to sentences with no verb, and, when there is a verb, to pronouns about who is doing the action.)

| | |
|---|---|
| *Gaba ngaya.* | I'm good. |
| *Yinggil nginda?* | Are you tired? |
| *Yawu, yinggil ngaya.* | Yep, I'm tired. |

(In the last example the second part can be considered a separate sentence.)

 **Audio:** GGU 4.5.mp3 is available in the electronic edition

*Ngaandi nginda?*
Who are you?

*Mary ngaya.*
I am Mary.

*Ngaandi nhama?*
Who is she/he?

*Kath.* Or *Kath nhama.*
She is Kath.

*Ngaandi ngaya?*
Who am I?

*Kim nginda.*
You are Kim.

*Ngaandi nhama?*
Who is that?

*Bubaa nhama.*
That is dad.

WIIDHAA

Sentences – pronoun and adjective:

 **Audio:** GGU 4.6.mp3 is available in the electronic edition

*Gagil ngaya.*
I am bad/no good.

*Yinggil nginda.*
You are tired. (remember: 'you – 1 person')

*Yuulngin=na,*
*yuulngin nhama.*
She/he is hungry.

## Questions

 **Audio:** GGU 4.7.mp3 is available in the electronic edition

Remember, you can ask yes/no questions using the tone of voice, or using *yaama*. All the following sentences are questions.

*Gagil ngaya?*
I am bad/no good?

*Yaama ngaya gagil?*
Am I bad/no good?

*Yinggil nginda?*
You tired? (remember: 'you – 1 person')

*Yaama nginda yinggil?*
Are you tired? (remember: 'you – 1 person')

*Yaama=nda yinggil?*
Are you tired? (remember: 'you – 1 person')

*Yuulngin nhama?*
She/he hungry?

*Yaama=nha yuulngin?*
Is she/he hungry?

## LESSON 4. WHO ARE YOU? ARE YOU GOOD?

*Gaba nhama miyay?*
That girl is good?

*Yaama gaba, nhama miyay?*
Is that girl good?

*Yuulngin nhama garrangay?*
That duck is hungry?

*Yaama nhama yuulngin, garrangay?*
Is that duck hungry?

*Burrul nhalay man.garr?*
This bag is big?

*Yaama burrul nhalay man.garr?*
Is this bag big?

*Yinggil nhalay birray?*
This boy is tired?

*Yaama yinggil, birray nhalay?*
Is this boy tired?

## Negatives – Is not

 **Audio:** GGU 4.8.mp3 is available in the electronic edition

To make a negative statement put ***gamil*** before the 'positive statement'.

*Gaba ngaya.*
I am well/good.

*Gamil ngaya gaba.*
I am not well/good.

## Word order

I assume you can change the order of the words after g*amil* to change the meaning.

*Gamil ngaya gaba* (not I good) is the normal order for 'I am not good'.

*Gamil gaba ngaya* is the unusual order, and puts the emphasis on 'not **good**?'

There are other ways of arranging this that will give different shades of meaning, but more research needs to be done on how Gamilaraay Yuwaalaraay and other Aboriginal languages convey these subtle differences.

*Gagil ngaya.*
I am bad.

*Gamil ngaya gagil.*
I am not bad.

*Yinggil nginda.*
You are tired. (remember: 'you – 1 person')

*Gamil nginda yinggil.*
You are not tired. (remember: 'you – 1 person')

*Yuulngin nhama. Yuulngin=na.*
She/he is hungry.

*Gamil nhama yuulngin. Gamil=na yuulngin.*
She/he is not hungry.

*Yuulngin nhama birray.*
That boy is hungry.

*Gamil nhama yuulngin, birray.*
That boy is not hungry.

## Practice

 **Audio:** GGU 4.9.mp3 is available in the electronic edition

Class sits in circle, each person introduces themselves.

*Kim ngaya, Bill ngaya, Sue ngaya …*

LESSON 4. WHO ARE YOU? ARE YOU GOOD?

Repeat, but after a person introduces themselves, the others answer:

| Kim: | *Kim ngaya.* |
| Ganugu: | *Yawu, Kim nginda.* |
| All: | Yes, you are Kim. |

Repeat, but each person turns to the one next to them and says:

*Kim nhama.*

In pairs:

A: *Yaama, Anne ngaya. Ngaandi nginda?*
B: *Yaama Anne, Beth ngaya.*

In threes: A talks to B, then B replies.

A: *Anne ngaya, Beth nginda, Charlotte nhama.*
B: *Yawu, Anne nginda, Charlotte nhama, Beth ngaya.*

Repeat, C talking to A, and so on.

Repeat using *Ngaandi.*

A: *Yaama Beth, ngaandi nhamalay?* (pointing to C).

🔊 **Audio:** GGU 4.10.mp3 is available in the electronic edition

Sit in a circle, each person does an action – rubs stomach for *yuulngin* 'hungry', looks angry for *gagil*, stands tall for *burrul* and so on.

1. All point to one person and say the appropriate adjective: *gaba* (thumbs up), etc. – go around the circle.

2. Use people's names, and go around the circle, describing each person.

*Gaba Garry. Gagil Graham. Yuulngin Yolanda. Burrul Belinda.*
Garry is good. And so on.

3. Comment on the quality of things.

| | |
|---|---|
| *Burrul nhalay man.ga.* | This table is big. |
| *Baadhal gaay.* | A small bottle. |
| *Gali gaba.* | Good water. etc. |

*Burrul nhalay, gaaybala nhamalay.*
This is big and that is small/this is bigger than that.

4. Questions.

Person A acts one of the adjectives, and asks:

| | | | |
|---|---|---|---|
| A: | *Gaba ngaya?* | | |
| B: | *Yawu, gaba nginda.* | or | *Gamilbala, yinggil nginda.* |
|    | Yes you are good. |    | No, you are tired. |

Use statements such as those in Activity 3 above to make intonation or *Yaama* questions.

| | |
|---|---|
| *?Burrul nhalay man.ga?* | This table is big? |
| *Yaama burrul, nhalay man.ga?* | Is this table big? |

5. *Ngaandi* questions.

| | | |
|---|---|---|
| *Ngaandi yinggil? Nginda?* | | Who's tired? You? |
| *Yawu, yinggil ngaya.* | or | *Gamil, gababala ngaya.* |

By now you will also have your own practice strategies. Important elements of practice are: repetition, working from simple to more complex language, using material from previous lessons, having fun, humour and developing good intonation patterns across groups of words.

## Conversations

 **Audio:** GGU 4.11.mp3 is available in the electronic edition

| | |
|---|---|
| Tim: | *Tammy, yaama nginda yinggil?* |
|      | Tammy, are you tired? |
| Tammy: | *Gamil Tim, yuulnginbala ngaya. Nginda?* |
|        | No Tim, (but) I am hungry. You? |

LESSON 4. WHO ARE YOU? ARE YOU GOOD?

| Tim: | *Giirr yuulngin ngaya.* |
| | *Gamilbala ngaya yinggil.* |
| | I am hungry, I'm not tired. |

| Betty: | *Yaama Bill. Ngaandi nhama?* |
| | Hi Bill, who is that? |
| Bill: | *Yaama Betty. Harry=nha.* |
| | Hi Betty, that is Harry. |
| Betty: | *Gaba=nha?* |
| | (Is) he good? |
| Bill: | *Yawu, gaba nhama.* |
| | Yes, he is good. |

*Yinggil nhama miyay.*
That girl is tired.

*Gamil yinggil nhama miyay.*
That girl is not tired.

*Gagil nhama man.ga.*
That table is no good.

*Gamil gagil nhama man.ga.*
That table is not bad.

*Yuulngin nhama garrangay.*
That duck is hungry.

*Gamil nhama yuulngin garrangay.*
That duck is not hungry.

## Pronunciation

For this lesson focus on the following:

| *ng* | as in singer, especially when it is the first sound in a word; *ngaya, nginda, yuulngin, garrangay* |
| *ngg* | as in 'finger'; *dhinggaa, yinggil* |
| *n.g* | as in 'sun.glasses'; *man.ga, man.garr*. Be careful to keep the stress on the first syllable in *man.garr*, and in other *arr* final words, such as *yinarr* 'woman'. |

## Extension

This includes some topics that will be covered later in *Garay Guwaala 1* or later materials.

*Ngaandi* is Nominative and Accusative case. Nominative case is used for questions such as *Ngaandi nhama?* 'Who is that?' and for the subject of intransitive verbs: e.g. *Ngaandi yanay?* 'Who will go?'. In GY it is also found asking a person's name. 'What is your name?' is said *Ngaandi nginda gayrr?*, literally 'who you name'. In Pitjantjatjara, it is also used to ask about any proper name – names that in English start with a capital letter. *Ngaandi nhama gundhilgaa?* 'What (is the name of) that town?' We have not found examples of GY asking this sort of question, and even if we did the GY of the informants could well have been influenced by English. English influence is seen in current Pitjantjatjara, with some people now using 'your' when asking about a name, not the traditional 'you'.

## *Winangala, garay guwaala, yawala.*
## Listen, say and read.

 **Audio:** GGU 4.12.mp3 is available in the electronic edition

*Gaba nhama miyay.*
That girl is good.
Those girls are good.

*Yuulngin nhama garrangay.*
That duck is hungry.
Those ducks are hungry.

*Burrul nhalay man.garr.*
This bag is big.
These bags are big.

*Yinggil nhalay birray.*
This boy is tired.
These boys are tired.

*Miyay nhama gaba.*
That is a good girl.
Those are good girls.

*Garrangay nhama yuulngin.*
That is a hungry duck.
Those are hungry ducks.

*Man.garr nhalay burrul.*
This is a big bag.
These bags are big.

*Birray nhama yinggil.*
That is a tired boy.
Those are tired boys.

> **Audio:** GGU 4.13.mp3 is available in the electronic edition

*Yinggil nhama miyay.*
That girl is tired.

*Gamil yinggil, miyay nhama.*
That girl is not tired.

*Gagil nhama man.ga.*
That table is no good.

*Gamil nhalay gagil, man.ga.*
That table is not bad.

*Yuulngin nhamalay garrangay.*
That duck is hungry.

*Gamil nhama yuulngin garrangay.*
That duck is not hungry.

*Yaama yuulngin bubaa?*
Is dad hungry?

*Yawu, giirr yuulngin.*
Yep, he sure is hungry.

*Yinggil gunii?*
(Is) mum tired?

*Gamil yinggil, gababala nhama.*
She is not tired, she is good.

WIIDHAA

*Yaama gaba dhaadhaa?*
Is grandpop well?

*Giirr gaba dhaadhaa,*
Grandpop is really well,

*badhiibala yinggil.*
but grandma is tired.

*Barry nhama?*
Is that Barry?

*Yawu, Barry nhama.*
Yep, that is Barry.

*Mary nhama?*
Is that Mary?

*Gamil Mary nhama, Suebala.*
That is not Mary, it is Sue.

🔊 **Audio:** GGU 4.14.mp3 is available in the electronic edition

| | |
|---|---|
| Don: | *Yaama Debbie, gaba nginda?* |
| | Hi Debbie, are you okay? |
| Debbie: | *Gamilbala. Yinggil ngaya, Don.* |
| | No, I'm tired Don. |
| Don: | *Ngarragaa. Yaamanda yuulngin, Debbie.* |
| | You poor thing. Are you hungry, Debbie? |
| Debbie: | *Gamil ngaya yuulngin, yinggilbala.* |
| | I'm not hungry, I'm tired. |
| | *Garriya garay guwaala. Gaabu.* |
| | Don't talk! Shush. |
| Don: | *Ngaayaybaay. Yaluu baawaa.* |
| | Okay, bye sister. |
| Debbie: | *Yaluu dhagaan.* |
| | Bye brother. |

LESSON 4. WHO ARE YOU? ARE YOU GOOD?

> **Audio:** GGU 4.15.mp3 is available in the electronic edition

| | |
|---|---|
| Mum: | *Yaama Mary.* |
| | Hi Mary. |
| Mary: | *Yaama gunii, gaba nginda?* |
| | Hi mum, you good? |
| Mum: | *Giirr ngaya gaba.* |
| | I'm really good. |
| | *Ngamila, ngaandi nhama?* |
| | Look, who's that? |
| Mary: | *Kim nhama. Gaba nhama.* |
| | That is Kim – a good guy. |
| Mum: | *Yaama miyay, nhama?* |
| | Is that (he/she) a girl. |
| Mary: | *Gamilbala gunii, birraybala nhama, Kim Jones.* |
| | No mum, that's a boy, Kim Jones. |
| Mum: | *Yaama gaba, birray nhama, Mary?* |
| | Is he a good bloke, Mary? |
| Mary: | *Yawu gunii, giirr nhama gaba.* |
| | Yes mum, he is really good. |
| Mum: | *Ngaayaybaay.* |
| | Okay. |
| Mary: | *Yaluu gunii.* |
| | See you mum. |
| Mum: | *Yaluu miyay.* |
| | See you daughter. |

# LESSON 5
# Verbs: *Y* class/ 'going to' (Allative) suffix

In this lesson, we look in some more detail at **verbs**. Verbs are 'doing' or 'being' words ('run, sleep, think, was, be, eat' are English verbs). In Gamilaraay Yuwaalaraay verbs fit into four groups or classes. This lesson is about *Y* class verbs, and we consider only one form of the verb – the simple command: e.g. Run! Walk! etc. We also learn about a Gamilaraay suffix, *-gu*, which has the meaning 'going to'. The technical term for this *-gu* is the **Allative suffix**.

## Vocabulary

 **Audio:** GGU 5.1.mp3 is available in the electronic edition

| *Garay* | Words |
|---|---|
| *yananga!\** | walk/go! |
| *banagaya!* | run! |
| *gubiya!* | swim! |
| *baraya!* | hop! |
| *barraya!\** | fly! |
| | |
| *dhayn\** | person |
| *Mari* | (Aboriginal) person |
| *giwiirr\** | man |
| *yinarr* | woman |
| *wanda* | white man |
| *wadjiin\** | white woman |
| *bubaa* | dad (father) |
| *gunii\** | mum (mother) |

| Garay | Words |
|---|---|
| *-gu\** | to (movement to) |
| *Minya ginyi?* | What happened? |

\**Yananga!* In previous editions, this verb was given as *yanaya*. However, a review of the sources shows that the command form of this verb is irregular – it does not follow the same pattern as other verbs.

\*The only information about the verb 'fly' is from written sources that generally do not distinguish *a*/*aa* and *r*/*rr*, so it is not clear if the traditional form is *baarraya*, *baaraya* or *barraya*, but the last is considered most likely. Yuwaalaraay 'fly!' is *baraya*.

\*The word *dhayn* has an interesting recent history. On the tapes, when a question is asked about a man or woman the informants distinguish between Aboriginal and non-Aboriginal. They are speaking Yuwaalaraay, and they use *dhayn* for 'Aboriginal man', *yinarr* for 'Aboriginal woman', *wanda* 'white man' and *wadjiin* 'white woman'. In the early stages of revival, it was decided that it would be good to have a general word for person, not based on race. Uncle Ted Fields pointed out that, before invasion, *dhayn* referred to all people, and it could be used again with that sense. *Dhayn* is now used with that meaning. In Yuwaalaraay it can mean 'Aboriginal person' or 'person', in Gamilaraay it just means 'person'.

\*It seems very likely that *giwiirr* meant something like 'man after a certain stage of initiation' and it is quite possible, from what we know of similar words in other languages, that *yinarr* was not the equivalent of English 'woman'. In Pitjantjatjara, *minyma* is 'woman who has had at least two children' (Eckert & Hudson, 1988, p. 105).

\*The word *wadjiin* is still sometimes used, but the current pronunciation is generally wadjən, influenced by English.

\*There is variation in the word for 'mum'. The older sources have *gunii*, but in some areas the pronunciation is Englishified to *guni*. This sort of change is common.

\*For more information about *-gu* (Allative suffix) see the *Dictionary*, pp. 264 and 270, and Giacon (2017). There is variation in the form of this suffix in some sources, but we will just use *-gu* in this course.

## Grammar: 'Command' verbs

The main use of the command form of a verb is to tell someone else to do something. Lesson 3 showed how to use *garriya* to **negate** commands.

 **Audio:** GGU 5.2.mp3 is available in the electronic edition

*Yananga!*
Go! Walk!

*Banagaya!*
Run!

*Garriya yananga!*
Don't go! Don't walk!

## -gu 'movement to'

*-gu* is added to nouns and adjectives to indicate 'movement.to'. Note: *-gu* is **not** added to pronouns and demonstratives.

The following sentences show the use of *-gu*. (These include a dash '-' to show the bits of the word. Later examples will not have the dash.)

| | |
|---|---|
| *Yananga!* | Walk! |
| *Yananga gunii-gu!* | Walk to mum! |
| *Girrinil-gu yananga!* | Walk to the door! |

The **word order** in these sentences can change, depending on what is being emphasised. This is particularly important in negative sentences.

> English often stresses the word being emphasised since it can't easily change the word order. Since Gamilaraay can signal emphasis by word order it does not need to stress individual words. In fact, it often groups a few words together, with the first word being loudest and having the highest pitch.

*Gunii-gu yananga!*
Walk to **mum**!

*Bubaa-gu yananga!*
Walk to **dad**!

WIIDHAA

*Garriya bubaagu banagaya!*
Don't run **to dad!**

*Garriya banagaya bubaagu!*
Don't **run** to dad!

 **Audio:** GGU 5.3.mp3 is available in the electronic edition

Remember (Lesson 3), *=bala* is suffixed to the first word of a phrase when there is a contrast. *=bala* follows *-gu*. Often it has no translation in the English. Study the following examples:

*Banagaya=bala! Garriya yananga!*
Run, don't walk.

*Garriya bubaa-gu yananga,*
*gunii-gu=bala banagaya!*
Don't go to dad, run to mum!

There are a number of ways of using *=bala*, and the difference in meaning is not currently understood. The following three sentences have the same English translation.

*Banagaya=bala!*
*Garriya yananga!*
Run, don't walk.

*Banagaya!*
*Garriya=bala yananga!*
Run, don't walk.

*Banagaya=bala!*
*Garriya=bala yananga!*
Run, don't walk.

**Social custom.** There are lots of ways of getting someone to do something. For example:

Take me fishing!
Will you take me fishing?
It's a nice day for fishing.

are all ways you might use to get someone to take you fishing. In this course, we do not give a lot of attention to that sort of social variation in language, we focus mainly on simpler grammar – what you can say in the language.

## Extension

Later you will learn more pronouns, such as *ngali* 'we(2)'. When commands/imperatives are used with *ngali* the are translated 'Let's'.

| | |
|---|---|
| *Yananga ngali!* | Let's go. |

## Pronunciation

For this lesson focus on the long vowel + *rr* at the end of a word. Listen and say: *bandaarr, giwiirr* and contrast those with *yinarr*. Use *Gayarragi, Winangali* to listen to traditional pronunciation of some of these words.

## Practice

 **Audio:** GGU 5.4.mp3 is available in the electronic edition

### Individually

Say a command and do the action: *Gubiya!* Swim.

### Group

One person says a command, others do the action.

All stand. One person says a command, others do the action. Anyone who does the wrong action, and/or the last person to do the right action sit down. Winner is the last standing.

### Pairs/group

One person says a command. The other does the wrong action.

| | | |
|---|---|---|
| A: | *B, banagaya.* | B flies. |
| A: | *B, Garriya barraya, banagaya=bala.* | B runs. |
| A: | *Gaba.* | |

Start simply, move to an object and say 'to X':

| | |
|---|---|
| *man.ga-gu* | 'to the table' |
| *Mary-gu.* | 'to Mary' |

WIIDHAA

**Individually, in pairs or as a group**

Give a command and do the action. If correct say *gaba*.

| | | |
|---|---|---|
| A: | *Man.gagu banagaya.* | Run to the table. |
| A: | (B complies) *Gaba* | or |
| A: | (B walks) *Banagayabala. Garriya yananga.* | |

Not that *garriya* is only used with verbs.

| | | |
|---|---|---|
| A: | *Man.gagu banagaya.* | Run to the table. |
| A: | (B complies) *Gaba* | or |
| A: | (B runs to bag) **Gamil** *man.garrgu, man.gagubala banagaya.* | |

This is a very good opportunity to use much of the vocabulary you have previously learnt, even if many of the sentences would not normally be used.

*Gaalagu baraya!*    Hop to the cup!

## *Winangala, garay guwaala, yawala.*
## Listen, say and read.

 **Audio:** GGU 5.5.mp3 is available in the electronic edition

*dhayn.gu*          to the person
*Dhayn.gu yananga!* Go to the person!

(Remember that *n.g* is two sounds, *ng* is one sound. Be careful to include the '.' before suffixes starting with '*g*' on words finishing with '*n*'.)

*marigu*
to the (Aboriginal) person

*marigu yananga*
go to the (Aboriginal) person

*giwiirrgu*
to the man

LESSON 5. VERBS: Y CLASS/ 'GOING TO' (ALLATIVE) SUFFIX

*Giwiirrgu yananga.*
Go to the man.

*yinarrgu*
to the woman

*Yinarrgu yananga.*
Go to the woman.

*wadjiin.gu*
to the white woman

*Wadjiin.gu yananga.*
Go to the white woman.

*wandagu*
to the white man

*Wandagu yananga.*
Go to the white man.

*bubaagu\**
to dad

*Bubaagu yananga.*
Go to dad.

*guniigu\**
to mum

*Guniigu yananga.*
Go to mum.

---

\*The curse of learning more. You do not need to apply this during this course, but you may be interested. Suffixes like *-gu* sometimes have a different form on some words, such as names. And when you say 'Dad' you are referring to a particular person, so it is like a name. It seems that the way you would say 'to mum/dad' is with the suffix *-ngunda*, not *-gu*. So, *Guniingunda, Bubaangunda*. There is a relatively small number of such examples in the GY sources, but the pattern is much clearer in some better-recorded Aboriginal languages.

**Audio:** GGU 5.6.mp3 is available in the electronic edition

*Buruma, banagaya galigu.*
Dog, run to the water.

*Dhigaraa, barraya galigu.*
Bird, fly to the water!

*Bandaarr, baraya galigu.*
Kangaroo, hop to the water!

*Gubiya Harry!*
Swim Harry.

*Harry, gubiya dhagaan.gu!*
Harry, swim to (your) brother.

*Gubiya Harry!*
Swim Harry.

*Harry, Garriya gubiya baawaagu!*
Harry, don't swim to (your) sister.

*Ngamila Billy, dhuru nhama. Banagaya bubaagu.*
(*nhama* is being used with a meaning like 'there'; *dhuru nhama* – 'snake there')
Look Billy, a snake. Run to dad.

 **Audio:** GGU 5.7.mp3 is available in the electronic edition

*Gunii, garriya gubiya.*
Mum, don't swim.

*Bandaarr, baraya bubaagu.*
Kangaroo, hop to dad.

*Garrangay, girrinilgu gubiya.*
Duck, swim to the door.

*Gamil guniigu, bubaagubala banagaya, Billy.*
Billy, don't run to dad, but to mum.

# LESSON 5. VERBS: Y CLASS/ 'GOING TO' (ALLATIVE) SUFFIX

🔊 **Audio:** GGU 5.8.mp3 is available in the electronic edition

| | |
|---|---|
| Cath: | *Kim, minya nhamalay?* |
| | Kim, what is that? (pointed to) |
| Kim: | *Girrinil nhama, Cath.* |
| | That's a door, Cath. |
| Cath: | *Kim, banagaya girrinilgu?* |
| | Kim, run to the door. |
| | 1. Kim runs to the door. |
| Cath: | *Gaba Kim.* |
| | 2. Kim runs to the table. |
| Cath: | *Gamil Kim, gamil man.gagu, girrinilgubala.* |
| | 3. Kim walks to the door. |
| Cath: | *Kim, garriya yananga, banagayabala.* |

# LESSON 6
# Verbs: *Y* class 'future' and 'past'

In this lesson, we look in some more detail at **Y class verbs**. In the last lesson, we saw the 'simple command forms' of the verbs. In this lesson, we consider the 'future' and 'past' forms.

## Vocabulary

 **Audio:** GGU 6.1.mp3 is available in the electronic edition

| *Garay* | Words |
|---|---|
| *ngarriya!* | sit! |
| *warraya!* | stand! |
| *dhuliya!* | bend/stoop! |
| *ginyi**  | happened |
| *dhalaa?** | where? |
| *dhalaagu?** | where to? |
| *barriyay* | window |
| *wilbaarr* | car |
| *dhulu* | tree, stick |
| *yanawaanha** | am/is/are walking |

*There is no English close equivalent of this verb. It sometimes translates become or get, and at other terms is a way of signalling tense. *Minya ginyi?* 'What happened?' is a recently developed phrase.

*Note that the English 'where' **must** be translated with *dhalaagu* (where to) if the question implies movement to somewhere, and with *dhalaa* if not. For 'Where are you going?' you must use *dhalaagu*. For 'Where are you?' use *dhalaa*.

*The 'present continuous' form of the verbs is complicated, so just one example is given here. This structure will be covered later.

## Grammar

### Past and future forms of Y class verbs

🔊 **Audio:** GGU 6.2.mp3 is available in the electronic edition

| Command | Future* | Past* |
|---|---|---|
| *yananga!* walk! | *yanay* will walk | *yananhi* walked |
| *banagaya!* run! | *banagay* will run | *banaganhi* ran |
| *baraya* (hop!) | *baray* | *baranhi* |
| *barraya* (fly!) | *barray* | *barranhi* |
| *warraya* (stand!) | *warray* | *warranhi* |
| *ngarriya* (sit!) | *ngarriy* | *ngarrinyi* |
| *gubiya* (swim!) | *gubiy* | *gubinyi* |
| *dhuliya* (bend down!) | *dhuliy* | *dhulinyi* |

*In the early stages, we will treat the past and future forms as if they had the same uses as English past (walk-ed, ate, did eat, etc.) and future (will walk, will eat, am going to eat). In reality, Gamilaraay Yuwaalaraay past and future have a number of differences from the English versions. For instance, what is labelled 'future' here actually means something like: 'this will likely happen'. GY future can be translated 'may x', as well as 'will x'. It is likely that future verbs in revived Gamilaraay will be used the same way as future English verbs are.

It is easy to form the **future** forms of *Y* class Gamilaraay verbs. If you know the command form, just leave the final '*a*' off, and you have the 'future' form (except for *yananga*). For example, *banagaya* is a command, 'run!', and *banagay* means 'will go'. *Gubiya* is the command 'swim' and *gubiy* is 'will swim'.

# LESSON 6. VERBS: Y CLASS 'FUTURE' AND 'PAST'

A useful concept is the **'verb stem'**. That is the part of the verb that is found in all verb forms. For 'go' the stem is *yana-*. The stem is never found by itself, there is always something following, but this bit of 'go' never changes.

An alternative way of thinking of future of *Y* class verbs is 'to form the future add "y" to the verb stem'.

The idea of a stem is also helpful when forming the past tense forms. The *Y* class rule for past tense is:

If the stem ends in ***a***:

| | |
|---|---|
| add *-nhi* to the stem | |
| *yana-nhi* | went |
| *banaga-nhi* | ran |

If the stem ends in ***i***:

| | |
|---|---|
| add *-nyi* to the stem | |
| *gubi-nyi* | swam |
| *dhuli-nyi* | bent over / did bend over |

(No *Y* (or *L*) class verb stems end in *u*.)

## Example sentences

 **Audio:** GGU 6.3.mp3 is available in the electronic edition

*Yana-nhi ngaya.*
walk-PAST I
I walked.

*Banagay buruma.*
The dog will run.

*Banaganhi miyay.*
The girl ran.

*Bandaarr baranhi.*
The kangaroo hopped.

*Barranhi dhigaraa, galigu.*
The bird flew to the water.

WIIDHAA

 **Audio:** GGU 6.4.mp3 is available in the electronic edition

*Bubaagu ngaya yananhi.*
dad-TO I walk-PAST
I walked to dad.

*Yananhi ngaya bubaagu.*
walk-PAST I dad-TO
I walked to dad.

*Guniigu ngaya yanay.*
mum-TO I walk-FUT
I will walk to mum.

*Yanay ngaya guniigu.*
walk-FUT I mum-TO
I will walk to mum.

*Ngaya yanay guniigu.*
**I** will walk to mum. (Having *ngaya* first is rare, and so creates a very strong emphasis.)

*Birray miyaygu banaganhi.*
**The boy** ran to the girl.

*Miyaygu birray banaganhi.*
The boy ran **to the girl**.

*Banaganhi miyaygu birray.*
The boy **ran** to the girl.

*Birraygu miyay banagay.*
The girl will run to the boy.

*Miyay birraygu banagay.*
The girl will run to the boy.

*Banagay miyay birraygu.*
The girl **will run** to the boy.

## Questions

Questions are formed by tone of voice or using *yaama*.

 **Audio:** GGU 6.5.mp3 is available in the electronic edition

*Yananhi ngaya?*
walk-PAST I
Did I walk?

*Yaama ngaya bubaagu yananhi?*
question I dad-TO walk-PAST
Did I walk to dad?

*Bubaagu ngaya yananhi?*
dad-TO I walk-PAST
I walked to dad?

*Yaama ngaya yanay guniigu?*
question I walk-FUT mum-TO
Will I walk to mum?

*Yanay ngaya guniigu?*
walk-FUT I mum-TO
I will walk to mum?

*Yaama birray miyaygu banaganhi?*
Did **the boy** run to the girl?

*Birray miyaygu banaganhi?*
**The boy** ran to the girl?

*Yaama miyaygu birray banaganhi?*
Did the boy run **to the girl**?
(Was it the girl the boy ran to?)

*Miyaygu=bala birray banaganhi?*
Was it the girl, the boy ran to?

*Yaama banaganhi miyaygu birray?*
Did the boy **run** to the girl?

*Banaganhi miyaygu birray?*
The boy **ran** to the girl?

WIIDHAA

## Pronunciation

For this lesson focus on **ng** at the start of a word. There are lots of words like that on *Gayarragi, Winangali* – use the option 'search for word starting' and then type in 'ng'. You can practise word-initial 'ng' by saying 'singing.ing.ing.ing' and then starting without the 'si'.

## Practice

Individually/in pairs.

Give a command: While not moving use the future verb; move, use the past tense.

🔊 **Audio:** GGU 6.6.mp3 is available in the electronic edition

| | | |
|---|---|---|
| A: | *B, banagaya.* | B, run. |
| B: | *Banagay ngaya.* | [runs] *Banaganhi ngaya.* |
| | I will run. | I ran. |
| A: | *Gaba, banaganhi nginda.* | |
| | Good, you ran. | |

A does action, e.g. sits, then asks question:

| | | |
|---|---|---|
| A: | *Minya ginyi?* | What happened. |
| B: | *Ngarrinyi nginda.* | You sat (down). |

A does action, e.g. sits, asks question:

| | | |
|---|---|---|
| A: | *Banaganhi ngaya?* | I ran? |
| B: | *Gamilbala. Ngarrinyi nginda.* | No, you sat (down). |
| | | |
| A: | *B, gubiy nginda?* | B, will you swim? |
| B: | *Yawu, gubiy ngaya.* | Yes, I'll swim. (swims) |
| | *Gubinyi ngaya.* | I swam. |
| A: | *Yawu, girrinilgu nginda gubinyi.* | You swam to the door. |

Repeat using different verbs and locations.

LESSON 6. VERBS: Y CLASS 'FUTURE' AND 'PAST'

🔊 **Audio:** GGU 6.7.mp3 is available in the electronic edition

In a group of three or more.

| A: | *B, banagaya.* | B, run. |
|---|---|---|
| B: | *Banagay ngaya.* | [runs] *Banaganhi ngaya.* |
| C *Adha*: | *Ngamila, B banaganhi.* | (*Adha*, speaking to A) |
| A *Cdha*: | *Yawu, banaganhi. //* | |
| | *Yawu, banaganhi=nha.* | |
| | Yes, she ran. | |

With *-gu*.

| A: | *B, girrinil-gu baraya.* | B, hop to the door. |
|---|---|---|
| B: | *Girrinilgu ngaya baray.* | *Girrinilgu ngaya baranhi.* |
| | I will hop to the door. | I hopped to the door. |
| A: | *Gaba, baranhi nginda.* | |
| | Good, you hopped. | |

🔊 **Audio:** GGU 6.8.mp3 is available in the electronic edition

Follow the previous conversation with:

| C: | *A, yananhi B girrinilgu.* | A, B walked to the door. |
|---|---|---|
| A: | *Yawu, giirrnha girrinilgu yananhi.* | (A has seen the event so can use *giirr*) |
| | Yes, she walked to the door. | |

| A *Bdha*: | *Dhalaagu nginda yanay?* |
|---|---|
| | Where will you go? |
| B: | *Wilbaarrgu. Wilbaarrgu ngaya yanay.* |
| | To the car. I'll go to the car. |

You can emphasise what you are asking about by putting it first after *yaama*.

| A: | *B, yaamanda girrinilgu barray?* |
|---|---|
| | *B, yaamanda barray girrinilgu?* |
| | B, will you fly to the door? |

79

WIIDHAA

## *Winangala, garay guwaala, yawala.*
## Listen, say and read.

You can do the exercises below in groups or pairs, or even by yourself. Then repeat the exercises using the verbs and nouns you have learnt so far. This will help you remember them. If you are by yourself you can take both roles in the conversation, perhaps using a doll or picture to do the actions of the other person.

 **Audio:** GGU 6.9.mp3 is available in the electronic edition

| | |
|---|---|
| Kim: | *Kath, girrinilgu banagaya.* |
| | Kath, run to the door. |
| Kath: | *Ngaayaybaay, girrinilgu ngaya banagay.* |
| | Okay, I will run to the door. |
| | (runs to door) |
| | *Girrinilgu ngaya banaganhi. Yinggil ngaya.* |
| | I ran to the door. I'm tired. |

| | |
|---|---|
| Kim: | *Kath, dhalaagu ngaya baray?* |
| | Kath, where will I hop to? |
| Kath: | *Man.gagu. Baraya man.gagu.* |
| | To the table. Hop to the table. |
| Kim: | *Ngaayaybaay, Man.gagu ngaya baray.* |
| | Okay, I will hop to the table. |
| Kath: | *Giirr maaru Kim, baranhi nginda man.gagu.* |
| | Well done Kim, you hopped to the table. |

# LESSON 7
# Where is it? The place (Locative) suffix

This lesson introduces the **place suffix**, also called the **Locative suffix**. The main use of this suffix is to tell where something is. It also has other uses, some of which are covered in this lesson.

## Vocabulary

 **Audio:** GGU 7.1.mp3 is available in the electronic edition

| *Garay* | Words |
|---|---|
| *dhawun* | ground |
| *wirri* | plate |
| *dhuwarr* | bread |
| *birralii* | child |
| *gundhilgaa* | town |
| *milimili* | mud |
| *dhalaa?* | where?* |
| *dhalaa=nda?* | where are you(1)? |
| *-Ga* | 'place' suffix (Locative) |

*Remember that the English 'where' is translated *dhalaa* (where at) or *dhalaagu* (where to), depending on the context.

## Grammar

The place/Locative suffix is -*Ga*. For more information see the *Dictionary*, pp. 265–66, 340, or Giacon (2017). Be careful to use the Gamilaraay suffix forms. Many of the examples in the *Dictionary* are from Yuwaalaraay, which has slightly different forms.

As with -*gu* from the previous lesson, this suffix occurs on nouns and adjectives, but **not** on pronouns and demonstratives.

Gamilaraay, like many Aboriginal languages, uses suffixes (bits attached to the end of words) where English would use prepositions ('pre-positions' are words that generally go in front of other words, e.g. '**in** Canberra', '**on** Monday', '**for** the baby'). The basic meaning of the -*Ga* suffix has to do with place. It has a wide range of translations into English: 'in, on, at, near' are just some of them. Gamilaraay has ways of making the meaning more exact if needed, but we will not be considering them now. When translating, use the English word that makes most sense in the context. So: 'He stood **near** the tree.' 'The plate is **on** the table.'

The capital '*G*' in -*Ga* shows that this part of the suffix can change, but it always has final *a*. The examples below show the form of the suffix after all seven letters found last in GY words: *a*(/*aa*), *i*(/*ii*), *u*(/*uu*), *n*, *rr*, *l* and *y*.

 **Audio:** GGU 7.2.mp3 is available in the electronic edition

| | |
|---|---|
| *buruma-ga* | on/at/near … the dog |
| *giidjaa-ga* | on/at/near … the ant/ants |
| *muru-ga* | on/at/near … the nose |
| *bundi-dha* | on/at/near … the bundi, the hitting stick |
| *gunii-dha\** | on/at/near … the mother |
| *gali-dha* | on/at/near … the water |
| *garrangay-dha* | on/at/near … the duck/ducks |
| *dhinawan-da* | on/at/near … the emu/emus |
| *barran-da* | on/at/near … the boomerang/s |
| *yarral-a* | on/at/near … the rocks/coins |
| *badjigal-a* | on/at/near … the bike |
| *bandaarr-a* | on/at/near … the kangaroo |
| *man.ga-ga* | on/at/near … the table |

## LESSON 7. WHERE IS IT? THE PLACE (LOCATIVE) SUFFIX

*yuruun-da*  on/at/near ... the road
*wilbaarr-a*  on/at/near ... the car/vehicle

*\*Gunii-dha.* Two GR versions of mother-Locative are found. One, *guniidha*, uses the normal form of the suffix. The other is *Gunii-ngunda*. The reason for the difference is not definite, but it seems likely that it is because, in the second version, *gunii* is being used like a name. In many Aboriginal languages the suffixes on names are different from those on other nouns, and on adjectives.

| Word ends | Suffix |
| --- | --- |
| a, u | -ga |
| i, y* | -dha |
| n | -da |
| rr, l | -a |

*\*For now add *-dha* to *y* final words. In fact a few *y*-final words follow a different rule: drop the *y* and add *-dha*, e.g. *yaraay* 'sun', *yaraa-dha* 'in the sun' (Giacon, 2017, p. 31).

> It is very likely there were other irregular locatives but they were not recorded, so revived GY will be more regular than traditional GY, it will have fewer irregular forms.

*Minya?* 'what?' has an irregular form of the suffix: *Minya-dha?* 'on/near ... what?'

Work out the Locative endings for the words below:

 **Audio:** GGU 7.3.mp3 is available in the electronic edition

| | |
| --- | --- |
| *girrinil* | door |
| *wiyayl* | pen |
| *biibabiiba* | book |
| *gaala* | mug |
| *dhigaraa* | bird |
| *dhuru* | snake |
| *man.garr* | bag |
| *dhinggaa* | meat |

WIIDHAA

| | |
|---|---|
| *bina* | ear |
| *mil* | eye |
| *mara* | hand |
| *dhina* | foot |
| *maliyaa* | friend |
| *dhagaan* | brother |
| *baawaa* | sister |
| *birray* | boy |
| *gundhi* | house |

The suffix goes on the word that in English would have 'in, on, near, …' in front of it.

*Girrinil-a*
Near the door.

*Man.garr girrinil-a.*
The bag is near the door.

*Girrinil-a man.garr?*
Is the bag near the door?

*Gundhi-dha nginda?* Or *Gundhidha=nda?*
Are you(1) at home?

*Man.garr-a ngay wiyayl wiimala.*
Put the pen in my bag.

*Dhalaa bubaa? Garrawala?*
Where is dad? At the shop?

*Minyadha nginda yananhi?*
What did you walk on?

## Noun + adjective

 **Audio:** GGU 7.4.mp3 is available in the electronic edition

When you use and adjective and a noun, the suffix must go on **both**.

*dhinggaa-**ga** gaba-**ga***
on the good meat

LESSON 7. WHERE IS IT? THE PLACE (LOCATIVE) SUFFIX

*Galidha gagila.*
In/near the bad water.

*Giwiirra gabaga.*
Near the good man.

*Yinggila burumaga.*
On the **tired** dog.

*Ngamila, giidjaa dhinggaaga gabaga.*
Look, the ant is on the good meat.

*Yaama nginda galidha warranhi gagila?*
Did you stand in the bad water?

*Dhinggaa gaba gundhidha?*
Is there good meat in the house?

In GY the noun and adjective do not need to be adjacent.

> Some other Aboriginal languages follow this pattern, while others, such as Pitjantjatjara, have the rules that the adjective follows immediately after the noun and only the last word in the group has the case marking.

## Other examples

 **Audio:** GGU 7.5.mp3 is available in the electronic edition

| | | |
|---|---|---|
| 1(a). | *Man.gaga wiimala wiyayl!* | |
| | table-on put-command pen | |
| | Put the pen on the table! | |
| 1(b). | *Garriya man.gaga wiimala wiyayl!* | |
| | not table-on put-command pen | |
| | Do not put the pen on the table! | |
| 2. | *Dhalaa giidjaa?* | |
| | where-at ant | |
| | Where is the ant? | |
| 3(a). | *Galidha garrangay.* | |
| | water-on duck | |
| | The duck is on the water. | |

3(b).   *Galidha garrangay?*
water-on duck
(rising inflection makes this a question)
Is the duck on the water?

Note the change in emphasis shown by change in word order in the following.

3(c).   Yaama galidha garrangay?
question water-on duck
Is the duck on the **water**?

3(d).   *Yaama garrangay galidha?*
question water-on duck
Is the **duck** on the water?
Is it the duck that is on the water?

3(e).   *Gamil garrangay galidha?*
not duck water-on
The **duck** is not on the water?
Is it not the duck that is on the water?

For a 'flash' answer to 3(c) you could say:

3(f).   *Gamil, dhurubala galidha.*
no, snake-but water-on
No, it's a snake in the water.

## Practice

 **Audio:** GGU 7.6.mp3 is available in the electronic edition

Touch various objects, say their name, and then add the place/Locative suffix.

*Bina, binaga; mil, mila; man.garr, man.garra.*
Ear, eye, bag.

Put your hand on objects, and describe the situation.

*Muru-ga mara.*
[My] hand is on my nose.

*Man.ga-ga mara.*
[My] hand is on the table.

> Note: The command verbs you have learnt that end in *-la* **cannot** be used for actions you do to yourself.
>
> *Wiyayl wiimala maraga.* 'Pen put hand-on' can **not** mean 'put the pen on your hand!' It can only be referring to someone else's hand. For more information, see 'Middle verbs' in Giacon (2017).

Put one object on another, and describe the situation.

*Nguuga wiyayl. Wiyayl nguuga.*
The pen is on the book.

**In pairs:** Tell your partner to put something somewhere.

*Gaalaga gali wiimala.*
Put the water in the cup.

Note: you can have these three words in any order. New information, or what is being emphasised, goes first. If there is no particular stress the verb will typically be last.

*Ngarriya gulabanda.*
**Sit** on the chair.

*Barriyaydha warraya.*
Stand near the window.

## Ask 'Where?'

 **Audio:** GGU 7.7.mp3 is available in the electronic edition

A: *Dhalaa Kim?*
   Where is Kim?
B: *Gundhidha. Gundhidha=nha. Gundhigu yananhi.*
   (She's) At home. She's at home. She went home.

(Note that he/she need not be translated into Gamilaraay if it is clear who is being spoken about.)

A: *Dhalaa ngaya ngarriy?*
Where will I sit?
B: *Dhawunda. Dhawunda ngarriya.*
On the ground. Sit on the ground.
A: *Gaba. Dhawunda ngaya ngarriy. Dhawunda ngaya ngarrinyi.*
Good. I will sit on the ground. I sat on the ground.
A: *Barriyaydha warraya.*
Stand near the window.
B: *Barriyaygu ngaya yanay. (yilaa) Barriyaydha ngaya.* or *Giirr ngaya barriyaydha.*
I will go to the window. (then) I am near the window.

## Other questions

| | |
|---|---|
| A, *yalduul-a:* | *?Gundhidha nginda?* |
| A, on the mobile: | You at home? |
| B: | *Gamilbala, schoola ngaya.* or *Gamil, schoolabala ngaya.* |
| | No, I'm at school. |

# Pronunciation

 **Audio:** GGU 7.8.mp3 is available in the electronic edition

We have covered a lot of the sounds, but you need to keep practising.

How are your **nh**, **ng** and **rr**?

Be especially careful of the difference in pronunciation of words that end in *arr* and *aarr*. With *arr* the stress will not be on *arr*: *yinarr*, whereas stress is on *aarr*: *ban**daarr***. Take care also to stress long vowels followed by a suffix: *mali**yaa**-ga* 'near, with a friend'.

You can also start focusing on the **sentence pattern**. There is a big difference between the way English and Gamilaraay stress words when they are put together. Listen to Arthur Dodd or Fred Reece on *Gayarragi, Winangali* and try to imitate them. Record yourself if you can and see how close you are to them.

## Extension

### Other Locative suffixes, Locative case

In this lesson, we have considered the Locative suffix on what can be called 'standard' nouns and adjectives.

Pronouns do not use the Locative suffix, but have a Locative form that is better thought of as one word, rather than as a word + a suffix. *Ngaya* is 'I' and the Locative form is *nganunda*, which will be considered in later lessons.

As mentioned earlier, there is a separate set of suffixes for use on proper nouns. Names – Jill, Jack, Chaquille, Canberra, etc. – are proper nouns. We will not use the proper noun forms in this course.

## *Winangala, garay guwaala, yawala.*
## Listen, say and read.

You can read further examples for Lesson 7 and listen to them as the sound files are made.

 **Audio:** GGU 7.9.mp3 is available in the electronic edition

*Dhalaa Billy?*
Where is Billy?

| *Giirr wilbaarra Billy.* | *Wilbaarra.* | *Wilbaarra=nha.* |
|---|---|---|
| Billy is in the car/near the car. | *or* Near/in the car. | *or* He's near/in the car. |

*Dhalaa gunii?*
Where is mum?

*Man.gaga gunii.*
Mum is near the table.

*Dhalaa Joe?*
Where is Joe?

WIIDHAA

*Gamil wilbaarra Joe.*
Joe is not near the car.

*Yaama gundhidha Joe?*
Is Joe in the house?

*Gamil. Giirrbala garrawala Joe.*
No. Joe is at the shops.

*Garrawala Mary?*
Is Mary at the shops?

*Gamil, gundhidhabala Mary.*
No, Mary is at home.

*Yaama Susan gundhidha?*
Is Susan at home?

*Gamil. Schoolgubala Susan yananhi.*
No. Susan went to school.

*Schoola Susan?*
Is Susan at school?

*Giirr schoola Susan.*
Susan **is** at school.

 **Audio:** GGU 7.10.mp3 is available in the electronic edition

A: *Dhalaa man.garr ngay?*
   Where is my bag?
   *Yaama gundhidha?*
   Is it at home?
B: *Yawu, gundhidha nhama.*
   Yes, it is at home.
A: *Yaama=nha man.gaga?*
   Is it on the table?
B: *Gamil, dhawundabala=nha.*
   No, it is on the ground.

LESSON 7. WHERE IS IT? THE PLACE (LOCATIVE) SUFFIX

🔊 **Audio:** GGU 7.11.mp3 is available in the electronic edition

A: *Dhalaa buruma? Yaama galidha?*
Where is the dog? Is it near the water?
B: *Giirr galigu buruma yananhi. Galidha nhama.*
The dog went to the water. It is near the water.
A: *Baawaa, gundhilgaaga bubaa?*
Sis, is dad in town?
B: *Yawu dhagaan, gundhilgaagu yananhi bubaa.*
Yes bro, dad went to town.

🔊 **Audio:** GGU 7.12.mp3 is available in the electronic edition

A: *Minya nhama man.gaga? Wirri nhama?*
What is that on the table? Is it a plate?
B: *Yawu, wirri nhama man.gaga.*
*Ngamila! Dhinggaa (nhama) wirridha.*
Yes, there is a plate on the table.
Look, there is meat on the plate.

🔊 **Audio:** GGU 7.13.mp3 is available in the electronic edition

A: *Billy, dhalaa nginda, dhalaanda?*
Billy, where are you, where are you?
B: *Nguwalay ngaya, Anna.*
I am here, Anna.
A: *Dhalaa Billy? Dhalaa nginda?*
Where Billy, where are you?
B: *Ngamila, gundhidha ngaya, Anna.*
Look, I am in the house Anna.
A: *Gaba, gundhigu ngaya yanay.*
Good, I will go to the house.
*Gundhidha ngaya ngarriy.*
I will stay (sit) at the house.

WIIDHAA

 **Audio:** GGU 7.14.mp3 is available in the electronic edition

M: *Joe, yananga dhagaan.gu, warraya dhagaanda.*
Joe, go to your brother. Stand near your brother.
J: *Gamil gunii, gamil ngaya yanay dhagaan.gu.*
No mum, I won't go to my brother.
*Gamil ngaya warray dhagaanda.*
I won't stand near my brother.

> I now suspect that traditional GY would have used the proper name suffixes here, because 'brother' and 'mum' refer to specific people. They are like names, words you would use to address someone. The sentences would then be:
>
> M: *Joe, yananga dhagaan-ngunda, warraya Dhagaanngunda.*
> J: *Gamil Guniidhi, gamil ngaya yanay Dhagaanngunda.*
> *Gamil ngaya warray Dhagaanngunda.*

 **Audio:** GGU 7.15.mp3 is available in the electronic edition

X: *Dhalaagu birralii yananhi?*
Where did the kid go?
X: *Yaama guniigu yananhi?*
Did it go to its mother?
Y: *Gamil guniigu yananhi.*
*Giirr milimilidha nhama birralii.*
*Milimilidha ngarrinyi.*
*Birralii, bubaagu yananga.*
It did not go to mum.
That kid is in the mud.
It sat in the mud.
Kid, go to your father.

# LESSON 8
# Possession

In this lesson, we look at some possessive pronouns, at the marking of possession on nouns and adjectives, and at some of the complexities associated with the idea of possession.

## Vocabulary

 **Audio:** GGU 8.1.mp3 is available in the electronic edition

| *Garay* | Words |
|---|---|
| *warraya* | stand! |
| *galiyaya!* | climb! |
| | |
| *ngay* | my |
| *nginu* | your(s)(1) |
| *ngurungu* | his/her(s)/its |
| *gulaban* | chair |
| *dhuwadi* | shirt |
| *gayrr* | name |
| *malawil* | shadow |
| *yira* | teeth |
| | |
| *yaamanda?* | *yaama nginda*\* |
| | |
| *-gu* | \*possessive/owning suffix (Dative) |

\*The phrase *yaama nginda* (question you(1)) is often abbreviated to *yaamanda*. It begins a question to which the answer is usually yes or no. Common translations include: 'Are you? Do you? Did you? Will you?' (see the *Dictionary*, p. 292). The abbreviated pronoun *=nda* occurs with other sentence initial words such as *dhalaa* 'where(at)'. *=nda* is common on words that finish with *a* and *u* and rarer with other words. Remember, the '=' means this generally goes on the first word of the sentence or clause.

\*The possessive suffix on standard nouns and pronouns is *-gu*. For the present always use that form. There is some variation in the form of this suffix in the sources. The proper name possessive is *-ngu*, but you do not need to use that.

Another name for this suffix is the **Dative** suffix. Dative has to do with 'giving to', and you will see this use of the suffix in later lessons.

This lesson has a limited amount of new material, and is a good opportunity to revise previous vocabulary and concepts. As well as using the new material in simple sentences incorporate it in negative (*gamil*) and question sentences.

# Grammar

## Simple possession

 **Audio:** GGU 8.2.mp3 is available in the electronic edition

This section has possessive pronouns (like English 'my' and 'your') and possessive nouns (like English 'child's'). Gamilaraay possessive words can, and mostly do, come after the noun, like adjectives. Here are some examples of possessive **pronouns**:

*dhinawan ngay*
emu my
my emu

*wilbaarr nginu*
car your(1 person)
your(1) car

*gulaban ngurungu*
chair his/her
her/his chair

*Dhalaa dhinawan ngay?*
Where is my emu?

## LESSON 8. POSSESSION

*Gundhidha nginu.*
house-at your(1)
At your house.

*Yananga schoolgu ngurungu.*
Go to her/his school.

Possessive **nouns** are formed by adding *-gu* to the basic noun.

*Dhinawan giwiirr-gu.*
The man's emu.

*Wilbaarr miyay-gu.*
The girl's car.

Possessive pronouns and nouns are like adjectives in that they most commonly follow immediately after the noun, but they can be separated from it, and occasionally occur before of the noun. Separation of the noun and possessive is common when a pronoun takes second position.

*Gulabanda nginda guniigu ngarrinyi.*
Chair-on you(1) mum-of sit-past.
'You sat on mum's chair.'

Possession is a complex and variable area of language – sometimes it is explicitly shown: **my** book, but at other times not: 'Here comes mum' (my/our mum). While these things vary subtly within languages, introductory courses necessarily take a fairly simple approach. Often Gamilaraay does not use possessives where English would (my hand, my mother). Sometimes the possessive pronoun is omitted entirely (*Bayn mara* (hand sore) = 'My hand is sore') or the simple pronoun is used (*Bayn mara ngaya* (hand sore I) = 'my hand is sore'/'I have a sore hand'). For more information about pronouns, see the *Dictionary*, pp. 286ff.

 **Audio:** GGU 8.3.mp3 is available in the electronic edition

1. *Wiyayl ngay.*
   pen my
   My pen.
2(a). *Nhalay wiyayl ngay.*
   pen this my
   This is my pen.

2(b). *Yaama ngay, nhalay wiyayl?*
question my, this pen
Is **this** pen mine?

2(c). *Gamil ngay, wiyayl nhama.*
not mine, pen that.
That pen is not **mine**.

3(a). *Yananhi giidjaa, dhinggaaga nginu.*
walked ant    meat-on    your
The ant walked on your meat.

3(b). *Gamil dhinggaaga nginu yananhi giidjaa.*
not    meat-on your    walked    ant
The ant did not walk on your meat. /
It wasn't your meat the ant walked on.

4. *Yaama nginda wiyayl wiima-li man.gaga ngay?*
*Yaamanda wiyayl nginu wiima-li man.gaga ngay?*
question-you(1) pen your(1) put-future table-on my
Will you put your pen on my table?

---

(In sentences like number 4 the *nginu* is often assumed rather than explicit.)

## Inalienable possession

This next section describes some patterns in GY about things that are 'owned' that are quite different from English. Linguists use the term 'inalienable possession' to describe the pattern, where possessive forms are not used indicate 'ownership'.

Languages have complex rules about possession and how it is expressed. For instance, in English you can say:

'The table leg is broken.' 'The car door is broken.'

But not: The boy leg is broken.

You say: 'The boy's leg is broken'.

'Possession' in Aboriginal languages, when talking of body parts, and in some other situations, often uses phrases like 'table leg', with no extra marker of possession. You say:

> **Audio:** GGU 8.4.mp3 is available in the electronic edition

*ngaya mara* (not *mara ngay*)
I hand
My hand

Apart from body parts, other important and personal things are 'inalienable possessed', for instance 'name' and 'shadow'. (It was a serious offence traditionally to step on someone's shadow.) Because of the limited GR records we do not know what else was traditionally inalienable possessed. This is an area where GR might look at other Australian languages to decide what it should do.

> Hawaiian has extensive use of inalienable possession. It is similar to Australian inalienable possession but there are differences. Things you ride on/in, such as a car or horse are inalienably possessed, whereas your cow is not. Wikipedia has a long article on the topic.

## More examples

*ngaya gayrr*
I name = my name

*ngaya dhinggaa*
I meat = my social section, meat

*ngaya malawil*
I shadow = my shadow

*ngaya yira*
I teeth = my teeth

Wangaaybuwan is closely related to Gamilaraay Yuwaalaraay and has much more extensive records of the traditional language. From these we can get indications of what GY was like. In Wangaaybuwan, if you are wearing something, you treat it like a body part to show possession. The pattern, using Gamilaraay words, is:

*ngaya dhuwadi*
I shirt = my shirt

(when you are wearing it), **but**

WIIDHAA

*dhuwadi ngay*
shirt my = my shirt

(when you are **not** wearing it)

And, if you have false teeth, sitting in a glass, you say:

*yira ngay*
teeth my = my teeth

But, when the teeth, false or not, are in your mouth, you say:

*ngaya yira*

### Inalienable possession and 'case'

In a phrase that uses inalienable possession, both elements must be the same case. For example:

'girl's hand' is *miyay mara*

'on the girl's hand' is *miyay-dha mara-ga* (with a place/Locative suffix on both).

## Practice

Sit in a group, each holding an object, a *wiyayl* to start with.

 **Audio:** GGU 8.5.mp3 is available in the electronic edition

Point to each *wiyayl* and say:

*Wiyayl ngay, wiyayl nginu, wiyayl ngurungu.*
My pen, your pen, his/her pen.

Then use possessive nouns:

*Wiyayl yinarrgu, wiyayl birraygu, wiyayl bubaagu, wiyayl Leegu, wiyayl maliyaagu.*
The woman's pen, the boy's pen, dad's pen, Lee's pen, the friend's pen.

## Questions

 **Audio:** GGU 8.6.mp3 is available in the electronic edition

**Intonation:** hold a book and say:

A: *?Nguu nhalay nginu?*
   (Is) this your book?
B: *Yawu, ngay nhama. Nguu nhama ngay.*
   Yes, it's mine. That's my book.
or
B: *Gamilbala. Gamil ngay. Gamil nhama ngay.*
   No. It's not mine. That is not mine.

Repeat, using *Yaama*:

A: *Yaama nginu, nhalay nguu?*
   Is this book yours? / Is this your book?

A: *Dhalaa yalduul ngay?*
   Where is my mobile?
B: *Nhalay. Man.garra Leegu.*
   Here it is, in Lee's bag.

## Commands

Do not use body parts in this exercise – see next section.

 **Audio:** GGU 8.7.mp3 is available in the electronic edition

*Wiimala man.garr nginu man.gaga.*
Put your bag on the table.

*Dhiyamala nguu ngay, wiimala man.garra nginu.*
Pick up my book and put it in your bag.

A: *Banagaya man.garrgu ngay, warraya man.garra ngay.*
   Run to my bag and stand near my bag.
B: *Yawu, banagay ngaya man.garrgu nginu, warray man.garra.*
   Yes, I will run to your bag and stand near the bag.
A: *Birray gaba. Banaganhi nginda man.garrgu ngay, warranhi man.garra.*
   Good boy. You ran to my bag and stood near the bag.

## Inalienable possession

Point to your body parts and name them:

| | |
|---|---|
| *Ngaya mil* | my eyes |
| *Ngaya mara* | my hand |

Do the same with other people.

| | | |
|---|---|---|
| *Nginda mil* | your eyes | |
| *Nginda mara* | your hand | |
| *Kim bina* | Kim's ear. | |
| A (Points to own hand): | *Minya nhalay?* | What is this? |
| B: | *Nginda mara.* | Your hand. |

We have not yet learnt place/Locative pronouns, i.e. how to say: 'on me', 'on you', etc., so we cannot say 'on my hand', but:

*Wiimala wiyayl, Bill-a mara-ga.*
Put the pen on/in Bill's hand.

## *Winangala, garay guwaala, yawala.*
## Listen, say and read.

 **Audio:** GGU 8.8.mp3 is available in the electronic edition

1. *Giirr nhama gundhi ngay.*
   That is my house.
2. *Gamilbala nhama gundhi nginu.*
   That is not your(1) house.

LESSON 8. POSSESSION

3. *Dhalaa baawaa?*
   Where is (my) sister?
4. *Giirr gundhidha baawaa nginu.*
   Your sister is at home (at the house).
5. *Giirr gundhidha ngay, baawaa nginu.*
   Your sister is at my house.
6. *Dhalaa buruma ngurungu?*
   Where is his/her dog?
7. *Giirr nhama galigu banaganhi, buruma ngurungu.*
   His dog ran to the water.

The last sentence shows a common feature of Gamilaraay sentences: first a general term (e.g. it, there) and later in the sentence the specific information.

🔊 **Audio:** GGU 8.9.mp3 is available in the electronic edition

8. *Ngaandi ngarrinyi, gulabanda ngay?*
   Who sat on my chair.
9. *Giirr Mary ngarrinyi, gulabanda nginu.*
   Mary sat on your(1) chair.
10. *Mary, yaamanda ngarrinyi gulabanda ngay?*
    Mary, did you sit on my chair?
11. *Gamil ngaya, Billybala gulabanda ngarrinyi.*
    Not me, it was Billy who sat on the chair.
12. *Shorty, dhalaa biibabiiba nginu?*
    Shorty, where is your book?
13. *Ngamila Irene, gulabanda nginu, biibabiiba ngay.*
    Look Irene, my book is on your chair.
14. *Joe, yaama nhama nginu, wilbaarr?*
    Shorty, is that car yours.
15. *Yawu, ngay nhama wilbaarr. Gaba nhama.*
    Yep, that is my car. It is a good one.
16. *Ngamila. Sue nhama, wilbaarr nhama ngurungu.*
    *Ngarragaa nhama wilbaarr.*
    Look, that's Mary, and that's her car.
    It's a hopeless car.

**Audio:** GGU 8.10.mp3 is available in the electronic edition

In the following, Gamilaraay uses *ngaya* 'I' or *nginda* 'you' where English uses the possessive 'my' or 'your'.

17. *Bayn dhina ngaya.*
    I've got a sore foot.
18. *Cecil, bayn nginda mubal?*
    (or *Cecil, yaama=nda bayn mubal?*)
    Cecil, have you got a gut-ache? /
    Is your stomach crook?
19. *Gamil=bala Trish. Gaba ngaya mubal.*
    No Trish. My stomach is good.

(There is still some question about the traditional position of the pronouns in such sentences.)

# LESSON 9
# To, From and At

This lesson introduces some new movement words and a new suffix, **-DHi** 'from', also called the **Ablative** suffix.

## Vocabulary

🔊 **Audio:** GGU 9.1.mp3 is available in the electronic edition

| *Garay* | Words |
|---|---|
| *-DHi* | from suffix (Ablative) |
| *gaanga!* | bring/take! |
| *dhaay\** | to here, to the place being talked about |
| *ngirilay/ngiilay\** | from here |
| *ngirima/ngiima\** | from there |
| *nguwalay\** | here |
| *nguwama\** | there |
| *yuruun* | road |
| *yarraaman\** | horse |
| *baawul* | chicken |
| *garrawal* | shop |
| *burruluu* | fly |
| *gundhi* | house |
| *dhalaa dhaay\** | where from? |
| *dhalaadhi\** | where from? |
| *giyal* | afraid |
| *gindama-y* | laugh **int** |

**Audio:** GGU 9.2.mp3 is available in the electronic edition

\*The ongoing examination of GY sources has led to a modification in the description of *dhaay*. Previously it was only described as 'to here', to the speaker. The description has been modified to include 'to the place being spoken about'.

\*For *ngirima/ngirilay/nguwama/nguwalay* see Extension at the end of this lesson.

> In the Gamilaraay sources there is one 'from' word based on *ngiri-* and one based on *ngii-* (Giacon, 2017, p. 195). Many GR words with *r* have Ø in Yuwaalaraay, e.g. *mara* GR, *maa* YR. Since YR has *ngii* it is likely that the GR used *ngiri-*, but it may have used both forms.

\*The word *yarraaman* 'horse' has many current pronunciations: *yaraman*, *yarəmən*, *yarraman*, *yarraamaan* and more. Such variation is typical of words that are still being used. The form *yarraamaan* is the most common in traditional sources. We made a mistake in having *yarraaman* as the dictionary entry.

\*The historical sources do not give clear information about how to say 'Where from?' as in 'Where did you just come from?' There seem to be at least two ways:

*Dhalaa nginda dhaay yananhi?* or *Dhalaa dhaay nginda yananhi?* or *Dhalaa=nda dhaay yananhi?*

Where.at to.here you came?
Where did you come from?

Even more commonly, the sentence would use the *L* class verb *dhurrali* 'come, appear', whose past tense is *dhurray*.

*Dhalaa nginda dhaay dhurray?* or *Dhalaa dhaay nginda dhurray?* or *Dhalaa=nda dhaay dhurray?*

Where.at to.here you came?
Where did you come from?

When the discussion is not about someone who is present, *dhalaa dhaay* is not appropriate and *dhalaadhi* should be used. For instance:

*Dhalaadhi Pemulwuy?*
Where was Pemulwuy from?

## Grammar

### *Dhaay* 'to here/to there'

This word often means 'to the person speaking' and occasionally means 'to (someone else)' or 'to the place being discussed'. It occurs with movement verbs like 'walk', 'run', 'bring' and 'give' and usually appears immediately before the verb.

*Dhaay banagaya.*
Run here.

It is also found in the expression:

*Nhama dhaay*, which can be translated as 'Watch out!' 'Be careful!' when something is approaching, e.g. a car.

*Nhama dhaay* would not be the appropriate translation of 'watch out' in other situations – for instance, if warning someone about a fire. Then the GR might be: *Bamba ngamila*. 'Look carefully'.

### *-DHi* 'from'

The main part of this lesson is the 'from' or Ablative suffix. Remember, the capital letters indicate that section of the suffix can vary. As for the 'go to'/Allative suffix *-gu*, the 'place'/Locative suffix *-Ga* and the possessive/Dative suffix *-gu*, this suffix can be used on most nouns and adjectives. It is not used on pronouns or demonstratives, and the proper name form is *-ngundi*. For this course use the standard form on names.

The simplest and most common use of this suffix is to indicate 'movement away from'. There are many other uses of the suffix. For more information about this see the *Dictionary*, p. 267, Giacon (2017) and the Extension section below.

The table shows the form of the suffix on all word-final letters.

🔊 **Audio:** GGU 9.3.mp3 is available in the electronic edition

| | |
|---|---|
| *buruma-dhi* | from the dog |
| *giidjaa-dhi* | from the ant |
| *muru-dhi* | from the nose |
| *bundi-dhi* | from the bundi |
| *gunii-dhi* | from mum |
| *gali-dhi* | from the water |
| *garrangay-dhi* | from the duck |
| *dhinawan-di* | from the emu |
| *barran-di* | from the boomeran |
| *yarral-i* | from the rock/coin |
| *badjigal-i* | from the bike |
| *bandaarr-i* | from the kangaroo |
| *man.ga-dhi* | from the table |
| *yuruun-di* | from the road |
| *wilbaarr-i* | from the car/vehicle |

The table from Lesson 7 is repeated here, with additional information for -DHi.

### Local Suffix* summary table

| Word ends | -*Ga* place | -*DHi* from | -*gu* to |
|---|---|---|---|
| a, u | -ga | -dhi | -gu |
| i, y* | -dha | -dhi | -gu |
| n | -da | -di | -gu |
| rr, l | -a | -i | -gu |

*GY has many suffixes. The term 'local suffix' refers to the three suffixes whose main meaning has to do with places – to a place, at a place, from a place.

There are summary tables in the *Dictionary*, pp. 266, 340, but some aspects of these may be out of date.

> After re-examining the Arthur Dodd and Fred Reece tape transcripts, it turns out that there is variation in the suffix on *y* final words. It seems that the words which drop the *y* before the Locative suffix also do so before the Ablative suffix. The two examples found are: *yaa-dhi* 'from the sun'; *yaay* 'sun', Yuwaalaraay (Fred Reece tape 2439A) and *baga-dhi* 'from the river bank' *bagay* (Arthur Dodd tape 5128). However, you can use the simpler description of the suffix in the table above.

### Movement from

 **Audio:** GGU 9.4.mp3 is available in the electronic edition

The simplest use of *-DHi* is to indicate 'movement from'.

*Gulaban-di ngaya warray.*
I will stand up from the chair.

*Buruma-dhi nginda banaga-nhi.*
You(1) ran away from the dog.

*Man.garr-i ngay wiyayl dhiyamala.*
Pick up the pen from my bag.

*Dhawundi man.garr dhiyamala.*
Pick up the bag from the ground/floor.

A noun and any associated adjective both have the suffix.

*Buruma-dhi=nha gagil-i banaga-nhi.*
He ran away from the bad dog.

## Other uses of Ablative case

Ablative/from forms have uses other than 'movement from'. They are used to show what something is made from, in comparisons and with a number of words.

### Made from
*Gidjiirri nhalay barran, malga-dhi=bala nhamalay bundi.*
This boomerang is (made from) Gidgee and that club is from Mulga.

## Comparison

*Giirrbala ngaya gaay, dhagaan-di.*
True=bala I small, brother-from
I am smaller than my brother.

This can also be said:

*Gaaybala ngaya, dhagaanbala burrul.*

 **Audio:** GGU 9.5.mp3 is available in the electronic edition

## Special words

With the adjective ***giyal*** 'afraid', what you are afraid of is in Ablative case. That is, in Gamilaraay 'I am afraid **from** someone'.

*Giyal nginda buruma-dhi?*
Are you afraid of the dog?

*Giyal nginda burumadhi ngirima?*
Are you afraid of that dog? (note: *ngirima* here is like an adjective, saying something about the noun)

*Giyal ngaya ngirima.*
Afraid I that-from.
I am afraid of that.

With the verb ***gindamay*** 'laugh', whom/what you laugh at is in Ablative case. You laugh **from** someone.

*Gindama-nhi ngaya birray-dhi ngarragaa-dhi.*
I laughed at the hopeless boy. (note the suffix on the noun and the adjective)

Ablative case is used with ***galiyay*** 'climb', marking what is climbed on.

*Garriya man.ga-dhi galiya-ya.*
Don't climb on the table.

*Garriya ngirilay galiyaya.*
Don't this-from climb.
Don't climb on this.

Less intuitively, when using the verb *wurugi* 'go in', what is gone into is in Ablative case (see Lesson 13).

*Gamil ngaya gundhi-dhi wurugi.*
I won't go into the house.

### Ngirima / ngirilay

(This may repeat some material from earlier discussion of demonstratives.)

 **Audio:** GGU 9.6.mp3 is available in the electronic edition

You have used the demonstratives *nhama* and *nhalay*, and even *nhamalay*. All with a common element: *nha-*. Our current definition of the other parts of those words is:

| | |
|---|---|
| *-ma* | The speaker expects the hearer to know what is being talked about. |
| *-lay* | The speaker is drawing attention to something, often by pointing. With simple use of *-lay* (that is, not *-malay* or *-gulay*) the thing being talked about is close to the speaker. |
| *-malay* | The thing is not close but is being pointed out. |

We will now consider two more sets of demonstratives:

### Ngirima, ngirilay

The first is based on *ngiri-* whose basic meaning is 'from', found in:

*ngirima* 'from there' and
*ngirilay* 'from here', the place the speaker is.

*Ngiri* is never found without a suffix. Presumably GR could also have *ngirimalay* 'from there (that place I am pointing out)'. *Ngiri-* can combine with other elements found in demonstratives; for instance, *-baa* 'up'. Ridley (1856) says 'Jesus came *ngiri-baa-dhaay gunagaladhi dhawun.gu.* from-up-to.here, from heaven to earth'.

*Ngirilay yananga. Ngirilay banagaya.*
Go away from here. Run away from here.

WIIDHAA

### *Nguwa, nguwalay, nguwama*

*Nguwa*, unlike *ngiri*, is found without other suffixes, but its meaning then is not clear.

*Nguwama* and *nguwalay* are 'there' and 'here', but are mostly found with verbs, in sentences like:

I will sit *nguwalay*/here and you stay *nguwama*/there.

*Nguwalaybala ngaya ngarriy, ngindabala nguwama ngarriya.*
I will sit here and you sit there.

## Practice

Work out what practice strategies work well for you. One way is to start with simpler practice, and gradually move to more complex practice, involving multiple sentences and conversations. Gradually expand the vocabulary you are using with each new structure.

 **Audio:** GGU 9.7.mp3 is available in the electronic edition

### Objects

Add the suffix to nouns from previous lessons, combining them with actions. For instance, put your hand on your ear, and as you lift it say: *binadhi*.

**Move from objects** (or 'finger walk' from pictures of objects)

| *Man.gadhi ngaya yanay.* | *Yilaa* | *Man.gadhi ngaya yananhi.* |
|---|---|---|
| I will walk away from the table. | Then | I walked from the table. |
| A: | B, *warraya gulabandi.* | |
| | B, stand up from the chair. | |
| B: | *Gaba, warray ngaya. Gulabandi ngaya warranhi.* | |
| | OK, I'll stand. I stood (up) from the chair. | |
| C Bdha: | *Warranhi nginda gulabandi.* | |
| (C, to B) | | |
| C Adha: | *Gulabandi warranhi B. // Gulabandi=nha warranhi. //* | |
| (C, to A) | *Gulabandi warranhi.* | |
| | B stood up from the chair. She stood up from the chair. | |

(*B-dha* and *A-dha* have the place/Locative suffix, with the form of the suffix based on the last sound of 'b' and 'a'. With *garay guwaali* 'talk', the one spoken to is Locative case.)

A: *Dhalaadhi burruluu barranhi?*
   Where did the fly fly from?
B: *Murudhi burruluu barranhi.*
   The fly flew from [my] nose.

## A range of suffixes

A: *B, gulabandi banagaya, girrinilgu. Warraya girrinila.*
   B, run from the chair to the door and stand at the door.
B: *Ngaayaybaay. Gulabandi ngaya banagay, girrinilgu, ngiyarrma ngaya girrinila warray.*
   OK. I will run from the chair to the door and I will stand at the door.

(GR often uses place words like *ngiyarrma* 'there' to join sentences and clauses, whereas English would typically use 'and'.)

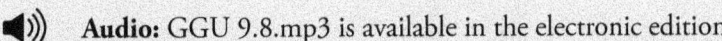 **Audio:** GGU 9.8.mp3 is available in the electronic edition

*Man.gadhi ngaya yanay, gulaban.gu, yilaa gulabanda ngaya ngarriy.*
I will go from the table to the chair, then I will sit on the chair.

A: *Ngirilay banagaya, dhulugabala warraya.*
   Run away from here and stand near the tree.
B: *Ngirilay ngaya banagay, dhulugabala ngaya warray.*
   I will run away from here and will stand near the tree.
*Yilaa*/then
B: *Ngirima ngaya banaganhi, dhulugabala ngaya warranhi.*
   I ran away from there and stood near the tree.

**Dhiyamala. 'Pick up!'**

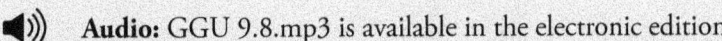 **Audio:** GGU 9.9.mp3 is available in the electronic edition

A: *B, wiyayl dhiyamala man.gadhi.*
   B, pick up the pen from the table.

(We have not done the other forms of *dhiyamala, gaanga* and some other verbs, so B cannot give a long answer, yet.)

A: *Girrinil-gu=nha gaanga.*
Take it to the door.
A: *Dhawundabala girrinila wiimala.*
And put it on the ground near the door.

**Ngirima, ngirilay, dhaay**

A: *Dhaay baraya, man.garri.*
Hop here, from the bag.
Then B, C and A can talk about it.
A: *B, gagil nginda. Ngirilay barraya, gundhi-dhi ngay.*
B, you are bad. Fly away from here, from my house.

# Questions

A: *?Gundhidhi nginda yananhi?*
You came from home? Did you come from home?
B: *Yawu, gundhidhi ngaya dhaay yananhi.*
Yep, I came here from home.

Or

B: *Gamil, garrawalibala ngaya yananhi.*
No, I came from the shops.

A: *Dhalaadhi nginda yananhi?*
Where did you come from?
B: *Gundhidhi ngaya maliyaagu dhaay yananhi.*
Yep, I came here from a friend's house.

**Dhiyamala – Wiimala**

You can use these verbs to give commands. In later lessons you will learn their past and future forms.

> **Audio:** GGU 9.10.mp3 is available in the electronic edition

*Dhiyamala wiyayl man.gadhi, nguuga wiimala.*
Pick up the pen from the table and put it on the book.

If you repeat the command the thing changing will be the object or location, so these will be mentioned first.

*Gaala dhawundi dhiyamala, man.gagabala wiimala.*
Pick up the cup from the ground and put it on the table.

*Gaala Billygu dhawundi dhiyamala, man.gagabala ngay wiimala.*
Pick up Billy's cup from the ground and put it on my table.

**Inalienable possession**

*Dhiyamala wiyayl Kimdhi maradhi, wiimala Bobga dhinaga.*
Pick up the pen from Kim's hand and put it on Bob's foot.

## -DHi, Ablative suffix, and Ablative case

## Cases

You will have noticed that some words have the 'from' meaning when a suffix is attached, e.g. *man.ga-dhi*, 'from the table'; other words have the 'from' meaning 'inbuilt', e.g. *ngirima* 'from here'. Other words have a special form with the 'from' meaning, e.g. *nganundi* is 'from me', and other words again can have a special (irregular) form of the suffix: *Lee-ngundi*, 'from Lee'. These all have the same job – the same function – in a sentence, and we can say they are all Ablative case. Using this terminology makes it easier to describe how the language works. You can say: in this instance use Ablative case, whether the word has the normal suffix, a special suffix, or is another sort of word, such as a pronoun or demonstrative.

The same situation arises with other suffixes. The standard 'place' suffix is *-Ga*, and there are proper noun forms, pronoun forms and demonstrative forms. So, it is simplest to talk about Locative case.

See Appendix 3 at the end of the book for a list of cases, case suffixes and other information.

There are other verbs where Ablative case is only used some of the time, and we do not yet all have the rules for this – we don't always know when to use -*DHi*/Ablative case and when to use something else. This last group of verbs include 'be in' and 'jump'.

Ablative case is also to mark 'selected body part': a situation where an action affects a **whole** thing, but is applied to a **part**. For instance:

Mum touched the **dog** on the **head**.

The **whole** is Accusative case and the **part** is Ablative.

*Ngambaagu **buruma dhaygal-i** dhamay.*

You may have noticed that upper case has been used for case names: Ablative, Locative. This is to distinguish between the case and its uses or functions. 'Movement from' is called 'ablative function'; the last example shows 'selected body part' function.

Interestingly, well it is to some, the 'from' ending in Latin and some other languages also has a wide range of uses that, like the uses of -*DHi*, do not look related.

## *Winangala, garay guwaala, yawala.*
## Listen, say and read.

 **Audio:** GGU 9.11.mp3 is available in the electronic edition

1. *Wiyayl dhiyamala dhawundi.*
   pick.up-command pen ground-from
   Pick up the pen from the ground.
2. *Dhaay gaanga!*
   to.here bring-command
   Bring it here!
   (Note: the 'it' can be omitted in GR)
3. *Wiimala man.gaga.*
   put-command table-on
   Put it on the table.

4. *Dhiyamala biiba ngurungu.*
   pick.up-command paper his
   Pick up his paper.
5. *Ngirilay gaanga!*
   from.here take-command
   Take it away.
6. *Yananhi ngaya garrawali, gundhigu nginu.*
   walked I shop-from house-to your
   I walked from the shop to your house.

🔊 **Audio:** GGU 9.12.mp3 is available in the electronic edition

*Banagaya gundhidhi.*
Run away from the house.

*Dhinawandi banagaya.*
Run away from the emu.

*Banagaya burumadhi.*
Run away from the dog.

*Wilbaarri yananga.*
Get away from the car.

*Dhaay yananga.*
Come here.

*Yananga ngirilay.*
Get away from here.

*Ngirilay banagaya.*
Run away from here.

*Dhigaraa, ngirilay barraya.*
Bird, fly away from here.

**Audio:** GGU 9.13.mp3 is available in the electronic edition

*Gaayli yuruundi gaanga.*
Take the kid away from the road.

*Dhaay banagaya, gundhigu.*
Run here, to home.

*Dhiyamala wiyayl man.gadhi.*
Pick up the pen from the table.

*Biibabiiba dhiyamala man.garri.*
Pick up the book from the bag.

*Ngaandi dhaay yananhi schooli?*
Who came here from school?

*Dhinggaa ngirilay gaanga. Gagil nhama.*
Take the meat away from here. It is bad.

*Dhaay yananga, galidhi.*
Come here, away from the water.

*Gaanga dhuru gaaylidhi.*
Take the snake away from the kid.

*Ngaandi banaganhi dhurudhi?*
Who ran away from the snake.

*Gamil ngaya banagay burumadhi.*
I won't run away from the dog.

 **Audio:** GGU 9.14.mp3 is available in the electronic edition

The text below is adapted from one created/written by Elena Anderson (a student in an earlier course)

A: *Yaama dhagaan.*
 Hi brother.
B: *Yaama baawaa.*
 Hi sister.
A: *Yaama gundhidha buruma?*
 Is the dog at home?

LESSON 9. TO, FROM AND AT

B: *Gamilbala, bubaaga nhama.*
No, he's with dad.
A: *Gaba nhama buruma.*
He's a good dog.
B: *Yawu.*
Yes.
A: *Yaamanda yinggil?*
Are you tired?
B: *Yawu. Giirr ngaya dhaay banaganhi.*
Yes, I ran here!

🔊 **Audio:** GGU 9.15.mp3 is available in the electronic edition

The text below is adapted from one created/written by Simon Ludowyk

S: *Yaama Mary. Gaba nginda?*
Hello Mary. Are you good?
M: *Yaama Simon. Giirr, gaba ngaya.*
Hello Simon. Yep, I am good.
S: *Ngamila! Yaama nhama bandaarr nginu?*
*Baranhi gundhigu ngay, bandaarr nhama.*
Look! Is that your kangaroo?
That kangaroo hopped to my house.
M: *Gamil, ngurungubala, bandaarr nhama.*
*Minya ginyi gundhidha nginu?*
No, that is his kangaroo.
What happened at your house?
S: *Bandaarr gagil baranhi man.gabididha.*
The bad kangaroo hopped on the big table.

🔊 **Audio:** GGU 9.16.mp3 is available in the electronic edition

Abdul: *Yaama baawaa.*
*Yaamanda yanay garrawalgu?*
Hi sister. Will you go to the shop?
Priscilla: *Yaama dhagaan. Giirr ngaya yanay.*
*Yuruunda ngaya yanay.*
Hi brother. I'll go. I will walk on the road.

117

Abdul: *Ngaayaybaay. Ngamila.*
*Dhigaraa nhama.*
*Burumadhi dhigaraa barranhi, gundhigu.*
OK. Look. There's a bird.
The bird flew away from the dog,
to the house.

Priscilla: *Yawu. Giirr gagil nhama buruma.*
*Yaamanda warray burumaga gagila?*
Yes. That dog is bad.
Will you stand near the bad dog?

Abdul: *Gamilbala;*
*Burumadhibala ngaya gagili banagay. Nginda?*
No. I will run away from the bad dog.
What about you?

Priscilla: *Giirr ngaya ngirilay yanay.*
*Ngamila, yarraaman nhama. Ngaandi nhama yarraamanda?*
I am going away from here.
Look, there's a horse. Who is that on the horse?

Abdul: *Giirr bubaa nhama.*
*Giirr dhaay banaganhi buruma, bubaadhi.*
That's (my) dad. The dog ran here,
it ran away from dad.

Priscilla: *Gundhigu ngaya yanay.*
*Baayandhu dhagaan.*
I'm going home. Bye brother.

Abdul: *Ngaayaybaay. Yaluu baawaa.*
OK. Bye sister.

# LESSON 10
# Adjectives – *Gayrrda*

This lesson introduces more Gamilaraay adjectives and discusses their use.

## Vocabulary

🔊 **Audio:** GGU 10.1.mp3 is available in the electronic edition

| *Garay* | Words |
|---|---|
| *minyangay?** | how many? |
| *maal* | one |
| *bulaarr* | two |
| *gulibaa* | three |
| *burrulaa* | many |
| *marayrr** | none |
| *burrul* | big |
| *-bidi** | big |
| *burrulbidi* | great big |
| *gaay* | small |
| *-DHuul* | small, one |
| *buluuy* | black |
| *banggabaa* | white |
| *guwaymbarra* | red |

 **Audio:** GGU 10.2.mp3 is available in the electronic edition

*\*Minyangay* is a 'Y2' word. In other words, the place/Locative form is *minyanga-dha*, and the from/Ablative form is *minyanga-dhi*.

Statements like 'How many children do you have?' are translated into Gamilaraay using possessives.

| | |
|---|---|
| *Minyangay nginu birralii?* | |
| *Gulibaa ngay, birralii.* | I have three, children. |

*Note that there are two ways of translating 'big' – with the adjective *burrul* or with the suffix *-bidi*. It is not clear at present if there is any difference in their meaning or use. The most common occurrence of *-bidi* is with another adjective, particularly *burrulbidi* – 'great big'. It also occurs in *wamu-bidi* 'big fat' and words such as *gagilbidi* 'bad-big', as well as on nouns. *-bidi* does not occur on *gaba* 'good'.

It is suggested that when there is an English way of doing things and a different Gamilaraay way of doing it – for instance, an adjective and a suffix that both mean 'big' – it is good to make sure the Gamilaraay way is often used.

The suffix *-DHuul* is more complex than *-bidi*. While it sometimes means 'small' it can at times mean 'one' and even 'just' – so *yinarr-duul* 'woman-DHuul' can mean a girl who has just become a woman. The *-DH* changes to *d* after words ending in *rr*, *l* and *n*. (In fact, words ending in *rr* are often pronounced without the *rr*, so *yinarr-duul* is often pronounced *yina-duul*.) The suffix is common in Yuwaalaraay place names, often written 'dool' in English. It is likely that we will learn more about this suffix with further investigation.

*\*Marayrr* is used to translate 'no + noun' phrases such as:

| | |
|---|---|
| *gali marayrr* | no water |
| *yarral marayrr* | no money |

It is also used to translate 'none'.

| | |
|---|---|
| *marayrr; gali marayrr* | none; no water |

## Grammar

This grammar section is mainly example sentences.

A question in Gamilaraay grammar is: What was the traditional practice for noun–adjective word order? The order in the sources varies, but is predominantly adjective–noun, especially for numbers. R.H. Mathews, writing around 1900 (Mathews 1902, 1903), said that the GR order is noun–adjective. It may be that the Gamilaraay sources have been influenced by English word order. For the present, use predominantly noun–adjective order. In many Australian languages the order is almost exclusively noun–adjective.

Remember, where a suffix is used on a noun it is also used on adjectives associated with the noun. In 10.1, *buluuy* and *buruma* go together – no suffix. In 10.2, *buluuy* and *man.ga* go together. Both have the Locative suffix, *-Ga*.

 **Audio:** GGU 10.3.mp3 is available in the electronic edition

---

10.1(a) *Buruma buluuy man.gaga.*
The black dog is on the table.
*Buluuy buruma man.gaga.*
The black dog is on the table.
10.2(a) *Buruma man.gaga buluuydha.*
The dog is on the black table.
*Buruma buluuydha man.gaga.*
The dog is on the black table.

---

In Gamilaraay the order for sentences like the next seems to be fairly fixed:

adjective–demonstrative–noun

*Gaba nhama yinarr.*
The woman is good.

> With further research, it turns out that the old sources do not have the clear patterns of adjective use given above. (The information comes from Yuwaalaraay, since there are very few Gamilaraay sentences recorded.) While numbers and words like 'many' are often case marked, phrases such as *wirridha gabaga* 'on the good plate' are quite rare. For the time being, stick with the process given in the grammar section, until someone finds how Gamilaraay actually used adjectives.

 **Audio:** GGU 10.4.mp3 is available in the electronic edition

In fact, in Gamilaraay an adjective and the noun it goes with do not have to be next to each other, so 10.1 could also be said:

10.1(b)   *Buruma man.gaga buluuy.*
          The black dog is on the table.

and you know that *buruma* and *buluuy* go together because they have the same suffix (in this instance 'zero'), so 10.2 can also be said:

10.2(b)   *Man.gaga buruma buluuydha.*
          The dog is on the black table.

Here *man.gaga* and *buluuydha* have the -Ga suffix and so go together.

Two women.
*Yinarr bulaarr*. Or, less regular:
*Bulaarr yinarr*.

> There is also a suffix *-gaali/-gaalay* that means something like 'a pair of', e.g. *yinarrgaali*.

*Gaay nhalay gundhi.*
This house is small.

*Man.gadhi girrinilgu baranhi bandaarr burrul.*
The big roo hopped from the table to the door.

*Ngamila, burumabidi gundhigu yananhi.*
Look, a big dog went to the house.

*Dhinaga warraya bulaarra.*
Stand on two feet.

*Giyal ngaya burumadhi burruli, gamilbala ngaya burumadhi giyal gaaydhi.*
I am afraid of the big dog but not of the small dog.

*Minyangay biibabiiba man.gaga?*
How many books are on the table?

*Giirr gaay nhama gulibaa dhuru.*
Those three snakes are really small.

*Yaama buluuy nhama gundhi nginu?*
Is your house black?

 **Audio:** GGU 10.5.mp3 is available in the electronic edition

Below are four translations of an English sentence.

Is the white horse on the road?

---

a) *Yaama nhama yuruunda, yarraaman banggabaa?*
   *Yuruunda, yarraaman ngaama banggabaa?*
b) *Yaama yarraaman banggabaa yuruunda?*
   *Yarraaman banggabaa, yuruunda?*

---

In a) the question is about where the horse is,
in b) it is about what is on the road.

*Burrulaa dhayn gundhidha.*
There are lots of people in the house.

*Giirr ngaya marayrr yarral.*
I've got **no** money. (note: *ngaya*)

*Gamil ngaya giyal burumadhi.*
I am not afraid of the dog.

*Yaama nginda giyal dhurudhi?*
Are you afraid of the snake?

*Gamil. Dhinawandibala ngaya giyal burruli.*
No. I am afraid of the big emu.

WIIDHAA

*Wiyayl bulaarr dhaay gaanga!*
Bring two pens here.

*Burrulaa burruluu dhinggaaga.*
There are lots of flies on the meat.

## Practice

### Just the adjective

 **Audio:** GGU 10.6.mp3 is available in the electronic edition

To get used to the words, just use an appropriate adjective.

Start with colours. Point to objects and say the colour. Do this for other adjectives – size, number and so on.

*Yilaa*/then sentences.

(Remember, the examples provide the pattern. You need to create many similar sentences using other vocabulary.)

*Banggabaa nhalay biiba.*
This paper is white.

*Wiyayl guwaymbarra.*
White paper.

---

A: *Man.garr buluuy?*  (pointing to a bag)
   Is it a black bag?
B: *Yawu, man.garr nhama buluuy. // Gamilbala. Banggabaa nhama man.garr.*
   Yes, that is a black bag. // No, that bag is white.
A: *Dhalaa baadhal?*
   Where is the bottle?
B: *Man.gaga baadhal gaaydha.*
   The bottle is on the small table.
A: *Minyangay wiyayl?*  (pointing to/holding *wiyayl*)
   How many pens?

B: (counts) *maal, bulaarr, gulibaa, burrulaa. Burrulaa wiyayl maraga.*
One, two, three, many pens. A lot of pens in (your) hand.

A: *Minyangay wiyayl buluuy?*
How many black pens?

## Commands

Gradually build up to sentences like:

A: *Wiyayl buluuy bulaarr dhiyamala man.gadhi, biibaga banggabaaga wiimala.*
Pick up two black pens from the table and put them on the white paper.

## *Winangala, garay guwaala, yawala.*
## Listen, say and read.

 **Audio:** GGU 10.7.mp3 is available in the electronic edition

*Yarraaman buluuy yananhi gundhigu.*
The black horse went to the house.

*Yarraaman yananhi gundhigu buluuygu.*
The horse went to the black house.

*Yarraaman yananhi gundhigu, buluuy.*
The black horse went to the house.
The horse went the house, the black one.

*Gundhigu yarraaman yananhi, buluuygu.*
The horse went to the house, to the black one.

*Yaama gundhigu banggabaagu buruma banaganhi?*
Did the dog run to the white house?

*Yawu, banggabaagu.*
Yep, to the white one.

**Audio:** GGU 10.8.mp3 is available in the electronic edition

| | |
|---|---|
| Sheila: | *Yaama Freida.* |
| | Hi Freida. |
| Freida: | *Yaama Sheila.* |
| | Hi Sheila. |
| Sheila: | *Yaamanda yanay gundhigu ngay?* |
| | Will you come to my place/house? |
| Freida: | *Ngaayaybaay. Dhalaa gundhi nginu?* |
| | OK. Where is your house? |
| Sheila: | *Yuruunda.* |
| | On the road. |
| Freida: | *Ngaayaybaay. Yaama nhama banggabaa?* |
| | OK. Is it white? |
| Sheila: | *Yawu, banggabaa nhama.* |
| | Yes, it is white. |
| Freida: | *Burrul?* |
| | Is it big. |
| Sheila: | *Gamil. Gaaybala gundhi ngay.* |
| | No. My house is small. |
| Freida: | *Minyangay birralii gundhidha?* |
| | How many kids at the house? |
| Sheila: | *Marayrr birralii. Guliirr maal.*   (*Marayrr* is first, since it is the new information, the answer.) |
| | No kids and one husband. |
| Freida: | *Ngaayaybaay. Yanay ngaya gundhigu.* |
| | OK, I will go to the house. |
| Sheila: | *Gaba.* |
| | Good. |

# LESSON 11
# *L* class verbs; transitivity; doer.to/Ergative suffix

This lesson introduces some other forms of *L* class verbs, describes the difference between transitive and intransitive verbs, and looks at some of the forms of nouns, pronouns and adjectives used with transitive and intransitive verbs. We will look at a range of sentences with transitive and intransitive verbs and then summarise the rules for nouns, pronouns and adjectives (collectively known as nominals).

There is a lot to learn in Lesson 11. Lesson 12 is considerably shorter.

A reminder: verbs can be thought of as '**doing/being**' words (cook, run, see, sleep, live). They can also be thought of as words that can be changed to things like a **past** form (cooked, ran, saw, slept, lived) and a **future** form (will cook, will run, will see, will sleep, will live) and generally **lots of other forms** (is cooking, has cooked, will be cooking, and more).

## Vocabulary

Below are the command forms of some new *L* class verbs.

 **Audio:** GGU 11.1.mp3 is available in the electronic edition

| *Garay* | Words | Transitivity |
|---|---|---|
| *baabila!* | sleep/lie | intransitive |
| *dhurrala!* | come, appear | intransitive |
| | | |
| *bumala!* | hit! | transitive |
| *garrala!* | cut! | transitive |
| *dhala!* | eat! | transitive |
| *yiila!* | bite! | transitive |
| *-Gu* | 'doer.to' | suffix (Ergative) |

*L* class verbs already learnt include:

*Winanga-la, ngamila, dhiyamala, wiimala, bawila, garay guwaala.*

There are very few intransitive *L* class verbs. You need only remember *baabila* and *dhurrala*.

There are very few transitive *Y* class verbs.

# Grammar

## Transitive and intransitive verbs

The difference between transitive and intransitive verbs is not relevant for English or for the vast majority of languages people in Australia learn, so study it carefully and be prepared to take a while to get used to it. The division is relevant to many languages including the vast majority of Australian languages, many languages in New Guinea, Inuit, some Indian languages, Basque and more. An introductory approach is:

With **intransitive verbs** only one thing needs to be involved, an ***actor/doer***:

*I* walked.

*You* slept.

*The wind* blew.

The *Y* class verbs in previous lessons are all intransitive. Most (but not all) *L* class verbs are transitive.

With **transitive verbs** two things are normally/mostly involved. For example, eat (eater and food), see (see-er and seen), drink:

**I** (actor/doer.to) ate (action) the meat (acted on/done.to).

**Mum** cooked the spaghetti.

**The dog** chased an emu.

**A wind** blew the house down.

The meaning of some verbs makes it obvious that they are transitive (eat, hit) or intransitive (sleep). Some verbs are not obvious. For example *bawi-li* 'sing' is transitive. The dictionary indicates which verbs are transitive (**tr**) and which intransitive (**int**).

In English the same form can be transitive and intransitive.

I cooked the meat. – transitive

*The meat* cooked. – intransitive

This does not happen in Gamilaraay – the verbs in those two sentences would be different.

Be careful to distinguish the core of the sentence from other bits. The core determines if a verb is transitive or intransitive. It is generally possible to add lots of other information to the sentence, but this does not change the core, the transitivity. The sentences above are now repeated, with more information that **does not** affect the transitivity.

I cooked the meat yesterday afternoon, for everyone who came to the party.

*The meat* cooked while we were talking about the weather on the patio.

## L class verbs

The simple forms of the *L* class verbs – command, future and past – are set out in the table below. The English translation is given for a few verbs. You can work out the others by following the pattern.

You have met the concepts of a verb root, the bit that does not change; and endings or suffixes, the bits that change. So, for *baabila!* the root is *baabi-*, and that must be followed by a suffix. The same suffixes or endings are used for all *L* class verbs.

🔊 **Audio:** GGU 11.2.mp3 is available in the electronic edition

| Command* | Future* | Past* | English, transitive/intransitive |
|---|---|---|---|
| *-la* | *-y* | *-li* | (Suffix) |
| *baabi-la* lie down! | *baabi-li* will lie down | *baabi-y* lay down | **int** also 'sleep' |
| *dhurra-la* come! | *dhurra-li* will come, appear | *dhurra-y* came, appeared | **int** |
| *bumala!* hit!beat/hit it! | *bumali* will hit/beat | *bumay* did beat/hit | **tr** |
| *dhala!* eat! eat it! | *dhali* will eat | *dhay* ate | **tr** |
| *yiila!* | *yiili* | *yiiy* | bite, **tr** |
| *dhiyamala!* | *dhiyamali* | *dhiyamay* | pick up, **tr** |
| *wiimala!* | *wiimali* | *wiimay* | put down, **tr** |
| *ngamila!* | *ngamili* | *ngamiy* | see, look at, **tr** |
| *winangala!* | *winangali* | *winangay* | hear, listen, **tr** |
| *garay guwaala!* | *garay guwaali* | *garay guwaay** | talk, **tr** |

*Command, or Imperative, is not actually a tense.

*The past tense has uses not found in English past tenses. It can be used for recent action that has current consequences, more commonly found in verbs of other classes, e.g. *balu-nhi* 'it died/it is dead'.

*As noted previously, the GY future indicates something may happen, but with less certainty than the English future does. GY future could be translated 'might X'.

*'Talk' in GR is a phrase, not one word. *Garay* is 'word, language' and *guwaali* something like 'tell/say'. The pronunciation of *guwaali/guwaay* is somewhat different from expected. The *aa* in *guwaali* is like English 'or' and the *guwaay* sounds like 'gwoi'. You can hear these words on *Gayarragi, Winangali*.

# LESSON 11. *L* CLASS VERBS; TRANSITIVITY; DOER.TO/ERGATIVE SUFFIX

The next six sentences have transitive verbs and intransitive verbs and nothing surprising. The pronouns and nouns are just as you have been using them.

 **Audio:** GGU 11.3.mp3 is available in the electronic edition

---

*Yananhi* ngaya.          intransitive verb
went       I
I went/walked.

*Yananhi* nginda.         intransitive verb
went you(1 person)
You(1) went/walked.

*Yananhi* buruma.         intransitive verb
went       dog
The dog went/walked.

*Yananhi* dhinawan.       intransitive verb
went       emu
The emu went/walked.

*Buruma ngaya ngamiy.*    transitive verb
dog        I     saw
I saw a dog.

*Buruma nginda ngamiy.*   transitive verb
dog you(1 person) saw
You(1) saw a dog.

---

It may help to practise the verb forms, as set out in part 1 of Practice, before going onto the next part of the grammar.

WIIDHAA

## The nouns and pronouns around transitive and intransitive verbs

> It would be more accurate to say the nominals around these verbs, including other types of words such as adjectives and nominal demonstratives.

 **Audio:** GGU 11.4.mp3 is available in the electronic edition

There is a range of terminology to refer to things involved with verbs, set out in the table below. Ignore the table if it is not helpful now. (This table sets out the Gamilaraay pattern, not the English.)

With Intransitive verbs there is fundamentally one thing involved. We will call it the **doer**, and say it is in Nominative case.

With Transitive verbs there are fundamentally two things involved. We will call one the **doer.to**, and say it is in Ergative case, the other is the **done.to** and it is in Accusative case.

> There is other terminology used. In languages, such as English and Latin, where there is no difference between the doer and doer.to they can be called 'subject'. The doer.to is sometimes called the 'agent'. The done.to is commonly called the 'object'.

The new rule you need to learn is when the **doer.to** with a transitive verb is represented by a noun – for instance, in the next two sentences – it must have the **doer.to/Ergative** suffix:

---

*Buruma-**gu** dhinawan ngamiy.*   transitive verb
dog-doer.to    emu    saw
The dog saw an emu.

---

*Dhinawan-**du** buruma ngamiy.*   transitive verb
emu-doer.to    dog    saw
The emu saw a dog.

---

In English, the 'doer.to' is the one that comes first in the sentence. Having a **doer.to/Ergative** suffix that shows who is doing the action means Gamilaraay can change the word order a lot, since **the suffix**, not the word order, **tells you who is acting**. This gives the language great flexibility to emphasise different things by putting them first in the sentence. The next five sentences can all have the same English translation, but have different emphases.

*Buruma-gu ngamiy dhinawan.*
dog-doer.to     saw     emu
**The dog** saw an emu.

*Dhinawan buruma-gu ngamiy.*
emu     dog-doer.to     saw
The dog saw **an emu**.

*Dhinawan ngamiy buruma-gu.*
emu     saw     dog-doer.to
The dog saw **an emu**.

*Ngamiy buruma-gu dhinawan.*
saw     dog-doer.to     emu
The dog **saw** an emu.

*Ngamiy dhinawan buruma-gu.*
saw     emu     dog-doer.to
The dog **saw** an emu.

## Ergative(doer.to) nouns

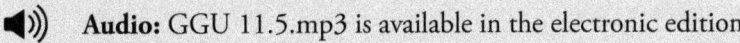
**Audio:** GGU 11.5.mp3 is available in the electronic edition

As with the place/Locative suffix, the actual shape or form of the **doer.to/Ergative** suffix varies, depending on the ending of the word it is attached to. Below is a list of words with the suffix. Remember, the **doer.to/Ergative** suffix is only used with transitive verbs.

| Noun+doer.to/Ergative suffix | English |
|---|---|
| *buruma-gu* | dog |
| *giidjaa-gu* | ant |
| *muru-gu* | nose |
| *gunii-dhu* | mum, mother |
| *gali-dhu* | water |
| *garrangay-dhu* | duck |
| *dhinawan-du* | emu |
| *barran-du* | boomerang |
| *badjigal-u* | bike |
| *bandaarr-u* | kangaroo |

The forms of the suffix is shown in the table below. Notice that the **doer.to/Ergative** suffix is the same as the **Locative** suffix, except that the final *a* is replaced by a *u*.

## Doer.to/Ergative and local suffixes*

| Word endings | *-Gu* (doer.to) | *-Ga* (place) | *-DHi* (from) | *-gu* (to) |
|---|---|---|---|---|
| **a, u** | -gu | -ga | -dhi | -gu |
| **i, y*** | -dhu | -dha | -dhi | -gu |
| **n** | -du | -da | -di | -gu |
| **rr, l** | -u | -a | -i | -gu |

*This is a slightly simplified version of GR. There are also so-called Y2 words, such as *yaraay* 'sun' and *bagay* 'creek' that form the Locative, Ablative and Ergative by dropping the *y* and adding -*dha*/-*dhi*/*dhu*: e.g. *yaraa-dha, yaraa-dhi, yaraa-dhu*. Only a few such words have been found in the GR sources, considerably more are found in the Yuwaalaraay sources.

Irregular case forms include *minya-dhu* Ergative and *minya-dha* Locative: *minya* 'what?'

There are summary tables in the *Dictionary*, pp. 266, 340, and a more up-to-date table in the appendices.

With first person pronouns and second person pronouns the **doer/Nominative** and the **doer.to/Ergative** pronoun is the same, whether the verb is intransitive or transitive. (Third person pronoun pronouns are treated in a later lesson.)

# LESSON 11. *L* CLASS VERBS; TRANSITIVITY; DOER.TO/ERGATIVE SUFFIX

 **Audio:** GGU 11.6.mp3 is available in the electronic edition

*Yananhi* ngaya. *Ngamiy* ngaya maliyaa.

I went. I saw a friend.

With nouns the **doer/Nominative** noun (intransitive verb) has no suffix, and the **doer.to/Ergative** noun (transitive verb) has the suffix.

*Yananhi* birralii. Birraliidhu maliyaa *ngamiy*. / Maliyaa birraliidhu *ngamiy*.

The child went. The child saw a friend.

Below are a few more sentences.

---

*Yanay gaayli.*  |  intransitive
will.walk child
The kid will walk.

---

*Gaayli-**dhu** bubaa ngamili.*  |  transitive
child-**doer.to** dad will.see
The kid will see dad.

---

*Gaayli bubaa-**gu** ngamili.*  |  transitive
child dad-**doer.to** will.see
Dad will see the child.

---

*Baabili gunii.*  |  intransitive
will. sleep mum
Mum will sleep.

---

*Gunii-**dhu** bubaa ngamili.*  |  transitive
mum-**doer.to** dad will.see
Mum will see dad.

---

*Gunii dhinawan-**du** ngamili.*  |  transitive
child emu-doer.to will.see
The emu will see mum.

## Summary

When the verb is transitive you need to decide the form of the doer.to (Ergative case) and the done.to (Accusative case).

The doer.to:

If the **doer.to** is **'I'** or **'you'** use the form you have already learnt, the same form that is used with intransitive verbs.

If the **doer.to** is a **noun** or **adjective**, you need to add an doer.to/Ergative suffix.

The **done.to** is the usual, simple form of the noun or adjective – no suffix.

# Extension

 **Audio:** GGU 11.7.mp3 is available in the electronic edition

You may have noticed some areas we have avoided. What if I/you are the done.to? What if the doer.to is third person? These will be covered fully in later lessons, but some instances are given in the table and sentences below.

| Case | Examples of case forms | | | | |
|---|---|---|---|---|---|
| | 1st and 2nd person pronouns follow the pattern of *ngaya* | 3rd person pronoun pattern | Other nominals | | Special (only some given here) |
| | | | marking | example | |
| Nominative/ doer | ngaya | =nha, nhama+ | Ø | yinarr | minya |
| Ergative/ doer.to | ngaya | nguru | -*Gu* | yinarr-u | minya-dhu |
| Accusative/ done.to | nganha | =nha, nhama+ | Ø | yinarr | minya |

LESSON 11. *L* CLASS VERBS; TRANSITIVITY; DOER.TO/ERGATIVE SUFFIX

*Yananhi=nha.*      intransitive verb
went **he/she**
she/he went/walked.

*Dhinawan nguru ngamiy.*      transitive verb
emu **he/she** saw
**She/he** saw an emu.

## Another approach

Another way of approaching this is:

When you are using a Gamilaraay verb **the first step** is to determine if the verb is **intransitive** or **transitive**.

**If the verb is intransitive** there is one thing that must be involved:

| | |
|---|---|
| I slept. | *Baabiy ngaya.* |
| The rock fell. | *Yarral bundaanhi.* |
| They walked. | *Yananhi ganunga.* |
| The bird is flying. | *Barawaanha dhigaraa.* |

The one thing can be called the doer (It is Nominative case).

**If the verb is transitive** there are generally two things involved: the doer.to (It is Ergative case.) and the done.to (It is Accusative case).

| | |
|---|---|
| I drank the water. | *Gali ngaya ngarunhi.* |
| The rock broke the stick. | *Yarral-u dhulu gamay.* |
| The bird heard the car. | *Dhigaraa-gu wilbaarr winangay.* |

Sometimes there is no 'done.to' word, but since the verb is transitive the doer.to is Ergative.

| | |
|---|---|
| I sang. | *Bawiy ngaya.* |
| The bird ate. | *Dhigaraa-gu dhay.* |

# Practice *maal*/1 – with pronouns

> **Audio:** GGU 11.8.mp3 is available in the electronic edition

Use the simple *L* class verb forms with the actor being *ngaya* or *nginda*. Then make longer sentences using other material from previous lessons.

A: *Baabila!*
Sleep!
B: *Baabili ngaya. Baabiy ngaya.*
I will sleep. (sleeps) I slept.

With the next practice use the first two sections, then gradually extend the conversation.

A: *Wiyayl dhiyamala!*
Pick up the pen!
B: *Yawu, dhiyamali ngaya wiyayl. Wiyayl ngaya dhiyamay.*
I will pick up the pen. (does it) I picked up the pen.
A: *Birray gaba. Wiyayl nginda dhiyamay!*
Good boy! You picked up the pen.
A: *Wiimala=bala=nga wiyayl nguuga!*
Now put the pen on the book!
B: *Ngaayaybaay. Wiimali ngaya wiyayl nguuga. Wiyayl ngaya (nguuga) wiimay.*
OK. I will put the pen down on the book. (does it) I put down the pen (on the book).

Start similar conversations with other phrases. A few examples are:

| | |
|---|---|
| *Man.ga bumala.* | Hit the table. |
| *Miyay winangala.* | Listen to the girl. |
| *Ngamila birray.* | Look at the boy. |

(Note: when translating listen **to** and look **at** you do not need any suffixes on the **done.to** in GY.)

> **Audio:** GGU 11.9.mp3 is available in the electronic edition

LESSON 11. *L* CLASS VERBS; TRANSITIVITY; DOER.TO/ERGATIVE SUFFIX

# Negatives

A: *Wiyayl dhiyamala!*
   Pick up the pen!
B: *Gamilbala. Gamil ngaya wiyayl dhiyamali.*
   No. I won't pick up the pen.   (note: *ngaya* stays in second position)

B does something, A tells them not to.
A: *Garriya man.ga bumala!*
   Don't hit the table!

# Questions

### Intonation

A: *?Wiyayl nginda dhiyamali?*
   You will pick up **the pen**? Will you pick up the pen?
B: *Gamilbala. Gamil ngaya wiyayl dhiyamali.*
   No. I won't pick up the pen.

Or:

B: *Yawu. Giirr ngaya wiyayl dhiyamali.*
   Yes. I **will** pick up the pen.   (note: *ngaya* stays in second position)
B: *Ngamila! Wiyayl ngaya dhiyamay.*
   Look! I picked up the pen.

Or start with:

A: *?Dhiyamali nginda wiyayl?*
   You will **pick up** the pen? Will you **pick up** the pen?

🔊 **Audio:** GGU 11.10.mp3 is available in the electronic edition

WIIDHAA

## Questions with *Yaama/Minya*, etc.

A: **Yaama** *nginda wilbaarr ngamiy? Yaama=nda wilbaarr ngamiy?*
Did you see the car?

---

A: **Minya** *nginda dhali?*
What will you will eat?
B: *Ngamila. Giirr ngaya apple dhali.* ... *Dhay ngaya apple.*
Look. I will eat an apple. ... I ate the apple.
A: **Dhalaa** *ngaya man.garr wiimali?*
Where will I put the bag?
B: *Man.ga-ga. Man.ga-ga man.garr wiimala.*
On the table. Put the bag on the table.

## Practice *bulaarr*/2: Nouns as doer, doer.to, done.to (Nominative, Ergative, Accusative)

It may help to label the role of all the nouns in this section: doer, doer.to, done.to.

Use the pattern below with the *L* class verbs you know.

A: *Baabila, dhagaan!*
Sleep, brother!
B: *Baabili dhagaan.* *Baabiy dhagaan.*
Brother will sleep. Brother slept.

With the next practice begin by just using the first two sentences, then gradually extend the conversation. You can then substitute other objects, or other verbs: *bumala, garrala, yiila, ngamila*, etc.

A: *Baawaa, wiyayl dhiyamala!*
Sister, Pick up the pen!
B: *Ngamila, wiyayl baawaa-gu dhiyamay.*
Look, sister picked up the pen.
A: *Baawaa, wiimala=bala=nga wiyayl nguuga!*
Sister, now put the pen on the book!
B: *Ngamila, wiimay baawaa-gu wiyayl nguuga.*
Look, sister put the pen down on the book.

Start similar conversations with other phrases. A few examples are:

| | |
|---|---|
| *Dhagaan, man.ga bumala.* | Brother, hit the table. |
| *Miyay winangala.* | Listen to the girl. |
| *Ngamila birray.* | Look at the boy. |

 **Audio:** GGU 11.11.mp3 is available in the electronic edition

## Negatives

Working in a group:

| | |
|---|---|
| A *Bdha*: | *Gamilbala C-dhu dhinggaa dhali.* |
| | C will not eat the meat. |
| B: | *Yawu, guniidhubala dhinggaa dhali.* |
| | Yes, but mum will eat the meat. |

> *Bdha* indicates A is talking **to** B; the Locative suffix has the form *-dha* because the letter B is said bee/be, ending with the same sound as Gamilaraay *i/ii*; so the suffix is *-dha*.

## Questions

**Intonation** (working in groups)

| | |
|---|---|
| A: | *?Wiyayl miyaydhu dhiyamali?* |
| | Will the girl pick up **the pen**? |
| B: | *Gamilbala. Gamil miyaydhu wiyayl dhiyamali.* |
| | No. The girl won't pick up the pen. |

Or

| | |
|---|---|
| B: | *Yawu. Yinarru wiyayl dhiyamali.* |
| | Yes. The woman will pick up the pen. |
| B: | *Ngamila! Wiyayl baawaagu dhiyamay.* |
| | Look! Sister picked up the pen. |

WIIDHAA

Or start with:

| | |
|---|---|
| A: | *?Dhiyamali nginda wiyayl?* |
| | You will **pick up** the pen? Will you **pick up** the pen? |

## *Winangala, garay guwaala, yawala.*
## Listen, say and read.

 **Audio:** GGU 11.12.mp3 is available in the electronic edition

1. *Giirr ngaya birralii burrulaa winangay.*
   I heard a lot of kids.
2. *Giirr miyaydhu birralii burrulaa winangay.*
   The girl heard a lot of kids.
3. *Man.garr nginda nhama ngay dhiyamay.*
   You picked up that bag of mine.
4. *Man.garr nhama ngay birraydhu dhiyamay.*
   The boy picked up that bag of mine.
5. *Giirr ngaya man.garr wiimay.*
   I put the bag down.
6. *Giirr bubaagu man.garr wiimay.*
   Dad put the bag down.
7. *Dhimbagu biiba dhay.*
   The sheep ate the paper.
8. *Birralii yarraamandu ngamiy.*
   The horse saw the child.
9. *Birraliidhu yarraaman ngamiy.*
   The child saw the horse.
10. *Dhurugu giwiirr yiiy, giwiirrubala gamil dhuru yiiy.*
    The snake bit the man, but the man did not bite the snake.
11. *Burumagu buluuydhu yinarr yiili.*
    The black dog will bite the woman.
12. *Gamilbala buruma buluuy yinarru yiili.*
    The woman will not bite the black dog.
13. *Bubaagu gunii ngamiy, gamilbala guniidhu bubaa ngamiy.*
    Dad saw mum, but mum did not see dad.

# LESSON 12
# Doer.to/Actor and instrument

This lesson introduces the instrumental use of Ergative case, *nguru* – Ergative 'she, he, it', and the Ergative question pronoun, *ngaandu*.

In Lesson 11 you saw the common form of the Ergative suffix on standard nouns and adjectives, but by now you will realise some other words such as pronouns do not have a suffix, just a special form.

## Vocabulary

 **Audio:** GGU 12.1.mp3 is available in the electronic edition

| Garay | Words |
|---|---|
| *gimubila!*\* | do/make! **tr** |
| *nguru*\* | she, he, it (Ergative) |
| *minyadhu?* | what with? |
| *ngaandu?* | who did it? (Ergative) |
| *nhaayba* | knife |
| *magal*\* | knife |
| *gula* | fork |
| *wirri* | plate |
| *dhiyarral* | spoon |
| *dhulu* | stick |
| *mungin* | mosquito |

*There are some English words, including 'make', that are particularly problematic to translate. You can use *gimubili* for creating something, but often other words would likely have been used. A few examples: 'cook' for 'make' a meal, 'cut' for make a boomerang, *burranba-li* for 'making happy/sad'.

\**Nguru* is doer.to/Ergative 'she/he/it', so is used to translate those words when they are the doer.to, the subject of a transitive verb. For example in:

*Man.garr nguru dhiyamay.*
She picked up the bag.

Like other subject and object pronouns it is predominantly in second position in the sentence or clause.

\**Magal* is a traditional word for knife and *nhaayba* is an adaptation of the English 'knife'. Some may prefer to use *magal* even if *nhaayba* has been used recently.

# Grammar

 **Audio:** GGU 12.2.mp3 is available in the electronic edition

### Instrumental function of Ergative case

You have seen how the Ergative suffix can show who or what is the **doer.to**, as in:

*Birraliidhu dhinggaa dhay.*
The child ate the meat.

The same suffix is used to show an instrument, something that is used to do something. For example:

*Birralii-dhu dhinggaa dhay, magal-u, gula-gu.*
The child ate the meat **with a knife and fork.**

*Dhiyamay ngaya wiyayl, mara-gu.*
I picked up the pen **with my hand.**

It is generally easy to distinguish the two functions of the suffix.

## LESSON 12. DOER.TO/ACTOR AND INSTRUMENT

A doer.to (also known as agent) is generally **animate** – a living thing.

Instruments are usually **inanimate** – non-living. The 'instrument' is also often after the verb, at the end of the sentence, whereas the doer.to is more often before the verb. The most common word order is:

Doer.to done.to verb; often with other words such as *giirr* (first word) and demonstratives.

Instruments are more commonly found in sentences with transitive verbs but are found with intransitive verbs.

| | |
|---|---|
| *Bumay ngaya dhawun, dhulu-gu.* I hit the ground with a stick. | transitive verb |
| *Yananhi ngaya dhulu-**gu**.* I walked with (using) a stick. | intransitive verb |

The Ergative suffix is used to translate 'with' when it means something is an instrument. It does not translate 'with' in other circumstances; for instance, 'I walked home with my sister'. 'I walked with a stick (on my shoulder)'. You will learn how to say that later.

Note a special form of the Ergative suffix on *minya*? 'what?'. *Minyadhu* means 'what with?' 'using what?' and 'what?(doer.to)'.

In the next sentences *minyadhu* refers to an **instrument**, it has **instrumental** function:

*Minyadhu nginda dhuru bumay?*
What did you hit/kill the snake with?

*Dhulugu ngaya dhuru bumay.*
I hit/killed the snake with the stick.

*Minyadhu=nda dhinggaa dhiyamay?*
What did you pick up the meat with?

*Maragu.*
With my hand.

In the next sentence, *minyadhu* refers to a **doer.to**, it has **ergative** function:

*Minyadhu buruma yiiy?*
What bit the dog?

**Audio:** GGU 12.3.mp3 is available in the electronic edition

Some more examples:

*Dhuru bumala dhulu-gu.*
Hit the snake with the stick.

*Garriya mara-gu yuul dhamala.*
Don't touch the food with your hand.

*Giirr=nha ngaya bumay, buruma, bundi-dhu.*
I hit the dog with a bundi/club.

(This example has a general term =*nha* 'it', then the specific *buruma*. This pattern is relatively common in Aboriginal languages.)

*Birraydhu buruma bumay, barran-du.*
The boy hit the dog with a boomerang.

*Dhiyamala dhinggaa gula-gu!*
Pick up the meat with the fork.

*Dhiyamala dhinggaa gula-gu, gamilbala maragu.*
Pick up the meat with the fork, not with your hand.

*Giirr dhaadhaa yananhi dhulugu.*
Grandad walked with a stick.

*Yaama dhaadhaagu giidjaa bumay, dhulugu burrul-u?*
Did granddad hit/kill the ant with a big stick?

## Nguru

*Nguru* is the doer.to/Ergative form of 'she/he/it'.

**Reminder:** When using verbs you need to start by knowing if the verb is transitive or intransitive.

If intransitive the only thing necessarily involved is the **doer**, which is in Nominative case.

If the verb is intransitive there is a **doer.to**/Ergative case and often a **done.to**/Accusative case.

The examples below show that the doer/Nominative and done.to/Accusative forms are the same for third person pronouns. The doer.to/Ergative is different.

| She ran. | Intransitive verb | so 'she' is =*NHa*, Ø, or *nhama*. | doer/Nominative |
|---|---|---|---|
| *Banaganhi**nha***. Or *Banaganhi*. Or, less commonly, *Banaganhi **nhama***. ||||
| I saw **her**. | Transitive verb | so 'she' is =*NHa*, Ø, or *nhama*. | done.to/Accusative |

*Ngamiy**nha** ngaya.* Or *Ngamiy ngaya.* Or, less commonly, *Ngamiy ngaya **nhama***.

For third person pronouns like 'he/she/it' the doer.to/Ergative is different.

She saw the car.   Transitive verb, doer.to/Ergative, so 'she' is *nguru*.
*Ngamiy **nguru** wilbaarr.* Or *Wilbaarr **nguru** ngamiy.*

## *Ngaandi / ngaandu* 'who, whom'

 **Audio:** GGU 12.4.mp3 is available in the electronic edition

Note also another GY pronoun that translates 'Who?'

*Ngaandi* is used when the verb is intransitive (**doer**), and *ngaandu* when the verb is transitive, and the question is about the **doer.to**. *Ngaandi* is **also used** for the **done.to** with a transitive verb.

Another way of putting this is that *ngaandi* is Nominative and Accusative case, *ngaandu* is Ergative case.

You may need to check this section a few times as this can be a difficult concept.

| Who? | (doer and done.to) | ***ngaandi?*** | For instance: |
|---|---|---|---|

***Ngaandi*** *dhaay dhurray?* (Intransitive verb, doer)
**Who** came here?

***Ngaandi*** *nginda ngamiy.*
**Who(m)** did you see?

| Who? (doer.to) | ***ngaandu?*** | For instance: |
|---|---|---|

***Ngaandu*** *dhinggaa dhay?*
**Who** ate the meat?

Further examples:

*Ngaandi yananhi?*
Who walked?

*Ngaandi banaganhi?*
Who ran?

*Ngaandi baabiy?*
Who slept?

*Ngaandu buruma bumay?*
Who hit the dog?

*Ngaandi burumagu yiiy?*
Who did the dog bite?

*Ngaandi nginda ngamiy?* (Transitive verb, done.to)
Who/whom did you(1) see?

*Ngaandu buruma yiiy?*
Who bit the dog?

*Ngaandu cake wiya-nhi?*
Who made the cake? (cooked)

*Ngaandi yananhi gundhi-gu?*
Who walked to the house? (using the *-gu* 'to' suffix)

Another way to describe the pattern is:

*Ngaandi* is not a first and second person pronoun, so the form of the doer (Nominative) and the done.to (Accusative) is the same. The doer.to (Ergative) is *ngaandu*, ending in *u* as most Ergatives do.

# Practice

 **Audio:** GGU 12.5.mp3 is available in the electronic edition

This is a good chance to revise vocabulary. Establish a pattern, then change just one thing.

*Dhama-li ngaya wirri gula-gu.*
I will touch the plate with a fork.

*Dhama-li ngaya wirri mara-gu.*
I will touch the plate with my hand.

*Dhama-li ngaya wirri wiyayl-u.*
I will touch the plate with a pen.

Then change more elements: the verb, the done.to, and so on.

*Dhama-y=nha ngaya gula-gu.*
I touched it with a fork.

 **Audio:** GGU 12.6.mp3 is available in the electronic edition

### In pairs/groups

| | |
|---|---|
| A: | *Buma-la man.ga maragu.* |
| | Hit the table with your hand. |
| B: | *Bumali ngaya man.ga maragu.* |
| | I will hit the table with my hand. |
| | *Bumay ngaya man.ga maragu.* |
| | I hit the table with my hand. |
| C *Adha*: | *Ngamiy nginda? Bumay Bdhu man.ga maragu.* |
| C to A: | Did you see? B hit the table with their hand. |
| A *Cdha*: | *Yawu, ngamiy ngaya. Man.ga nguru bumay.* |
| A to C: | Yes, I saw. She hit the table. |

### Questions

*Minyadhu ngaya biiba dhiyamali?*
What will I pick up the paper with?

---

A: *Magalu nginda dhinggaa garray?*
   Did you cut the meat with a knife?
B: *Yawu, magalu ngaya banggabaagu dhinggaa garray.*
   Yep, I cut the meat with the white knife.

---

## Winangala, garay guwaala, yawala.
## Listen, say and read.

It may help to first revise the *L* class verbs forms in the Lesson 11 table:

| Command | Future | Past | |
|---|---|---|---|
| *dhiyama-la!* | *dhiyama-li* | *dhiyama-y* | pick up |

 **Audio:** GGU 12.7.mp3 is available in the electronic edition

*Minya nguru gimubiy?*
What did he/she do/make?

*Biiba garray yinarru nhaaybagu.*
The woman cut the paper with a knife.
(paper cut-PAST Woman-ERG knife-INST)

*Ngaandu dhinggaa dhay?*
Who ate the meat?

*Ngaandi nginda ngamiy?*
Who/whom did you see?

*Ngaandi yinarru winangay?*
Who did the woman hear?

*Ngaandi burumadhi banaganhi?*
Who ran away from the dog?

## LESSON 12. DOER.TO/ACTOR AND INSTRUMENT

**Audio:** GGU 12.8.mp3 is available in the electronic edition

*Minyadhu nginda gaala bumay?*
What did you hit the cup with?

*Minyadhu giwiirru gaala bumay?*
What did the man hit the cup with?

*Minya gimubiy giwiirru?*
What did the man do? (to something)

(The Gamilaraay here feels like English, but I do not know a better way to say this. In Pitjantjatjara there is a verb 'do what?', based on *nyaa?* 'what?'. It might be better to use a pattern found in another Aboriginal language rather than use an English pattern. The next sentence does that, using *minyaba-li* 'do.what?', transitive.)

*Minyabay giwiirru?*
What did the man do? (to something)

*Biiba ngaya garray nhaaybagu.*
I cut the paper with the knife.

*Buruma giwiirru bumay bundidhu.*
The man hit the dog with a bundi.

*Yaama dhimba Maridhu bumay?*
Did the Murri hit the sheep?

*Yaama bundidhu Maridhu bumay dhimba?*
Did the Murri hit the sheep with a bundi?

*Yaama bundidhu Maridhu dhimba bumay?*
Was it a stick that the man hit the sheep with?

You might like to speak and act out the following:

 **Audio:** GGU 12.9.mp3 is available in the electronic edition

*Dhulu ngaya dhiyamali.*
I will pick up a stick.

WIIDHAA

*Dhulu ngaya dhiyamay.*
I picked up a stick.

*Buruma nhalay.*
This is a dog.

*Gagil nhama buruma.*
That dog is bad.

*Buruma ngaya bumali dhulugu.*
I will hit the dog with a stick.

*Buruma ngaya bumay dhulugu.*
I hit the dog with a stick.

*Banagay ngaya burumadhi.*
I will run away from the dog.

> **Audio:** GGU 12.10.mp3 is available in the electronic edition

(It may help to be holding a photo and talking to a person or maybe your dog.)

*Yaama.*
Hello.

*Maliyaa ngay nhalay, Clyde.*
This is my friend Clyde.

*Dhinawan ngaya ngamiy.*
I saw an emu.

*Clydegubala bandaarr ngamiy.*
Clyde saw a kangaroo.

*Clydegu bandaarr bumay barrandu.*
Clyde hit the kangaroo with a boomerang.

*Bandaarrubala Clyde yiiy.*
The kangaroo bit Clyde.

*Banaganhi Clyde bandaarri.*
Clyde ran away from the kangaroo.

*Gamil yaluu Clydegu bandaarr bumali.*
Clyde won't hit kangaroos again.

 **Audio:** GGU 12.11.mp3 is available in the electronic edition

Then answer the questions based on GGU 12.10.mp3.

*Ngaandi nhalay* (pointing to Clyde)
Who is this?

*Ngaandu dhinawan ngamiy?*
Who saw the emu?

*Yaama Clydegu dhinawan ngamiy?*
Did Clyde see the emu?

*Ngaandu bandaarr bumay, minyadhu?*
Who hit the kangaroo; what with?

*Ngaandi bandaarru yiiy?*
Who did the kangaroo bite?

*Ngaandi bandaarri banaganhi?*
Who ran away from the kangaroo?

# LESSON 13
# Verbs: *NG* class, *RR* class

This lesson introduces the last two of the four Gamilaraay verb classes. These are relatively small classes, known as the *NG* and *RR* classes. Both have a number of transitive and intransitive verbs. It also introduces the concept of three-place verbs.

## Vocabulary

 **Audio:** GGU 13.1.mp3 is available in the electronic edition

| *Garay* | Words | |
|---|---|---|
| Some *NG* class verbs | | |
| *ngarunga!* | drink! | tr |
| *bundaanga!* | fall! | int |
| *ginga!\** | become! | int |
| *yulunga!\** | dance, play, enjoy! | int |
| *gaanga!* | bring/take! | tr |
| *wurunga!\** | go.in! | int |
| Some *RR* class verbs | | |
| *wuuna!* | give! | tr |
| *dhuna!\** | poke! | tr |
| *dhuuna!* | crawl! | int |

The command or imperative forms of the verbs are given above. The *Dictionary* gives the future form of verbs, for example *ngaru-gi* 'drink' and *wuu-rri* 'give'.

*\*Ginga* can be translated 'get' as in 'get happy', but not as in 'get a hamburger' or 'get a joke'.

*Yulunga*, in the *Dictionary*, is 'play, dance, gamble'. It is possible these are specific examples of its actual, broader meaning, something like 'have fun', and that GY did not have more specialised words.

*Wurunga*. This verb is not in the *Dictionary*, but the Yuwaalaraay *wuu-gi* is, so that form was used in Gamilaraay classes for many years. Recent research has found the verb *wuru-gi* a number of times in the Gamilaraay sources, so it is now used.

Note: when using *wuru-gi* the location entered is in the 'from' form, i.e. in Ablative case. See below in the Grammar section.

*Dhuna* has a wide range of uses. See the *Dictionary* entry. A number of GY verbs (and other words) have a wide range of uses and no simple translation in English. The concept of a 'gloss' is useful. It is used where a one-word equivalent is needed, but any translation needs a very careful consideration of the context. For instance, *dhuna* can be translated with 'spear, stab, poke' and with other words. It has also been used for 'write', as have similar words in other Aboriginal languages. To make this use explicit use *dhurri wiyayl-u* or *wiyaylu dhurri* 'poke using pen' (pen-instrument poke).

## Grammar

By now you might be getting used to the idea that there are a number of simple verb forms – a command form ('Do it!'), a future form ('Will do it') and a past form ('Did it'). The table below shows these forms for some *NG* class verbs.

 **Audio:** GGU 13.2.mp3 is available in the electronic edition

### *NG* class verbs

| Command | Future | Past | |
|---|---|---|---|
| *yulunga* dance! | *yulugi* will dance | *yulunhi* danced | dance/play/have.fun **int** |
| *gaanga* bring it! | *gaagi* will bring | *gaanhi* brought | bring/take **tr** |

## LESSON 13. VERBS: *NG* CLASS, *RR* CLASS

| Command | Future | Past | |
|---|---|---|---|
| *ngarunga* | *ngarugi* | *ngarunhi* | drink **tr** |
| *bundaanga* | *bundaagi* | *bundaanhi* | fall **int** |
| *wurunga* | *wurugi* | *wurunhi* | go in **int** |
| *ginga* | *gigi* | *ginyi* | become, get **int** |

Remember the idea of 'verb root', the part of the verb that stays the same – for instance, *yulu* for 'dance/play' – which is followed by suffixes. Can you work out what the Command suffix is for *NG* class verbs? The bit that comes after the root? *yulu-nga, gaa-nga, ngaru-nga*... The future suffix for *NG* class verbs: (*yulu-gi, gaa-gi*) is *-gi* and the past tense suffix (*yulu-nhi, gaa-nhi, gi-nyi*) is *-nhi* after *a* or *u*, and *-nyi* after *i*.

Sometimes verbs are written with dashes to show how they are made up (*yulu-nhi*) but this is only to help you to learn. It would be like separating English words (cook-ed, cook-ing, cook-s) to help people understand the processes of the language.

The last group of Gamilaraay verbs are *RR* class and some verbs are shown in the table.

 **Audio:** GGU 13.3.mp3 is available in the electronic edition

### *RR* class verbs

| Command | Future | Past | |
|---|---|---|---|
| *wuuna* | *wuurri* | *wuunhi* | give **tr** |
| Give (it)! | will give | gave | |
| | | | |
| *dhuna* | *dhurri* | *dhunhi* | poke **tr** |
| | | | |
| *dhuuna* | *dhuurri* | *dhuunhi* | crawl **tr** |

Notice again that there are patterns. The Command ending is *-na*, the future ending is *-rri* and the past ending is *-nhi*. The past ending is the same as for *Y* and *NG* class. Work out the roots of the *RR* class verbs above.

WIIDHAA

## Simple Gamilaraay verbs

You have now seen all four Gamilaraay verb classes and the simple forms are given in the table below. You might like to copy it and have it for handy reference. Being able to use the four verb classes is a major step in learning Gamilaraay.

 **Audio:** GGU 13.4.mp3 is available in the electronic edition

### Gamilaraay verbs – simple forms

| Command | Future* | Past* | English |
|---|---|---|---|
| *Y* Class | | | |
| yana**nga**\* | yana**y** | yana**nhi** | walk/ come/ go |
| gubi**ya** | gubi**y** | gubi**nyi** | swim |
| | | | |
| *L* Class | | | |
| buma**la** | buma**li** | buma**y** | hit |
| | | | |
| *NG* Class | | | |
| yulu**nga** | yulu**gi** | yulu**nhi** | dance |
| gi**nga** | gi**gi** | gi**nyi** | become (get) |
| | | | |
| *RR* Class | | | |
| wuu**na** | wuu**rri** | wuu**nhi** | give |

*Note: We have used the labels 'future' and 'past' since they are simple and give a lot of information about the verb forms in that column. That is appropriate for an introductory course and given our knowledge of traditional Gamilaraay. However, the reality is a bit more complex, for instance the 'future' form is sometimes translated 'might' or 'could'. Be prepared for some adjustments in your understanding of these if you continue in your Gamilaraay study.

## *Wuurri, dhurri, wurugi* – complex verbs

You have learnt about simple intransitive (which basically involve one thing) and transitive verbs (two things, mostly). You will be excited to know things can get more interesting, more complicated.

### *Wuu-rri* 'give'

 **Audio:** GGU 13.5.mp3 is available in the electronic edition

It generally takes some practice to use this verb correctly. You need to remember that generally there are three things involved:

| | | |
|---|---|---|
| 1. | the giver | **doer.to/Ergative** |
| 2. | the given | **done.to/Accusative** |
| 3. | the receiver/given.to | **possessive/Dative case** |

(*Wuurri* can be called a 'three-place' verb.)

*I₁ gave the **book**₂ to **you**₃.*

The table below shows some nouns and pronouns to use with *wuurri* and the case of each of the three involved. Make sure you understand the cases used in the sentences that follow.

| 1. giver: **doer.to/Ergative** | 2. given: **done.to/Accusative** | 3. receiver/given.to: **possessive/Dative** |
|---|---|---|
| *ngaya* 'I' | *gali* 'water' | *miyay-gu* '(to the) girl' |
| *gunii-dhu* 'mum' | *banggul* 'money' | *birralii-gu* '(to the) child' |
| *dhagaan-du* 'brother' | *minya* 'what' | *gunii-gu* '(to) mum' |
| *ngaandu?* 'who?' | *man.garr* 'bag' | *ngay* 'to me' (my) |
| *giwiirr-u* 'man' | *wirri* 'plate' | *nginu* 'to you(1)' (your) |

🔊 **Audio:** GGU 13.6.mp3 is available in the electronic edition

| *Gali*₂ | *ngaya*₁ | *miyay-gu*₃ | *wuu-rri*. |
|---|---|---|---|
| Water | I | girl-to | give-will. |

I will give water to the girl. // I will give the girl water.

*Guniidhu*₁ *banggul*₂ *birraliigu*₃ *wuunhi*.
Mum gave the child money. // Mum gave money to the child.

*Minya*₂ *dhagaandu*₁ *guniigu*₃ *wuunhi?*
What did brother give mum? // What did brother give to mum?

*Bubaa-gu*₁ *birralii-gu*₃ *dhuwarr*₂ *wuu-nhi*.
Dad gave the child bread.

*Bubaagu*₁ *ngay*₃ *gali*₂ *wuunhi*.
father-ERG my(to.me) water give-PAST
Dad gave me water.

*Wuu-na dhinggaa₂ dhayn.gu₃.*
give-IMP    meat    person-to
Give that guy some meat.

(Imp = Imperative = Command verb)

*Ngaandu ngurungu gali wuurri.*
Who₁ will give her₃ some water₂?

## Common phrases

 **Audio:** GGU 13.7.mp3 is available in the electronic edition

*Dhaay wuuna.*
Give it here.

*Ngay wuuna.*
Give it to me.

The verb **dhurri** 'poke' can be used as a simple transitive verb, but most often an instrument is mentioned, so there are three nominals used:

| | |
|---|---|
| The poker | (doer.to/Ergative) |
| The poked | (done.to/Accusative) |
| The instrument | (Ergative, but with instrumental use) |

*Giirr ngaya dhagaan dhurri!*
I will poke my brother. (simple use, two things)

*Giirr ngaya dhinggaa gulagu dhurri!*
I will poke/stab the meat with my fork. (instrument explicit, three things)

*Dhunhi giwiirr-u bandaarr bilaarr-u.*
Poked    man-ERG    kangaroo    spear-ERG.instrument
The man speared the kangaroo.

*Birraydhu=nha dhunhi wiyaylu.*
The boy poked her with a pen.

*Minyadhu ngaya biiba dhurri?*
What will I write with?

# LESSON 13. VERBS: *NG* CLASS, *RR* CLASS

***Wurugi*** 'go.in' is an intransitive verb, but mostly a place is named, and that is in Ablative/from form.

*Ngaandi gundhi-dhi wurunhi?*
Who   house-from   go.in-past
Who went into the house?

*Gamil ngaya wilbaarri wurugi.*
I will not get into the car.

*Garriya ngirima wurunga.*
Don't go in there.

## Practice

 **Audio:** GGU 13.8.mp3 is available in the electronic edition

These can be done in pairs or groups, or adapted for individual practice. Repeat the pattern of each exercise using different verbs and other elements. Start by using all the new *NG* and *RR* class verbs.

A:  *B, yulunga.*
    B, dance!
B:  *Yawu, yulugi ngaya.*    (dances)    *Yulunhi ngaya.*
    Yes, I will dance.                   I danced.

A:  (Drinks) *Minya ginyi?*
    What happened.
B:  *Gali nginda ngarunhi.*
    You drank water.
A:  *Yawu, gali ngaya ngarunhi.*
    Yep, I drank water.

A:  *Gali-wadhaay dhaay gaanga.*
    Water(please) to.here bring.
B:  *Gamil, gamilbala ngaya gali gaagi.*
    No. I won't bring the water.

WIIDHAA

A: *Dhurri ngaya man.garr, gula-gu.*
   I will poke the bag with a fork.

---

A: *Gayrr dhuna wiyaylu.*
   Write (your) name.
B: *Ngaayaybaay. Gayrr ngaya wiyaylu dhurri, biibaga.*
   *Gayrr ngaya dhunhi.*
   OK. I will write my name on the paper. I wrote my name.

🔊 **Audio:** GGU 13.9.mp3 is available in the electronic edition

*Guniigu man.garr wuuna.*
Give the bag to mum.

*Yaama nginda ngay gali wuurri?* (or *Yaama=nda ...*)
Will you give me some water?

*Minya bubaagu miyaygu wuunhi?*
What did dad give the girl?

*Gamilbala ngaya dhagaan.gu wiyayl wuunhi.*
I did not give my brother a pen.

*Ngaandu burumagu dhinggaa wuunhi?*
Who gave the dog the meat?

Create more sentences using the words in the table, and other words you have learnt.

## *Winangala, garay guwaala, yawala.*
## Listen, say and read.

 **Audio:** GGU 13.10.mp3 is available in the electronic edition

*Giirr nguru gali burrulaa ngarunhi.*
really s/he   water   a.lot   drink-Past
He drank a lot of water.

LESSON 13. VERBS: *NG* CLASS, *RR* CLASS

*Dhaay nhama wuuna, yarral.*
Give that money here.

*Ngaandu nginu wiyayl wuunhi?*
Who gave you the pen?

*Birraliidhuul/gaaylidhuul ngambaagu dhuunhi.*
The baby crawled to mum.

*Yaamanda badha gali ngay ngarunhi?*
(*badha/badha gali/gali badha* 'beer')
Did you drink my beer?

*Maridhu bandaarr bilaarru dhunhi.*
(*bilaarr* 'spear')
The Murri speared the kangaroo.

🔊 **Audio:** GGU 13.11.mp3 is available in the electronic edition

*Gamil ngaya bundaagi galidha.*
I will not fall in the water.

*Giirr burumaga dhuunhi gaaylidhuul/birraliidhuul.*
The baby crawled on the dog.

*Yaamanda dhaay yanay?*
Will you come here?

*Gaaylidhu yarral dhiyamay, gaanhi.*
The kid picked up the money and took it.

*Minyanda ngarugi, dhali?*
What will you eat and drink?

*Dhalaagu dhuru dhuunhi?*
Where did the snake crawl to?

# LESSON 14
# What for/Whose/Who for?

This lesson further considers the possessive/Dative case, the purpose use (purposive use) of Dative case, including the purposive forms of verbs. The extension looks at the use of pronouns/nouns when a transitive verb is followed by in intransitive, or vice versa.

## Vocabulary

 **Audio:** GGU 14.1.mp3 is available in the electronic edition

| Garay | Words |
|---|---|
| *dhiyamala!* | pick up! **tr** |
| *dhamala!* | touch! **tr** |
| | |
| *yilaa\** | then, short time |
| *=nga* | then, now |
| *-gu\** | possessive/purpose (Dative) |
| *minyagu?\** | what for? why? |
| *ngaanngu\** | whose? for who(m)? |
| *minya-gu-waayaa\** | I don't know what for\* |

\*See below.

## Grammar

 **Audio:** GGU 14.2.mp3 is available in the electronic edition

*Yilaa* can mean 'soon' or 'a little time before or after now'. It is also used to link sentences, when 'then' is a better translation. It will not generally occur in the first sentence of a passage. It is generally the first word in the sentence. There is still some uncertainty about its meanings and uses. =*nga*, with current analysis, is more like 'immediately after', whereas *yilaa* is 'short time'.

> There is still more to be learnt about Gamilaraay linkage words. English tends to use time words extensively to link sentences and clauses – words such as 'then, afterwards, soon'. GY does use *yilaa* and =*nga* 'then' as time 'linkers', but very frequently uses *ngiyarrma*, whose meaning seems to have changed from 'there' to being a general linker. For *Gamilaraay 1* use *yilaa* and =*nga*.

*Wiimala dhinggaa dhawunda.*
put.down-Com meat ground-On
Put the meat on the ground.

*Yilaa yinarru dhinggaa dhiyamali, wiyagi.*
then women-Erg meat pick.up-Fut cook-Fut
Then the women will pick up the meat and cook it.

*Nginda, wii wiimala, yilaa ngaya bandaarr gaagi.*
You, make the fire and later I will bring a kangaroo.

**'I don't know'** in Gamilaraay is most commonly a suffix. It is actually a two-stage suffix. Interrogatives, question words, can have a suffix added that adds (mostly) the meaning 'some'. Three examples are given below.

| *Minya?** | What? | *minyagaa* | something |
| *Dhalaa?* | Where (at)? | *dhalaawaa* | somewhere |
| *Ngaandi?** | Who? | *ngaandiyaa* | someone |

As you can see, the form of the suffix varies. The common form is -*Waa*, i.e. -*waa* after *a* and *u*, -*yaa* after *i*. *Minya-gaa* is irregular. Adding a further -*yaa* changes the meaning to 'I don't know'.

> It may be that -*Waa* and -*gaa* have different functions – a topic for further research.

| *Minyagaayaa.* | I don't know what. |
| *Dhalaawaayaa.* | I don't know where. |
| *Ngaandiyaayaa.* | I don't know who. |

*By now you would realise that word lists with one word in each language by no means have full information. Here, for instance, *minya* and *ngaandi* are Nominative and Accusative case. Nominative is used with intransitive verbs, and the done.to or object is Accusative case. For a sentence such as 'Who drank my water?' you would use the doer.to/Ergative form.

*Ngaandu gali ngay ngarunhi?*
Who drank my water?

*Ngaanduwaa.*
Someone.

## Possessive/purposive

 **Audio:** GGU 14.3.mp3 is available in the electronic edition

So far we have used Dative case in two ways. The first use, shown in the next example sentence, is to indicate the owner or possessor. The second use, seen in the subsequent sentence, is to show the recipient when using the verb *wuurri* 'give'.

*Gundhi **maliyaa-gu**.*
The friend's house.

*Gali **birralii-gu** wuuna.*
Give the child some water.

Possessive/Dative case can also indicate purpose, as in the next two sentences. The first has a Dative noun, so with the *-gu* suffix. The second has a Dative pronoun.

*Yananhi ngaya **dhuwarr-gu**.*
went      I       bread-*gu*
I went for some bread.

*Gali ngaya **nginu** gaanhi.*
Water I you.for/you.of brought.
I brought some water for you.

Remember, Dative pronouns do not have a suffix, but a special form ending in *-ngu* apart from *ngay* 'my' and *nginu* 'your(1)'.

The next two sentences show the purposive suffix on a verb. It is only found on the future form of verbs.

*Yananhi ngaya dhali-gu.*
I went to eat.

*Wiimala gali gaalaga, birraliidhu ngarugi-gu.*
Put the water in the cup, for the child to drink it.

The suffix form *-gu* has a number of uses: movement to, possession and 'purpose'. This may seem confusing, but there are clues as to the use. The movement.to/Allative use is usually with a motion verb. The possessive/Dative use is usually in a two noun phrase, for instance *wiyayl guniigu* 'mum's pen', and the noun with the purpose suffix is often at the end of the sentence.

## Summary

- 'For me' is *ngay*, which also translates 'my/mine'.
- 'For you(1 person)' is *nginu*, which is also 'your/yours(1 person)'.
- 'For her/him/it' is *ngurungu*, which is also 'her/his/its'.

Other possessive pronouns are used the same way, for instance:

*Ngaanngu?* is:

- possessive (whose?),
- dative/giving to (to who(m)?) and
- purpose (for who(m)?).

Since possessive and purposive nominals have the same form there is potential ambiguity. With nouns that form is also used for Allative case, so potentially more interpretations of the one statement. However, the context will generally indicate the meaning.

*Dhiyamala wiyayl Marygu.*

This could be translated:

Pick up Mary's pen.
Or
Pick up the pen for Mary.

I suspect that the way the sentence is said would make the meaning clear. In Pick up Mary's pen, *wiyayl Marygu* would likely be said as one unit; in Pick up the pen for Mary, I suspect there would be a pause after *wiyayl*.

*Yananhi ngaya gali-gu.*

This could be translated:

I went for some water.
Or
I went to the water.

 **Audio:** GGU 14.4.mp3 is available in the electronic edition

## *Ngaanngu, minyagu*

*Ngaanngu nhalay buruma?*
Whose dog is this? (possessive)

*Ngaanngu nginda nhalay buruma wuurri? / Ngaanngu=nda nhalay buruma wuurri?*
Who will you give this dog to? (giving to)

*Ngaanngu nginda nhalay nguu dhaay gaanhi.*
Who did you bring this book here for? (purposive)

*Minyagu* means 'for what purpose?'. It is the first word in the sentence. It often translates English 'why? what for?' (see below for other translations of 'Why?'). *Minyagu* can be used in sentences like:

---

*Minyagunda (minya-gu=nda) dhaay yananhi?*
what.for-you(1) to.here came.
What did you come here for?

---

*Minyagunda birray ngamiy?*
What did you look at the boy for?

*Minyagu miyay dhaay yananhi?*
What did the girl come here for?

*Minyagu nhama garrawalgu yananhi?*
What did she go to the shop for?

*Minyagu=ndaay buruma bumay?*
Why did you(>2) hit the dog?

**Audio:** GGU 14.5.mp3 is available in the electronic edition

Some answers might include:

*Giirr nguru bamba garay guwaay.*
He talked really loud.

*Giirr nhama gaba ngulu.*
He is really good looking.

*Dhinggaagu.*
For meat.

*Maliyaa ngamiligu.*
To see her friend.

*Gagil nhama buruma.*
That dog is bad.

*Giirr burumagu dhinggaa ngay dhay.*
The dog ate my meat.

Other translations of 'Why?' include:

*Minyadhi*, for instance in 'Why are you afraid?', 'Why did you laugh/ What did you laugh at?'.

*Minya-nginda* (see Lesson 18 for *-nginda*) 'what-wanting', in 'Why is the baby crying?'.

# Extension

 **Audio:** GGU 14.6.mp3 is available in the electronic edition

For transitive and intransitive verbs 'near one another', the rule is:

When there is a change in verb transitivity it must be signalled by a pronoun or noun or other nominal. When there is no change in transitivity there is no need for pronouns, especially in the second phrase.

In English and Gamilaraay you can say:

*Yananhi(=nha), banaganhi.*
She walked and ran.

And in English you can say: 'She walked and sang'.

But in Gamilaraay *yana-y* 'walk' is intransitive and *bawi-li* 'sing' is transitive. There needs to be a Nominative noun or pronoun with 'walk', and an Ergative one with 'sang'.

*Yananhi=nha, bawiy nguru.*
She walked and (she) sang.

*Yananhi miyay, bawiy nguru.*
The girl walked and (she) sang.

'She' with an intransitive verb can be Ø, *=nha*, *nhama* or have other forms.

She with a transitive verb is Ø or *nguru*. However, when there is a change in transitivity Ø is rarely used.

## Examples of change in transitivity

 **Audio:** GGU 14.7.mp3 is available in the electronic edition

*Giirr=nha banaga-nhi, winanga-y nguru.*
true she(Nom) walk-PAST, sang-PAST she(Erg)
She ran and listened.

Compare:

*Giirr nguru bawi-y, yana-nhi nhama.*
She sang and walked.

*Marygu bawi-y, yana-nhi=nha.*
Mary sang and walked.

*Yana-nhi Mary, bawi-y nguru.*
Mary walked and sang.

WIIDHAA

## No change in transitivity

 **Audio:** GGU 14.8.mp3 is available in the electronic edition

Both verbs intransitive:

*Giirr=nha yana-nhi, bara-nhi.*
true she walk-PAST, hop-PAST
She walked and hopped.

or

*Giirr yana-nhi, bara-nhi.*
true walk-PAST, hop-PAST
She walked and hopped.

Both verbs transitive:

*Giirr nguru ngaru-nhi, dha-y.*
true she drink-PAST, eat-PAST
She drank and ate.

or

*Giirr ngaru-nhi, dha-y.*
true drink-PAST, eat-PAST
She drank and ate.

# Practice

 **Audio:** GGU 14.9.mp3 is available in the electronic edition

A: *Man.gagu yananga, wiyaylgu.*
   Go to the table, for a pen.     (vary the place, object: *gali, yuul, nguu, man.ga, gaala*)
B: *Wiyaylgu ngaya man.gagu yanay.*
   I will go to the table for a pen.
B: *Yananhi ngaya man.gagu, wiyaylgu.*
   I will go to the table for a pen.
A: *Man.gagu nginda yananhi, wiyaylgu.*
   You went to the table for a pen.

A: *Dhaay=wadhaay gulaban gaanga, ngarriygu ngaya.*
   (Please) Bring a chair here, for me to sit down.
B: *Ngamila, dhaay ngaya gulaban gaanhi, ngarriygu nginda.*
   Look, I brought a chair for you to sit on.

---

A: *Minyagu nhalay gali?*
   What's this water for?
B: *Ngarugigu.*
   To drink.

---

A: *Minyagu=nda garrawalgu yananhi?*
   What did you go to the shop for?
B: *Dhuwarr ngaya dhiyamaligu.*
   To pick up/get some bread.

---

A: *Ngaanngu nginda gali dhaay gaanhi?*
   Who(m) did you bring the water for?
B: *Nginu. Giirr ngaya nginu gali gaanhi.*
   For you. I brought the water for you.

Or

B: *Ngaannguwaa.*
   For someone.

---

A: *Ngaanngu nhalay yuul.*
   Who is this food for? // Whose food is this?
B: *Ngaannguwaayaa. Ngaannguwaayaa nhalay yuul.*
   I don't know. I don't know who this food is for. // I don't know whose food this is.

WIIDHAA

## *Winangala, garay guwaala, yawala.*
## Listen, say and read.

> 🔊 **Audio:** GGU 14.10.mp3 is available in the electronic edition

*Ngaanngu nhama wiyayl man.gaga?*
Whose is that pen on the table?

*Giirr ngaya burrulaa dhay, yilaa ngaya gagil ginyi.*
I ate a lot, and then I got/felt bad.

*Minyagu wandagu burrulaa dhinggaa dhay?*
What did the whitefella eat a lot of meat for?

*Garriya nhama dhamala biibabiiba ngay.*
Don't touch that book of mine.

> 🔊 **Audio:** GGU 14.11.mp3 is available in the electronic edition

*Ngaandu dhamay nhama man.garr Billygu? (or Billyngu)*
Who touched Billy's bag?

*Ngaanngu nhalay wiyayl guwaymbarra?*
Whose is this red pen?

*Dhuru ngamiy yinarru, yilaa-nha gundhigu banaganhi.*
The woman saw the snake and ran to the house.

*Yilaa ngaya gunii ngamili.*
I will see my mother soon.

*Banagaya gundhigu, galigu.*
Run home for some water.

*Ngaandi yanay man.gagu, wiyaylgu?*
Who will go to the table for a pen. (to get a pen)

---

A: *Minyadhiyaayaa nguru bamba gagay.*
I don't know why she talked loudly.
B: *Giirr burumagu=nha yiiy.*
A dog bit her.

# LESSON 15
# More Pronouns: Singular

This lesson introduces the **other case forms** of singular pronouns: the Accusative case, Locative/Allative case and Ablative case. It also looks at instances where Gamilaraay need not express third person singular pronouns (he, she, it, her, him). There are many other pronouns in later lessons.

We have been using the term 'case' since it makes it possible to formulate quite concise rules, but the idea, the concept, can be hard to get your head around. Appendix 3 has further discussion, and you may find it helpful to consult introductory linguistics texts.

## Vocabulary

 **Audio:** GGU 15.1.mp3 is available in the electronic edition

| *Garay* | Words |
| --- | --- |
| *nganha* | me (done.to) (Accusative) |
| *ngay* | my/mine (Dative) |
| *nganunda* | to/at/on/near me (Locative **and** Allative) |
| *nganundi* | from me (Ablative) |
| | |
| *nginunha* | you(1) (done.to) (Accusative) |
| *nginu* | your/yours(1) (Dative) |
| *nginunda* | to/at/on/near you(1) (Locative **and** Allative) |
| *nginundi* | from you(1) (Ablative) |
| | |
| *=nha, Ø, nhama\** | she/he/her/him/it (Nominative **and** Accusative) |
| *nguru* | she/he//it (doer.to) (Ergative) |
| *ngurungu* | her(s)/his/its (Dative) |
| *ngurungunda* | to/at/on/near her/him/it (Locative **and** Allative) |
| *ngurungundi* | from her/him/it (Ablative) |

| *Garay* | Words |
|---|---|
| *wamba** | mad, silly |
| *ngarragaa* | hopeless, sad |
| *bamba** | with energy |

*The words *wamba* and *ngarragaa* are common in the Aboriginal English of the Gamilaraay Yuwaalaraay area. *Ngarragaa* is generally pronounced *naragaa* because people have got used to English sounds, which do not include *rr*, or *ng* at the start of a word.

**Bamba* is used with lots of verbs, for example:

| | |
|---|---|
| *bamba* run | run hard |
| *bamba* eat | have a big feed |
| *bamba* hit | hit hard |
| *bamba* look | stare |
| *bamba* listen | listen carefully. |

By now you will be well aware that:

- the meanings/uses of *nhama* are quite complex – many more than listed here
- *nhama* is just one of many ways of translating English 'she/he/her/him/it'.

## Grammar

Remember that, for first person and second person pronouns, the Nominative (doer) and Ergative (doer.to) forms are the same: *ngaya* 'I' and *nginda* 'you(1)'.

For third person pronouns, nouns, adjectives and other case marked words, the Nominative (doer) and the Accusative (done.to) are the same. For example:

=*nha*, Ø and ***nhama*** are used for **she, he, it** (doer) and **her, him, it** (done.to).

**Accusative case** is used for the 'done.to' in sentences with a transitive verb. English has some distinctive forms for this role (in **bold** below).

He/she saw **me**. I saw **him/her**.

## LESSON 15. MORE PRONOUNS: SINGULAR

With second person, however, English uses '**you**' whether it means 'doing the action' (**You** ran. **You** ate it.) or the 'done.to' (The car hit **you**.).

The 'done.to' or **Accusative pronouns** are in bold in the following sentences.

 **Audio:** GGU 15.2.mp3 is available in the electronic edition

*Giirr burumagu **nganha** yiiy.*
The dog bit **me**.

*Giirr burumagu **nginunha** yiiy.*
The dog bit **you(1)**.

*Giirr **nhama** burumagu yiiy.*
The dog bit **her/him**.

*Giirr nginda **nganha** ngamiy.*
You(1) saw **me**.

*Giirr ngaya **nginunha** ngamiy.*
I saw **you(1)**.

*Giirr=**nha** ngaya ngamiy.*
I saw **her/him**.

Remember, with third person pronouns you need to distinguish between the doer (=*nha*, Ø and *nhama* for singular pronouns) and the doer.to (*nguru* for singular pronouns), in other words you need to check whether the verb is intransitive (doer) or transitive (doer.to). Look at the following sentences.

 **Audio:** GGU 15.3.mp3 is available in the electronic edition

*Banaganhi=nha. Banaganhi. Banaganhi nhama.*

| **She/he** ran. | *banaga-y* **intransitive** |
|---|---|

*Giirr nguru nganha ngamiy.*

| **She/he** saw me. | *ngami-li* **transitive** |
|---|---|

*Giirr=nha ngaya ngamiy. Giirr ngaya ngamiy. Giirr ngaya nhama ngamiy.*
I saw **her/him**.

*Giirr **nguru** nganha ngamiy.*
**She/he** saw me.

Pronouns (and proper nouns/names) are different from standard nominals in that the **Locative and Allative have the same form**, as seen below.

| Locative | | |
|---|---|---|
| *dhinawan-da* | *ngurungunda* | *Bubaa-ngunda* |
| on/*at/near the emu | on/at/near him/her/it | on/at/near Dad |
| **Allative** | | |
| *dhinawan.gu* | *ngurungunda* | *Bubaa-ngunda* |
| *to the emu | to him/her/it | to Dad |

For simplicity, when talking of pronouns and proper nouns we will sometimes use Locative rather than Locative/Allative. Note that some older pronoun charts do not describe Allative pronouns.

*'to' here means 'movement to'. Allative case is not used to translate 'to' in 'give to', 'listen to' or 'talk to'. Similarly with 'at'/Locative case. Locative is not used to translate 'look at'. The general principle: don't expect translation to be simple.

## Locative/Allative pronouns

These are used where nouns have the Locative (*-Ga*: 'on/at/in/near') or Allative (*-gu*: 'going to') suffixes: see Lesson 7 for uses of the Locative case and Lesson 5 for Allative.

**Locative use**

 **Audio:** GGU 15.4.mp3 is available in the electronic edition

*Warranhi Kim **bubaa-ga.***
Kim stood on/near/with her father.

The Locative pronoun is used the same way: the pronoun is generally second.

*Warranhi nganunda Kim.*
Kim stood near/with me.

*Warranhi nginunda Kim.*
Kim stood near/with(on) you(1).

Allative use:

*Yananhi Kim gunii-gu.*
Kim went to/walked to mum.

Locative/Allative pronouns also have this role:

*Yananhi nganunda Kim.*
Kim came to me.

*Yananhi nginunda Kim.*
Kim came to you(1).

The main point here is that Locative and Allative pronouns have the same form, unlike nouns.

## Another challenging verb

English speakers are used to having a verb 'talk/speak'. In GR (and in some close languages), 'talk/speak' is translated by a phrase: *garay guwaali*. It is something like 'words tell'. The person 'spoken to' is in place/Locative case.

*Garay ngaya guwaa-li maliyaa-**ga**.*
Word    I    tell-will    friend-At.
I will talk to my friend.

*Ngaandu nginunda garay guwaay?*
Who talked to you?

*Birray-dhu garay guwaay miyay-dha.*
The boy spoke to the girl.

(Note that *guwaali* is pronounced like gu-or-li and *guwaay* is pronounced like gwoi – listen to them on *Gayarragi, Winangali*.)

However, *guwaali* also has another use, 'telling' someone to do something. With that use the 'told.to' is in done.to/Accusative case and the verb is purposive, i.e. future+*gu*.

*Ngaandu **nginunha** guwaay yanay-gu?*
Who told you to go?

*Guwaala birray warray-gu.*
Tell the boy to stand up.

## Ablative pronoun use

You have already seen many uses of Ablative nouns. Ablative pronouns are used in the same circumstances: movement from, fear of/laugh at, and with some verbs.

 **Audio:** GGU 15.5.mp3 is available in the electronic edition

*Giirr **nganundi** buruma banaganhi.*
The dog ran away from me.

*Minyagu nginda man.garr **ngurungundi** gaanhi?*
Why did you take the bag from her?

*Yaamanda **nganundi** giyal?*
Are you(1) scared of me?

*Ngaandi **nginundi** gindama-nhi?*
Who laughed at you?

*Giirr giidjaa **nganundi** galiya-nhi.*
An ant climbed on me.

**Reminder:**

The possessive/**Dative** pronouns (and nouns) are used for a number of things:

**Owning**

*Buruma **ngay**.*
My dog.

*Buruma **nginu**.*
Your dog.

*Buruma **ngurungu**.*
Her/his dog.

## Giving to

*Guniidhu nhama **ngay** wuunhi.*
Mum gave me that.

*Guniidhu nhama **nginu** wuunhi.*
Mum gave you(1) that.

*Guniidhu nhama **ngurungu** wuunhi.*
Mum gave her/him that.

## Purpose

*Guniidhu **ngay** nhama gaanhi.*
Mum brought that for me.

*Guniidhu nhama **ngurungu** gaanhi.*
Mum brought that for him/her.

# Extension 1

Remember, this is for when you have understood the earlier material.

## Body parts and inalienable possession

In Lesson 8 there was a discussion of 'inalienable possession'. This is an interesting topic for Gamilaraay since there is little information, and perhaps some of the historical material has already been influenced by English. So, it is not clear what the rules of traditional Gamilaraay were. For expressions like 'my hand', many Aboriginal languages do not use the possessive pronoun but instead the pronoun is the same case as 'hand'. The following pairs of sentences show Gamilaraay alternatives – one closer to most Aboriginal languages, one more like English.

 **Audio:** GGU 15.6.mp3 is available in the electronic edition

*Giirr nginda **nganha mara** dhamay.*
You touched my hand.
(using *nganha mara* 'me hand')

WIIDHAA

*Giirr nginda **mara ngay** dhamay.*
You touched my hand.
(using *mara ngay* 'my hand')

*Giirr ngaya **nginunha bina** dhamay.*
I touched your ear.
(using *nginunha bina* 'you ear')

*Giirr ngaya **bina nginu** dhamay.*
I touched your ear.
(using *bina nginu* 'your ear')

*Giirr ngaya **nhama mara** yiiy.*
I bit his/her hand.
(using *nhama mara* 'her/him hand')

*Giirr ngaya **mara ngurungu** yiiy.*
I bit his/her hand.
(using *mara ngurungu* 'her/his hand')

It would be a pity if Gamilaraay moved more towards English, at least I think so, so my preference is for the first sentence in each pair.

The sentences below show inalienable possession using a range of cases.

*Wiimala yarral nganunda maraga.*
Put the money in my hand.
(*nganunda* and *maraga* are Locative case)

*Yarral nganundi maradhi dhiyamala.*
Pick up the money from my hand.
(*nganundi* and *maradhi* are Ablative case)

*Gagil ngaya mara.*
My hand is sore.
(*ngaya* and *mara* are Nominative case)

*Maraga ngurungunda wiyayl wiimala.* // *Maraga wiyayl ngurungunda wiimala.*
Put the pen in her/his hand.

A: *Wiyayl nganunda maraga wiimala.*
Put the pen on/in my hand.
B: *Yawu, wiyayl ngaya wiimali nginunda maraga. Wiimay ngaya nginunda maraga.*
Yep, I will put the pen in your hand. I put it in your hand.
C, to A: *Giirr Bdhu wiyayl wiimay nginunda maraga.*
B put the pen in your hand.
C, to B: *Giirr nginda wiyayl wiimay ngurungunda maraga.*
You put the pen in her hand.

*Wiyayl **mara-dhi** gaanga **nganundi**.*
Take the pen from my hand.
(inalienable possession: 'from my hand' in GY is 'from-me hand-from')

*Giirr giidjaa nganundi bina-dhi wuru-nhi.*
An ant went in my ear.
(inalienable possession: '(go) in my ear' in GY is '(go) me-from ear-from')

# Extension 2

Remember, this is for when you have understood the earlier material.

In Gamilaraay, and many Aboriginal languages, you can leave out the 'she, he, him, her' words on many occasions, generally when the identity of who you are talking about is clear from the situation you are in or from the previous conversation.

 **Audio:** GGU 15.7.mp3 is available in the electronic edition

*Billy dhaay yananhi.*
Billy came here.
(so we are talking about Billy)

*Giirr ngaya ngamiy.*
I saw him.
(no **him** in Gamilaraay)

*Giirr ngaya burumagu wuunhi.*
I gave (it) to the dog.
(the conversation was about some meat)

The following are all good Gamilaraay, but again they presume the people know who or what is being referred to, they know who 'she/he/him/her/it' means.

| | |
|---|---|
| *Bumala.* | Hit (it/him/her). |
| *Dhala.* | Eat (it). |
| *Dhay.* | He ate it. |
| *Balunhi.* | (She/he/it) died. |

# Practice

 **Audio:** GGU 15.8.mp3 is available in the electronic edition

Practice in pairs is good for learning the first and second person pronouns, with three in the group it is easy to practise third person pronouns as well.

## Accusative

### *Bulaarr/2*

| | | |
|---|---|---|
| A: | *Dhamala nganha.* | |
| | Touch me. | |
| B: | *Giirr ngaya nginunha dhamali.* | *Giirr ngaya nginunha dhamay.* |
| | I will touch you. | I touched you. |
| A: | *Giirr nginda nganha dhamay.* | |
| | You touched me. | |

Repeat with other verbs: *Ngamila, winangala, bumala, garrala,* etc.

### *Buligaa+*, 3 or more

| | | |
|---|---|---|
| A: | *Dhamala nganha.* | |
| | Touch me. | |
| B: | *Giirr ngaya nginunha dhamali.* | *Giirr ngaya nginunha dhamay.* |
| | I will touch you. | I touched you. |
| C, to A: | *Giirr nguru nginunha dhamay.* | |
| | She touched you. | |

## LESSON 15. MORE PRONOUNS: SINGULAR

A, to C: *Yawu, dhamay nguru nganha.* // *Giirr nguru nganha dhamay.*
Yes, she touched me.
B, to C: *Giirr ngaya dhamay.* Or *Giirr=na ngaya dhamay.*
I touched her. (=*nha* can be =*na* after *rr*)

And so on. Repeat with other verbs as above.

 **Audio:** GGU 15.9.mp3 is available in the electronic edition

## Locative/at.near/with

With 'at/near/with' use.

A: *Warraya nganunda.*
Stand near/with me.
B: *Yawu, warray ngaya nginunda.*
Yep, I will stand with/near you.
C: *B, warranhi nginda ngurungunda.*
B, you stood near/with him.

Develop your own conversations. Some starting points are:

A: *Garriya ngurungunda ngarriya.*
Don't sit near him.
A: *Yaamanda nganunda ngarriy?*
Will you sit with me?

## Allative/go.to

A: *Banagaya nganunda.*
Run to me.
B: *Yawu, banagay ngaya nginunda.*
Yep, I will run to you.
C: *B, banaganhi nginda ngurungunda.*
B, you ran to him.

 **Audio:** GGU 15.10.mp3 is available in the electronic edition

WIIDHAA

## Ablative/from

With movement function:

A: *Banagaya nganundi.*
   Run away from me.
B: *Yawu, banagay ngaya nginundi. Banaganhi ngaya nginundi.*
   Yep, I will run away you. I ran away from you.
C: *B, banaganhi nginda ngurungundi.*
   B, you ran away from him.

Then use questions, *garriya* 'don't', *gamil* 'not', and other verbs.

Use both Allative and Ablative in one sentence.

A, to B: *Bamba nganundi banagaya, ngurungunda.*
   Run quickly away from me, to him.
B, to A: *Yawu, wamba nginda. Bamba ngaya nginundi banagay, maliyaagu.*
   Yes, you are mad. I will race away from you to my friend.

You can make many similar sentences.

With other functions:

*Giyal* 'afraid'

A: *B, giyal nginda nganundi?*
   B, are you afraid of me?
B: *Giirr ngaya nginundi giyal. Gamilbala ngaya nginunda warray.*
   I am afraid of you. I won't stay near you.

🔊 **Audio:** GGU 15.11.mp3 is available in the electronic edition

*Gindama-y* 'laugh' (intransitive)

A: *Ngaandi nganundi gindamanhi?*
   Who laughed at me.
B: *Giirr ngaya nginundi gindamanhi. Ngarragaa nginda.*
   I laughed at you. You are hopeless/pitiful.
C: *B, gagil nginda, garriya ngurungundi gindamaya.*
   B, you are bad. Don't laugh at him.

*Wuru-gi* 'go in' (intransitive)

A: *Giirr burruluu nganundi murudhi wurunhi.*
A fly went up my nose.
B: *Dhalaadhi wurunhi? Murudhi?*
Where did it go? In your nose?

## *Winangala, garay guwaala, yawala.*
## Listen, say and read.

 **Audio:** GGU 15.12.mp3 is available in the electronic edition

*Ngaandu nginunha ngamiy?*
Who saw you(1)?

*Chris-gu nganha ngamiy.*
Chris saw me.

*Ngamiy=nha dhigaraagu.*
The bird saw him.

*Yaama nguru dhigaraa ngamiy?*
Did he see the bird?

*Ngaandi nginda ngamiy?*
Who did you see?

*Gamil ngaya nginunha ngamiy.*
I did not see you.

*Yaamanda nganha ngamiy?*
Did you see me?

*Bamba nginda garay guwaay.*
You talked loudly.

*Yaamanda nganha winangay?*
Did you hear me.

*Giirr ngaya nginunha winangay.*
I sure heard you.

**Audio:** GGU 15.13.mp3 is available in the electronic edition

*Dhalaa nhama buruma?*
Where is that dog?

*Giirr nginda nhama bamba bumay.*
You really hit him.

*Yaama nguru nginunha yiiy?*
Did it bite you?

*Gamilbala, gamil nguru nganha yiiy.*
No, it didn't bite me.

*Banaganhibala nhama.*
He ran away.

*Bamba banaganhi.*
He really ran. (He really took off)

*Ngaandi yananhi gundhigu, baabiligu?*
Who went home to sleep?

*Giirr nguru nginunha ngamiy, gamilbala nginda nhama ngamiy.*
She saw you, but you did not see her.

*Man.garr ngay gaanga, wuuna ngurungu.*
Take my bag and give it to him.

*Giirr wamba nginda.*
You are **mad**.

*Birray ngarragaa bundaanhi galidha.*
That hopeless boy fell in the water.

*Yarral wuuna birraygu ngarragaagu.*
Give that sad kid some money.

# LESSON 16
# Verbs: Continuous – non-moving

This lesson introduces some further Gamilaraay verb structures. Verbs in Aboriginal language typically incorporate information that English uses separate words for, as you will see in Lessons 16 and 17. This is an important area but can take a while to absorb, so give yourself time.

For a somewhat technical article on continuous Gamilaraay verbs go to 'Associated Eating and Movement' (Giacon, 2008, pp. 107–14) available at tinyurl.com/jgpublications, or the later treatment in Giacon (2017). A summary of information on verbs is being prepared for yuwaalaraay.com.

## Vocabulary

 **Audio:** GGU 16.1.mp3 is available in the electronic edition

| *Garay* | Words |
|---|---|
| *yaliwunga* | always |
| *yilaadhu* | now |
| *gunhugunhu dhu-rri* | cough (verb phrase) **tr** |
| *gunhugunhu* | cough (noun) |

## Grammar

Gamilaraay verbs, and Aboriginal language verbs generally, can have many suffixes. You are used to some already: *-li* and *-y* 'future tense', *-nhi* 'past tense', *-gu* 'purpose', and so on. The suffixes introduced in this lesson have a number of functions, but the basic one is to show that the action is continuous. English would generally use a verb ending with -ing.

*Warra-**y.la-nha** ngaya.*
I am standing.

stand-*y*.CONT-PRES
(CONT = continuous, PRES = present tense)

We can think of the bits of the word *Warra-**y.la-nha*** as carrying different information:

| | |
|---|---|
| *warra-* | This the root of the verb *warra-y* 'stand' – it indicates what the 'action' is. |
| *-y.la-* 'continuous' | This tells you that the action is ongoing, it continues. *-y.la-* corresponds to the **-ing** in 'stand**ing**'. |
| *-nha* 'present tense' | This tells you the action is happening now. It corresponds to the '**am**' in English. |
| *-y-* | This tells you it is a *Y* class verb. |

You can easily form other similar *Y* class verbs.

*Ngarri-y.la-nha ngaya.*
I am sitting.

**But**, and this is a big but, there is another continuous suffix used for verbs that involve 'moving along', and you will learn about that in the next lesson. So you **cannot** use the suffix *-y.la-nha* to say 'I **am walking**' or 'I **am running**' or 'the bird **is flying**' because those involve 'moving along'.

*-y.la-* is the **continuous (non-moving)** suffix for *Y* class verbs. (There have been various names for the suffix.) There are similar suffixes for the other verb classes, shown in the table below.

 **Audio:** GGU 16.2.mp3 is available in the electronic edition

## Continuous (non-moving) verb examples

| Command | Future | Present | Past |
|---|---|---|---|
| **Y** Class | | | |
| *warra-y.la-ya* | *warra-y.la-y* | *warra-y.la-nha* | *warra-y.la-nhi* |
| keep standing | will be standing | is/am/are* standing | was standing |
| | | | |
| **L** Class | | | |
| *dha-lda-ya* | *dha-lda-y* | *dha-lda-nha* | *dha-lda-nhi* |
| keep eating | will be eating | is eating | was eating |
| | | | |
| **NG** Class | | | |
| *ngaru-gi.la-ya* | *ngaru-gi.la-y* | *ngaru-gi.la-nha* | *ngaru-gi.la-nhi* |
| keep drinking | will be drinking | is drinking | was drinking |
| | | | |
| **RR** Class | | | |
| *wuu-dha-ya* | *wuu-dha-y* | *wuu-dha-nha* | *wuu-dha-nhi* |
| keep giving | will be giving | is giving | was giving |

*Make similar adjustments as appropriate.

Non-moving continuous suffixes have a number of uses.

1. To show **continuous action** when it is (more or less) **on the one spot**, it does **not** involve 'moving along'.
   'I am standing.' 'You are sitting.' 'They were eating.' 'She will be drinking.' 'He is sleeping.' 'Keep talking.', etc.
   The suffix is used with verbs that would typically be moving verbs ('walk, run', etc.) if there is no 'linear movement'.
2. To show **habitual action.** That is, something that regularly happens. For example:
   'I walk (every day).' 'She reads books.' 'They eat (spinach).' 'He is sick (all the time).' 'We go to the pictures.'
3. To show **ability** and occasionally to show preference:
   'I **can** talk Gamilaraay.' 'She **can** swim.' 'He **knows how to** cook prawns.'
   'I **like to** (eat kebabs).'
   For 'like' you can also use the suffix *-nginda*, see Lesson 18.

## Translation

 **Audio:** GGU 16.3.mp3 is available in the electronic edition

When the action being referred to is continuous GY more commonly uses a continuous verb, whereas English tends to use simple verb forms: e.g. 'I slept' (all night) has a non-continuous verb in English, but would mostly be translated with *baabi-lda-nhi*, the continuous verb, in GR.

GY continuous verbs like 'stand, sit, lie'* often translate English 'is/are'. (*These are sometimes called stative verbs.)

The present tense sentence can be verb-less, but otherwise tense is shown using a stative verb.

*Dhulu gundhi-dha.* or *Dhulu gundhi-dha warra-yla-nha.*
Tree     house-at      stand-continuous-present.
The tree is near the house.

*Dhulu gundhi-dha warra-yla-**nhi**.*
Tree house-at stand-continuous-past.
The tree **was** near the house.

> We do not know which stative verb GR used for various things, e.g. does a house 'stand', 'sit' or 'lie'? Information from other Aboriginal languages could inform future GY usage.

A similar principal applies to command/imperative verbs. If the meaning is do x, and keep doing it, use the continuous command form.

If you wanted someone to listen you would say:

*Bamba winanga-lda-ya.*
Listen carefully (and keep listening).

Look at the sentences below. They show the alternative translations of verbs with the continuous non-moving suffix.

## LESSON 16. VERBS: CONTINUOUS – NON-MOVING

🔊 **Audio:** GGU 16.4.mp3 is available in the electronic edition

*Warraylanha nhama.*
He is standing. / He stands.

*Dhaldanha nguru.*
She is eating. / She eats.

*Ngarugilanha nguru.*
He is drinking. / He drinks.

*Wuudhanha nguru.*
She is giving. / She gives.

*Ngarriylanha dhawunda.*
She/He is sitting on the ground. / She/He sits on the ground.

*Ngarriylanha nhama dhawunda.*
He is sitting on the ground. / He sits on the ground.

 **Audio:** GGU 16.5.mp3 is available in the electronic edition

*Gamil ngaya bandaarr dhaldanha.*
I am not eating kangaroo. / I don't eat kangaroo.

*Giirr ngaya gabi ngarugilanha.*
I am drinking coffee. / I do drink coffee.

*Yaamanda Coke ngarugilanha?*
Are you drinking Coke? / Do you drink Coke?

*Giirr ngaya Coke ngarugilanhi,*
I used to drink Coke,

*gamilbala ngaya yaliwunga Coke ngarugilanha.*
but I don't drink Coke now.

*Yaamanda Gamilaraay guwaaldanha?*
Do you talk Gamilaraay?

WIIDHAA

## Practice

 **Audio:** GGU 16.6.mp3 is available in the electronic edition

You can practise with any verb. With non-moving verbs the meaning often refers to current action.

In a group of three, A talks to B, pointing in turn to A, B and then C.

*Warraylanha ngaya. Warraylanha nginda. Warraylanha=nha.*
I am standing. You(1) are standing. He/she is standing.

Then B talks to C, then C to A.

Repeat with A, B and C in different positions.

*Warraylanha ngaya. Ngarriylanha=bala nginda. Baabildanha=nha=bala.*
(note the order *=nha=bala*)

Repeat with a range of verbs. Make sure you cover all verb classes: e.g. *Ngamildanha, winangaldanha, ngarugilanha, dhudhanha, wuudhanha, bundaagilanha.*

| *Ngaru-gila-nha ngaya.* | *Ngarugilanha nginda.* | *Ngarugilanha Marydhu.* |
|---|---|---|
| I am drinking. | You(1) are drinking. | Mary is drinking. |

*Giirr ngaya nginunha ngamildanha.*
I am looking at you.

*Gamilbala nginda nganha ngamildanha.*
You are not looking at me.

Use *ngarriy* 'sit' for 'live', as in:

*Dhalaa=nda ngarriylanha?*
Where do you live?

*Canberraga ngaya ngarriylanha, Coomagabala ngaya ngarriylanhi.*
I live in Canberra, but I used to live in Cooma.

Use the non-moving suffix with any verb to indicate ability or habitual action.

## LESSON 16. VERBS: CONTINUOUS – NON-MOVING

 **Audio:** GGU 16.7.mp3 is available in the electronic edition

A:  *Gabi=nda ngarugilanha?*
    Do you drink coffee?
B:  *Giirr ngaya gabi ngarugilanha. Burrulaa.*
    I drink coffee. Lots of it.
    *Giirr ngaya badha burrulaa ngarigulanhi.*
    I used to drink a lot of beer.
    *Yilaadhubala ngaya gamil badha ngarugilanha.*
    But now I don't drink beer.

Start conversations with sentences like:

*Dhinggaa nginda dhaldanha?*
Do you eat meat?

*Mandarin ngaya guwaaldanha, ngindabala?*
I can talk Mandarin, and you?

*Gamil ngaya Mandarin guwaaldanha\*.*
I don't talk Mandarin.
(*\*guwaal…* is pronounced like g+wall, i.e. English 'wall'.)

*Gamil ngaya banagaylanha.*
I don't run. (continuous non-moving suffix on a moving verb)

Look at the verb lists from previous lessons and practice the continuous form. Then use longer sentences:

*Giirr birraliidhu gabagu gali dhigaraagu wuu-dha-nha.*
The good boy is giving water to the bird.

## Commands

 **Audio:** GGU 16.8.mp3 is available in the electronic edition

A:  *Nganha winangaldaya.*
    Listen (and keep listening) to me.
B:  *Giirr ngaya nginunha winangaldanha.*
    I am listening to you.

A *Bdha*: *Dhaldaya.*
A to B:  Eat, and keep eating.
B:  *Dhaldanha ngaya.*
 I am eating.
A:  *Garriya dhaldaya.*
 Don't keep eating. / Stop eating.

## *Winangala, garay guwaala, yawala.*
## Listen, say and read.

There are also many examples of these suffixes on *Gayarragi, Winangali*. Remember that the examples are Yuwaalaraay, so the actual root may be different (e.g. *yanaa-* 'go' in YR and *yana-* 'go' in Gamilaraay) but the rest of the structure is the same.

 **Audio:** GGU 16.9.mp3 is available in the electronic edition

A: *Giirr nginunda burruluu warraylanha.*
 There are flies on you.
B: *Gamil, marayrrbala nganunda burruluu warraylanha.*
 No, there are no flies on me.

*Giirr ngiyaningunda guniidhu garay guwaaldanha.*
Mum is talking to us.

*Gamil ngiyani yulugilanha.*
We are not playing. / We don't play/gamble.

*Yaama nginaalinya yarraamandu ngamildanhi?*
Was the horse looking at you(2)?

*Gamil ngalinya giwiirru winangaldanha.*
The man is not listening to us(2).

*Dhalaa nginda baabildanhi?*
Where were you living?

## LESSON 16. VERBS: CONTINUOUS – NON-MOVING

🔊 **Audio:** GGU 16.10.mp3 is available in the electronic edition

*Nginunha burumagu ngamildanha.*
It's you(1) the dog is looking at.

*Gamil nganunda Marygu garay guwaaldanhi.*
Mary was not talking to me.

*Ngaandi yuruunda baabildanha?*
Who is sleeping on the road?

*Garriya warraylaya dhuruga.*
Don't keep standing near the snake.

*Yaamanda ngarriylay gundhidha?*
Will you be at the house?

*Gamil garrawalgu yanaylanha gaayligal.*
The kids don't go to the shop. / The kids are not going to the shop.

*Giirr nginda bamba gunhugunhu dhudhanhi.*
You were really coughing badly.

# LESSON 17
# Verbs: Continuous – moving

This lesson introduces the continuous **moving** suffix. Any continuous verb in Gamilaraay has either this suffix or the continuous non-moving suffix.

## Vocabulary

 **Audio:** GGU 17.1.mp3 is available in the electronic edition

In previous vocabularies verbs have been given in command form. In this and subsequent lessons they are given in future form. This is the citation form found in the *Dictionary*.

| *Garay* | Words |
|---|---|
| *giiri-gi* | itch **int** |
| *dhurra-li\** | come **int** |
| *gambaay* | sweetheart |
| *walgan* | aunt |
| *garruu* | uncle |
| | |
| *wiibi-li* | be sick **int** |
| *balu-gi* | die **int** |
| *wuru-gi\** | go in; set (sun/moon) **int**; + Ablative |
| *yaraay* | sun |
| *gilay* | moon |

\**Dhurra-li* – see the *Dictionary* – it has many uses, including of 'sun rising'.

\**Wuru-gi* – Note that the location entered is in Ablative case.

## Grammar

The table below sets out the suffix for each verb class.

 **Audio:** GGU 17.2.mp3 is available in the electronic edition

### Moving continuous verbs

| Command | Future | Present | Past |
|---|---|---|---|
| **Y Class** | | | |
| *yana-waa-ya* keep walking | *yana-waa-y* will be walking | *yana-waa-nha* is/am/are* walking | *yana-waa-nhi* was walking |
| *gubi-yaa-ya* keep swimming | *gubi-yaa-y* will be swimming | *gubi-yaa-nha* is swimming | *gubi-yaa-nhi* was swimming |
| **L Class** | | | |
| *dhurra-laa-ya* keep coming | *dhurra-laa-y* will be coming | *dhurra-laa-nha* is coming | *dhurra-laa-nhi* was coming |
| **NG Class** | | | |
| *gaa-waa-ya* keep bringing | *gaa-waa-y* will be bringing | *gaa-waa-nha* is bringing | *gaa-waa-nhi* was bringing |
| *gi-yaa-ya* keep getting | *gi-yaa-y* will be getting | *gi-yaa-nha* is getting | *gi-yaa-nhi* was getting |
| **RR Class** | | | |
| *dhuu-rraa-ya* keep crawling | *dhuu-rraa-y* will be crawling | *dhuu-rraa-nha* is crawling | *dhuu-rraa-nhi* was crawling |

 **Audio:** GGU 17.3.mp3 is available in the electronic edition

The 'continuous moving' verb suffixes have two main uses. The first use is to show 'linear motion', 'moving along'. Look at some *Y* class examples:

LESSON 17. VERBS: CONTINUOUS – MOVING

*Yana-**waa**-nha ngaya.*
I am walking.

*Banaga-**waa**-nha buruma.*
The dog is running.

*Bara-**waa**-nha bandaarr.*
The kangaroo is hopping.

*Gubi-**yaa**-nha guduu.*
The cod (*guduu*) is swimming.

Examples from other verb classes include:

*Dhurra-**laa**-nha gilay.*
The moon is coming/rising.

*Gabi nginda gaa-**waa**-nha.*
You(1) are bringing the coffee.

*Dhuu-**rraa**-nha birraliidhuul.*
The baby is crawling.

These sentences all involve words where 'moving along' is a normal part of the meaning of the verb.

As with other verb suffixes, the word used to describe it does not convey the full use of the form. While the *-nha* suffix on verbs is called present tense, it is likely that these forms can also be used to indicate future action in some circumstances (yet to be carefully described). For instance, it seems likely that the present continuous *yana-waa-nha ngaya* 'I am going', can refer to future action, as it can in English ('I am going to Goodooga (tomorrow).').

**Note:** all the continuous moving suffixes have a **double 'a' (*aa*)** (*-laa-*, *-waa-*, *-yaa-*, *-rraa-*) and all the continuous non-moving suffixes have a **single 'a'** (*-lda*, *-y.la-*, *-gi.la-*, *-dha-*).

If you are finding this pretty strange it is okay – it probably indicates your mind has been strongly influenced by English. You may be like lots of monolingual people and not used to languages doing things very differently from English.

The continuous moving suffixes can be used on 'non-movement' verbs. Look at the examples below.

🔊 **Audio:** GGU 17.4.mp3 is available in the electronic edition

*Miyay bubaaga ngarri-yaa-nha.*
The girl is 'sitting(-moving)' on her father.

(Said, in Yuwaalaraay, of a girl sitting on dad's shoulders as he walks. You would use the same suffix if talking about someone sitting in a moving car.)

*Maridhu dha-laa-nha.*
The man is eating(-moving).

(Arthur Dodd said this when asked to translate: 'The man is eating while walking along'.)

Fred Reece (tape 2439, in Giacon, 2017) describes a dog (*maadhaay* in Yuwaalaraay) chasing a goanna:

*Maadhaay dhaay banaga-waa-nha,* **gula-laa-nha**.
The dog is running here and barking.

*Ngaarrima nguu* (GR *nguru*) **gula-lda-nha**.
He's barking over there now (at the base of the tree the goanna ran up).

The verb *gula-li* 'bark', has the continuous moving form when the dog is running and the continuous non-moving form when it is standing.

So, one use of the continuous moving suffix on **non-movement** verbs is to show that there is 'linear' movement. The other use shows a different kind of movement. Look at the next sentences, all with 'moving' suffixes.

*Buruma balu-waa-nha.*
The dog is dying.

*Gaba ngaya gi-yaa-nha.*
I am getting good.

*Giirr nginda wiibi-laa-nha.*
You(1) are getting sick.

All three sentences indicate a kind of movement: from alive to dead, from bad to good, from healthy to sick. This 'movement' is shown by the use of the continuous-moving suffix.

Compare the following sentences, which use the 'non-moving' suffix.

*Gaba ngaya gi-**gi.la**-nha.*
I am (always/often) good.

*Giirr nginda wiibi-**lda**-nha.*
You(1) are (always/often) sick.

Finally, a different use for the **non-moving** continuous suffix with verbs that usually show 'movement along'. On the Yuwaalaraay tapes there are many examples of kangaroos hopping: *bara-waa-nha*. But when Arthur Dodd talks of fish flopping in the bottom of the canoe he uses *bara-y.la-nha* – same verb root (*bara-* 'hop'), but different suffix – because the fish is not going anywhere. (The Gamilaraay version of the verb has been used here.) This use of the non-moving suffix is not all that common. Below are some further examples.

 **Audio:** GGU 17.5.mp3 is available in the electronic edition

*Birralii burumaga baraylanha.*
The kid is jumping on the dog.

*Banagaylanha nhama baawul-guwaay gawugaa-dhalibaa-guwaay.*
(*gawugaa* 'head')
He's running around like a headless chook.
(I wonder what the Gamilaraay simile was.)

## Practice

 **Audio:** GGU 17.6.mp3 is available in the electronic edition

You can follow the patterns used in Lesson 16.

Perform a 'moving' action, and describe it.

*Yanawaanha ngaya, yanawaanha nginda, yanawaanha=nha.*
I am walking, you are walking, she is walking.

## WIIDHAA

Use other verbs: *gubi-y, banaga-y, bara-y, barra-y*, etc.

Give a command, then use a range of verb forms.

A: *B, banagawaaya.*
B, run (and keep running).
B: *Banagay ngaya, banagawaanha ngaya, banaganhi ngaya.*
I will run, I am running, I ran.

Expand the range of verb forms to include:

*Banagawaay ngaya* and *Banagawaanhi ngaya*.
I will be running. ... I was running. (while pointing to the place of the action)

A: *Minya nhalay.*
What is this?
B: *Gubiyaanhi nginda.*
You were swimming.

Perform action while still and then while moving.

A: *Dhaldanha ngaya, dhalaanha=nga ngaya.*
I am eating (standing), I am eating (walking along) now.

Commands.

A: *Gamilaraay guwaaldaya.*
Talk (and keep talking) Gamilaraay.
B: *Gamilbala ngaya Gamilaraay guwaaldanha.*
I can't speak Gamilaraay.
C: *Giirrbala ngaya maaru Gamilaraay guwaaldanha.*
But I talk Gamilaraay well.
C: *Giirr ngaya Gamilaraay guwaalaanha.*
I am talking Gamilaraay (while walking).

Do something complex.

A: *Wuudhanha ngaya nginu gali.*
I am giving you some water.
B: *Yawu, Wuudhanha nginda ngay gali.*
Yes, you are giving me water.

A: *Gamilaraay ngaya nginunda guwaalaanha.*
   I am talking Gamilaraay to you (while walking).
B: *Yawu, Gamilaraay nginda nganunda guwaalaanha.*
   Yes, you are talking Gamilaraay to me.
B: *Winangalaanhabala=nga ngaya nginunha bamba.*
   And I am listening carefully to you now (while walking).

## *Winangala, garay guwaala, yawala.*
## Listen, say and read.

You can read further examples for Lesson 17 and listen to them, and again there are lots of Yuwaalaraay examples in *Gayarragi, Winangali*.

 **Audio:** GGU 17.7.mp3 is available in the electronic edition

A: *Giirr burruluu nginunda yanawaanha.*
   There are flies (walking) on you.
   *Gamil, giidjaabala nganunda banagawaanha.*
   No, there are ants running on me.

*Minya dhaldanha nhama birraydhu?*
What is that boy eating?

*Gamil dhaay barrawaanha dhigaraa.*
The bird is not flying here.

*Dhuludhi ngindaali gubiyaanhi?*
Were you(2) swimming away from the tree?

*Yaamandaali gubiylanha?* ( =*ndaali* – short for *ngindaali*)
Do you(2) swim?

*Minyangay burruluu girrinili galiyawaanha?*
(previous versions had *girrinila*)
How many flies are climbing on the door?

**Audio:** GGU 17.8.mp3 is available in the electronic edition

*Dhalaagu barawaay bandaarr?*
Where will the kangaroo be hopping to?

*Giirr nginaayngundi banagawaanhi buruma.*
The dog was running from you(3+).

*Garay nhama guwaalaanhi giwiirru.*
The man was talking. (as he walked)

*Ngaandi yuruunda dhuurraanha?*
Who is crawling on the road?

*Wiibilaanha gaayli dhinggaadhi.*
The kid is getting sick from the meat.

*Ngarriylay nginda wilbaarra ngay?*
Will you sit in my car? (while it is still)

*Gamil, ngarriyaaybala ngaya wilbaarra nginu.*
No, but I will go for a drive. (sit in it while it moves)

*Ngamila, yaraay dhurralaanha, wuuwaanhabala gilay.*
Look, the sun is rising, but the moon is setting.

# LESSON 18
# Further Suffixes

## Vocabulary

 **Audio:** GGU 18.1.mp3 is available in the electronic edition

| Garay | Words |
| --- | --- |
| -Baraay | having |
| -DHalibaa | without |
| -nginda* | wanting |
| -guwaay (and -giirr) | like |
| -galgaa | plural |
| -gal | plural on birralii, gaayli |
| -gaali* | dual |

*The suffix *-nginda* is sometimes also used to translate the verb 'like'.

*The suffix *-gaali* was not included in previous versions of this list. Perhaps an unconscious bias to the common European system of having singular and plural forms, but not duals. Duals are common in Australian languages and very prominent in Gamilaraay pronouns. We know little about other dual forms, nouns and adjectives, for instance, probably because they were not investigated to any extent when GY was being collected. *-gaali* seems to have an alternative *-gaalay*, and is found in names such as *gulayaali* 'pelican' (*gulay* 'net') and *mangun.gaali* 'goanna'.

## Grammar

 **Audio:** GGU 18.2.mp3 is available in the electronic edition

Examples of suffixed nouns.

| Noun | having | without | wanting |
|---|---|---|---|
| buruma | -baraay | -dhalibaa | -nginda |
| muru | -baraay | -dhalibaa | -nginda |
| yarraaman | -baraay | -d(h)alibaa | -nginda |
| wiyayl | -araay | -d(h)alibaa | -nginda |
| bandaarr | -araay | -d(h)alibaa | -nginda |
| gaayli/birralii | -baraay | -dhalibaa | -nginda |
| dhalay | -baraay | -dhalibaa | -nginda |

For example, *buruma-baraay* = 'having a dog/dogs', etc.

Remember, the capital letters in the suffix means that part can change, depending on the word it is attached to. Also, the 'translation' given ('having, without …') is only an **indication** of the meaning. The suffix **does not** correspond precisely with that English word.

For more information on these suffixes see the *Dictionary*, pp. 273–77, the dictionary entries for the suffixes and Giacon (2017, pp. 81ff). The *-Baraay* suffix occurs in many Gamilaraay place names: Narrabri, Collarenebri, Boggabri and Yalaroi. There are a number of places called *Wii Dhalibaa* 'no fire/firewood' (Written Weetaliba, and other spellings).

One modification of previous analysis concerns *-DHalibaa*. The form of this suffix is uncertain, but it is very unusual for *dh* to occur after word final *n*, *rr* or *l*, so *-dalibaa* is now the preferred form there.

There are many examples of most of these suffixes in *Gayarragi, Winangali* – but not of *-Baraay* since it is Gamilaraay and the tape material is Yuwaalaraay, which uses *-Biyaay* with the same meaning.

## -Baraay 'having'

 **Audio:** GGU 18.3.mp3 is available in the electronic edition

This suffix is *-baraay* except when a word ends in *l* or *rr*, when it is *-araay*. It is mostly translated 'with' or 'having'. It is not used to translate 'with' if that means 'instrument'. So, use it for: 'I walked down the street <u>with</u> a hammer' (carrying a hammer) but **not** for 'I hit the nail <u>with</u> the hammer'. Some examples are:

**Words:**

*Guliirr-araay*
partner-having = married

*gali-baraay*
water-having = wet

**Sentences:**

*Dhawun nhama milimili-baraay.*
That ground is muddy. = (mud-having)

*Mari yananhi bilaarr-araay.*
The man walked along with his spear.

*Burriin-baraay ngaya warraylanhi.*
I stood with my shield.

*Yaama nginda water bag-baraay?*
Have you got a water bag?

*Yaama=nda birralii-baraay?*
Have you(1) got any kids?

*Giirr ngaya birralii-baraay, bulaarr.*
Yes, I've got two kids.

> The suffix occurs in the name Gamil**araay**. There are similar suffixes in Yuwaalaraay (*-Biyaay*), Wangaaybuwan (*-buwan*), Wayilwan (*-wan*, almost certainly a modified form of *-buwan* after *l*), Wiradjuri (possibly *-dhurraay*), *(Pitjantja)-tjara* and many other Australian languages. Gamilaraay has many place names which use the *-Baraay* suffix. Yuwaalaraay does not use the corresponding *-Biyaay* suffix on place names, but many use *-DHuul*. The other 'no-with' languages also use their 'having' suffix on place names. The Wiradjuri suffix, *-dhurraay*, occurs as -dry and fairly modified as -dra (Cootamundra and Cootamundry creek). Wangaaybuwan and Wayilwan *-buwan* is found in Gulargambone.

## Extension

 **Audio:** GGU 18.4.mp3 is available in the electronic edition

The suffix is not generally used in phrases like 'I went with Chris'. The most likely way to translate that is with Locative case:

*Chris-ga ngaya yananhi.*

A similar meaning can be conveyed by the following, which has a structure that is common in Australian languages but strange to English ears.

*Yananhi ngali-Chris.*

Chris and I went. (The structure is: We(2) including Chris went.)

The language might have used Chris-*baraay*, but I suspect that implied something like: 'I am in charge of/responsible for/senior to Chris'.

## *-DHalibaa* 'without'

 **Audio:** GGU 18.5.mp3 is available in the electronic edition

The form of the suffix is described above. It means 'a lack of something'. Many Aboriginal languages have a similar suffix.

*Dhawun nhama milimili-dhalibaa.*
That ground hasn't got any mud.

## LESSON 18. FURTHER SUFFIXES

*Yananhi Mari bilaarr-dalibaa.*
The man walk along without his spear.

*Burriin-dalibaa ngaya warraylanhi.*
I stood without my shield.

---

A: *Yaama nginda water bag-baraay?*
   Have you got a water bag?
B: *Gamilbala, water bag-dhalibaa ngaya.*
   No, I've got no water bag.

---

A: *Yaama=nda birralii-baraay?*
   Have you(1) got any kids?
B: *Birralii-dhalibaa=bala ngaya.*
   I've got no kids.

---

*Yarral-dalibaa ngaya.*
I've got no money.

At times *DHalibaa* behaves like a suffix, but at times it is like a separate word.

## -nginda 'wanting, needing'

 **Audio:** GGU 18.6.mp3 is available in the electronic edition

This suffix is attached to nouns or the future forms of verbs, indicating that the thing or action is wanted.

*Guliirr-nginda ngaya.*
I want a wife/husband/spouse.

---

A: *Yaamanda yarral-nginda?*
   Do you(1) want any money?
B: *Giirr ngaya yarralnginda.*
   Sure, I want some money.

---

*Galinginda ngaya.*
I want some water. / I'm thirsty.

*Gamil ngaya yanay-nginda.*
I don't want to go.

WIIDHAA

*Gamil ngaya nginunha ngamili-nginda.*
I don't want to see you.

Some useful phrases:

*Minya-nginda=nda?*
What do you want? (What-wanting-you?)

*Minya-nginda=ndaali?*
What do you(2) want?

*Minya-nginda=ndaay?*
What do you(>2) want?

## Extension

At times the suffix has the form *ngin* or *ngindi*, as in *yuulngin* 'hungry'. The significance of the differences is not fully understood.

## -guwaay 'like'

Most of our information about this suffix comes from the corresponding Yuwaalaraay suffix, *-giirr*. There is also one Gamilaraay example of *-giirr*. In future we may learn more by investigating the Wangaaybuwan cognate, *-gulaay*.

 **Audio:** GGU 18.7.mp3 is available in the electronic edition

This suffix is still used by people in Walgett and Lightning Ridge in phrases like:

She swims fish-*giirr*.
She swims like a fish.

This the same as the traditional use.

*Baranhi nhama bandaarr-giirr.*
He hopped like a kangaroo.

*Giirr ngaya banagawaanhi dhinawan.giirr.*
I ran like an emu.

The remaining examples will use *-guwaay*.

*yinarr-guwaay*
like a woman

*mari-guwaay*
like a murri

*Giirr nguru dha-y buruma-gu-guwaay.*
He ate like a dog. (greedily)

## Extension

It actually turns out that *-guwaay* has different properties from most other suffixes. Details in later courses.

## -*galgaa* 'plural'

 **Audio:** GGU 18.8.mp3 is available in the electronic edition

In English, plural nouns are almost always different from the singular. **Men/man**, **dogs/dog**, and so on (with exceptions like 'sheep' and 'fish'). This is not so in Gamilaraay and in most Aboriginal languages. We do not know the Gamilaraay rules well, so the following may be modified after more study of Gamilaraay and other languages.

The plural is often or generally shown on people words.

So *yinarr-galgaa* 'women', *giwiirr-galgaa* 'men'. The plural is *-gal* for *birralii* 'child', so *birralii-gal* 'children'. (Other languages, including Wangaaybuwan, have a different plural for 'little things'.)

*Yinarrgalgaa dhaay yananhi.*
The women came here.

*Birraliigal yinarrgu yananhi.*
The children went to the women.

*Mari-galgaa ngaya ngamiy.*
I saw the Murris.

Other suffixes come after the plural suffix.

*Mari-galgaa-gu nganha ngamiy.*
The Murris saw me.

*Yinarrgalgaa-gu dhinggaa dhay.*
The women ate the meat.

*Birraliigal-araay ngaya.*
I've got lots of kids.

All nouns, including people nouns, can have plural meaning without suffixing *-galgaa*.

*Yinarr-u dhinggaa dhay.*
The women ate the meat.

## Extension

Some of the sources also have a dual suffix, *-gaali*. (This is only for your information. You do not need to use this suffix.)

*Yinarr-gaali-dhu dhinggaa dhay.*
The (2) women ate the meat.

As with many other areas, there may be slight changes or additions to this part of Gamilaraay grammar.

## Noun + adjectives

With the case suffixes studied earlier, if there is a noun and an associated adjective, the suffix is on both, e.g. *man.ga-ga burrul-a* 'on the big table'. We have not found examples of the suffixes from this lesson in such situations, but for the present follow the same rule as for earlier suffixes.

| | |
|---|---|
| *Man.garr-nginda ngaya burrulnginda.* | I need a big bag. |

# Practice

 **Audio:** GGU 18.9.mp3 is available in the electronic edition

## Conversations

These suffixes are very useful in conversations.

---

A: *Guliirr-araay nginda?*
   You married/partnered?
B: *Yawu, guliirr-araay ngaya. Kim. Gaba=nha.*
   Yes, I've got a partner, Kim. S/he is good.
A: *Birralii-baraay nginda?*
   You got kids?
B: *Birraliidhalibaabala ngaya, birraliingindabala ngaya.*
   I've got no kids, but I want kids.
A: *Yaamanda burumabaraay?*
   Do you have a dog/dogs?
B: *Gamilbala. Burumadhalibaa ngaya.*
   No. I don't have a dog.
A: *Buruma-nginda=nda?*
   Do you want a dog/dogs?
B: *Yawu. Burumanginda ngaya.*
   Yes. I want a dog/like dogs.
A: *Minyangay-nginda=nda?*
   How many do you want?

---

Use as many words as you can from the previous lessons, including verbs.

*Banagay-nginda ngaya.*
I need to run.

*Gunii, yarraldalibaa ngaya, yarralnginda ngaya, nguugu, schoolgu.*
*Yarral ngay wuuna.*
Mum, I've got no money, and I need money for books, for school.
Give me some money.

WIIDHAA

A: *Minya nhalay?* (hops like a kangaroo)
   What's this.
B: *Barawaanhi nginda, bandaarr-guwaay.*
   You were hopping like a kangaroo.

## Games

If you have cards of say six vocabulary items you can shuffle, give everyone six cards; people ask for cards using formulas like:

*Bandaarraraay nginda? Bandaarrnginda ngaya.*
The first person to get all six wins.

Use normal playing cards, first person to get a full set wins. You may need to use some English and adapt the rules.

*Kingnginda ngaya, guwaaymbarranginda.*
I need a red king.

## *Winangala, garay guwaala, yawala.*
## Listen, say and read.

 **Audio:** GGU 18.10.mp3 is available in the electronic edition

*Burumabaraay nhama yinarr.*
That woman has a dog.

*Giwiirr nhama dhigaraaguwaay barranhi.*
That man flew like a bird.

*Galinginda ngaya.*
I need water.

*Gaaylidhalibaa nhama giwiirr.*
That man has no kids.

*Giirr ngaya yarraldalibaa. Yaamandaay yarralaraay?*
I've got no money. Have you(>2) got any money?

*Giirr ngaya yarralaraay. Gamilbala ngaya yarral nginu wuurri!*
I've got some money, but I'm not going to give you any money.

## LESSON 18. FURTHER SUFFIXES

🔊 **Audio:** GGU 18.11.mp3 is available in the electronic edition

*Galinginda ngaya. Ngaandu ngay gali wuurri?*
I am thirsty (water-wanting). Who will give me some water?

*Burumaguguwaay nginda dhay.*
You(1) ate like a dog/greedily.

*Gaayligalaraay ngaya.*
I've got lots of kids.

*Yaama galibaraay nhama man.ga?* (*galibaraay* = wet)
Is that table wet?

*Dhaay banagaya, wiyaylaraay.*
Run here with the pen.

*Bundaanhi nhama giwiirr, yarralguwaay.*
That man fell like a stone.

*Gamil garrawalgu yanay guniidhalibaa gaayligal.*
The kids will not go to the shop without their mother.

*Yaama nginaalingunda gaayligalu garay guwaay?*
Did the kids talk to you(2)?

*Dhulugalgaa dhiyamala!*
Pick up sticks!

# LESSON 19
# More Pronouns: Dual and Plural

This lesson introduces more pronouns – more first person (I, we) and second person (you) pronouns. Lessons 19–21 all have more pronouns. They fit into patterns already done in previous lessons, so you are learning more vocabulary, but not new structures.

These take most people a while to learn, so try, for a start, to understand the system and see the patterns. Also practise the pronunciation – a good way to do that is to listen to and repeat these words on *Gayarragi, Winangali*, especially when they are in sentences from the old tapes.

The vocabulary includes a Case column, to help you to know when to use the form.

## Vocabulary

 **Audio:** GGU 19.1.mp3 is available in the electronic edition

| *Garay* | Words | Case |
|---|---|---|
| *ngali* | we two | Nominative/doer and |
| *ngiyani* | we mob(>2) | Ergative/doer.to |
| *ngalinya* | us two | Accusative/done.to |
| *ngiyaninya* | us mob(>2) | |
| *ngalingu* | our(s) two | Dative/possessive/owning |
| *ngiyaningu* | our(s) mob(>2) | |
| *ngindaali* | you two (doer) | Nominative/doer and |
| *ngindaay* | you mob(>2) (doer) | Ergative/doer.to |
| *nginaalinya*\* | you two (done to) | Accusative/done.to |
| *nginaaynya* | you mob(>2) (done to) | |

| *Garay* | Words | Case |
|---|---|---|
| *nginaalingu* | your(s) two | Dative/possessive/owning |
| *nginaayngu* | your(s) mob(>2) | |

*This and the following forms starts with *ngina*, not *nginda*.

## Grammar

**Reminder:** Pronouns are, most of the time, the second word in the sentence. However, interrogative (question) pronouns, like other interrogatives, are first in the sentence.

These pronouns are used the same way as the corresponding singular pronouns introduced in previous lessons; that is, you need to know what case is used in a particular situation. An important distinction is between **dual** and **plural** pronouns. Dual pronouns refer to two people: 'us(2)', 'you(2)', etc. English does not have dual pronouns, but they are found in many languages including Māori. When speaking of Gamilaraay, **plural** refers to **3 or more**, whereas in English **plural** refers to **2 or more**. (The symbol > means 'more than', so >2 means 'more than 2'; that is, 3 or more.) You might like to look at the pronoun table in Appendix 5 or in the references section of yuwaalaraay.com as you read this section.

### Doer/doer.to

 **Audio:** GGU 19.2.mp3 is available in the electronic edition

You have already learnt most of the patterns for these pronouns. You have learnt how to use the doer/doer.to pronouns *ngaya* and *nginda*, starting in Lesson 4.

| | | |
|---|---|---|
| *Gaba ngaya.* I am good. | (no verb) | |
| *Gaba nginda.* You(1) are good. | (no verb) | |
| *Yananhi ngaya.* I went. | (doer) | |

## LESSON 19. MORE PRONOUNS: DUAL AND PLURAL

*Yananhi nginda.*
You(1) went. (doer)

*Gali ngaya ngarunhi.*
I drank the water. (doer.to)

*Gali nginda ngarunhi.*
You(1) drank the water. (doer.to)

Some may by now be comfortable with using Nominative case for 'doer', Ergative case for 'doer.to' and Accusative case for 'done.to'.

*Ngaya* refers to 1 person: 'I'.

The new **doer/doer.to** pronouns are used the same way, but they refer to different groups.

| | | |
|---|---|---|
| *ngali* | 'we' | refers to 2 people: me and someone else |
| *ngiyani* | 'we' | refers to more than 2 people: me and someones else |
| *ngindaali* | 'you' | refers to 2 people |
| *ngindaay* | 'you' | refers to >2 people |

Remember, these are for Nominative and Ergative case, doer/doer.to, and follow the pattern above for *ngaya* and *nginda*. Anywhere there is a *ngaya* or *nginda* you can use *ngali, ngiyani, ngindaali, ngindaay*. Compare these sentences with the ones above.

 **Audio:** GGU 19.3.mp3 is available in the electronic edition

*Gaba **ngali**.*
We(2) are good. (no verb)

*Gaba **ngindaay**.*
You(>2) are good. (no verb)

*Yananhi **ngindaali**.*
You(2) went. (doer/Nominative)

*Yananhi **ngiyani**.*
We(>2) went. (doer/Nominative)

*Gali **ngindaay** ngarunhi.*
You(>2) drank the water.    (doer.to/Ergative)

*Gali **ngali** ngarunhi.*
We(2) drank the water.    (doer.to/Ergative)

(Remember, the symbol > means 'more than', so >2 means 'more than 2' – 3 or 4 or …)

## Done.to

(Accusative case)

 **Audio:** GGU 19.4.mp3 is available in the electronic edition

You have already seen how *nganha* 'me' (done.to/Accusative, first person) and *nginunha* 'you(1)' (done.to/Accusative, second person) pronouns are used in Lesson 15:

*Giirr **nganha** burumagu yiiy.*
The dog bit **me**.

*Giirr **nginunha** burumagu yiiy.*
The dog bit **you(1)**.

The other done.to/Accusative pronouns are used the same way.

*Giirr **ngalinya** burumagu yiiy.*
The dog bit **us(2 people)**.

*Giirr **nginaalinya** burumagu yiiy.*
The dog bit **you(2)**.

*Giirr **ngiyaninya** burumagu yiiy.*
The dog bit **us(>2 people)**.

*Giirr **nginaaynya** burumagu yiiy.*
The dog bit **you(>2)**.

## Owner/Dative

(Dative = given.to, and other uses)

 **Audio:** GGU 19.5.mp3 is available in the electronic edition

'Owner' (or 'Possessive case' or 'Dative case') was introduced in Lesson 8. You can use all the possessive pronouns the way *ngay* is used in:

*Buruma ngay.*
My dog.

So you can say:

*Dhalaa buruma **ngay**?*
Where is **my** dog?

*Dhalaa buruma **ngalingu**?*
Where is **our(2)** dog?

*Dhalaa buruma **nginaayngu**?*
Where is **your(>2)** dog?

Remember, possessive pronouns are also used for 'given.to'. Another way to say this is that recipients, with the verb *wuurri* 'give', are Dative case. The pattern is the same for all Dative/possessive/owner pronouns. (They are in one row or column in pronoun tables.)

*Bubaagu **ngay** yarral wuunhi.*
Dad gave **me** money.

*Bubaagu **ngiyaningu** yarral wuunhi.*
Dad gave **us(>2)** money.

*Bubaagu **nginaalingu** yarral wuunhi.*
Dad gave **you(2)** money.

## Practice

There is a lot in this lesson, so do not try to absorb it all in one go. Gradually build up your knowledge.

 **Audio:** GGU 19.6.mp3 is available in the electronic edition

**In a group:** *gayadha*/in turn each one *guwaali*/says:

| | |
|---|---|
| *ngaya* | and points to themselves. |
| *ngali* | and puts their arm around other person. |
| *ngiyani* | and puts their arms around a few people. |

When you have got that, start on *nginda, ngindaali, ngindaay*, pointing to one, two and more than two people in turn. Notice that the words all start with *nginda*.

Describe actions.

Similar to the previous exercise.

While sitting:

*Ngarriylanha ngaya, ngali, ngiyani.*
I, we(2), we(>2) are sitting.

Then

*Ngamildanha nginda, ngindaali, ngindaay.*
You(1), you(2), you(>2) are looking.

### Accusative case

 **Audio:** GGU 19.7.mp3 is available in the electronic edition

Use a similar pattern. This works well in a bigger group, or you need to have some 'pretend people' around.

*Ngamildanha nginda nganha.*
*Ngamildanha nginda ngalinya.*
*Ngamildanha nginda ngiyaninya.*
You(1) are looking at me, us(2), us(>2).

Then change the number of people looking: *ngindaali, ngindaay.*

Then change who is doing the looking: *ngaya, ngali, ngiyani.* You will also need to change the 'looked at'.

Or if you have a pet or toy dog:

*Burumagu nginunha ngamildanha.*
*Burumagu nginaalinya ngamildanha.*
*Burumagu nginaaynya ngamildanha.*
The dog is looking at you(1), you(2), you(>2).

With a little imagination you will create other variations, so having the repetition that is essential to language learning.

## Dative/possessive

 **Audio:** GGU 19.8.mp3 is available in the electronic edition

Holding an item (1 person, then 2, then more)

*Man.garr ngay, man.garr ngalingu, man.garr ngiyaningu.*
My bag, our(2) bag, our(>2) bag.

*Man.garr nginu, man.garr nginaalingu, man.garr nginaayngu.*
Your(1) bag, your(2) bag, your(>2) bag.

**With *wuurri* 'give'**

Have two groups, the number in each group needs to change from time to time.

One person A is giving pens to group B, to one person, then to two and three people.

| | | |
|---|---|---|
| A: | *Wiyayl ngaya nginaalingu wuurri.* | *Wiyayl ngaya nginaalingu wuunhi.* |
| | I will give you(2) pens. | I gave you(2) pens. |
| B: | *Wiyayl nginda ngalingu wuudhanha.* | *Wiyayl nginda ngalingu wuunhi.* |
| | You(1) are giving us(2) pens. | You(1) gave us(2) pens. |

WIIDHAA

A: *Ngaandu nginaalingu wiyayl wuunhi?*
   Who gave you(2) pens?
B: *Nginda.*
   You.

## Extension

This course does not look at another important distinction, **inclusive–exclusive,** which is shown by dual and plural first person pronouns (we, us, our, etc.) in Gamilaraay and in many Aboriginal languages.

**Inclusive** means that the person(s) spoken to are included. So 'we' then includes both the speaker(s) and listener(s) (we = me and you(s)).

**Exclusive** pronouns exclude the listeners (we = me and she/he/they, but not you). Exclusive 'we' includes the speaker(s) but not the listener(s). This distinction only refers to first person dual and plural pronouns. The distinction is also found in other languages, for instance Māori. See Giacon (2014, 2017).

For recent analysis of pronouns see Appendix 5 and Giacon (2017). The information there on third person Nominative/Accusative singular and third person dual pronouns has been updated, so has some differences from earlier sources, including the Dictionary (pp. 286ff) and *Gaay Garay Dhadhin* (the *Picture Dictionary*).

## *Winangala, garay guwaala, yawala.*
## Listen, say and read.

 **Audio:** GGU 19.9.mp3 is available in the electronic edition

*Giirr ngali gundhigu yananhi.*
We(2) went to the house.

*Yaama nginaalingu nhama gundhi?*
Is that house yours(2)?

*Gamil ngalingu nhama, Billgubala.*
It is not ours(2), it is Bill's.

## LESSON 19. MORE PRONOUNS: DUAL AND PLURAL

*Giirr burumagu ngiyaningu nginaaynya yiili.*
Our(>2) dog will bite you(>2).

*Giirr ngaya nginaalinya ngamiy.*
I did see you(2).

*Yaama, ngindaay.*
Hello to you(>2).

You can listen to Arthur Dodd and Fred Reece say many of these pronouns on *Gayarragi, Winangali*. Remember that they are speaking Yuwaalaraay. These pronouns are the same in Yuwaalaraay and Gamilaraay, but other pronouns and words may not be.

# LESSON 20
# Pronouns: Locative/Allative and Ablative

This lesson introduces more Locative/Allative and Ablative pronouns including Locative/Allative and Ablative question pronouns. See Lesson 15 for the uses of these pronouns.

## Vocabulary

 **Audio:** GGU 20.1.mp3 is available in the electronic edition

(singular forms are repeated from Lesson 15)

| Garay | Words | Case |
|---|---|---|
| *nganunda* | to, at, on me | |
| *ngalingunda* | to, at, on us(2) | |
| *ngiyaningunda* | to, at, on us mob(>2) | Locative (at, on, near, with) and Allative case (movement.to) |
| *nginunda* | to, at, on you(1) | |
| *nginaalingunda* | to, at, on you(2) | |
| *nginaayngunda* | to, at, on you mob(>2) | |
| *ngurungunda* | to, at, her/him | |
| *nganundi* | from me | |
| *ngalingundi* | from us(2) | |
| *ngiyaningundi* | from us(>2) | |
| *nginundi* | from you(1) | Ablative/from |
| *nginaalingundi* | from you(2) | |
| *nginaayngundi* | from you(>2) | |
| *ngurungundi* | from him, her | |

| *Garay* | Words | Case |
|---|---|---|
| *ngaandi?* | who?/whom? | Nominative and Accusative |
| *ngaandu?* | who? | Ergative |
| *ngaanngu?* | whose? (give) to who? | Dative/possessive |
| *ngaanngunda?* | to, at, on who(m)? | Locative and Allative |
| *ngaanngundi?* | from who(m)? | Ablative |

# Grammar

This lesson introduces the last two sets of pronouns – the **'Locative/Allative' (place/movement.to)** and **Ablative (source, from)** pronouns.

There is a pronoun chart in Appendix 5 that may help you to see the patterns. The pronouns will be a lot easier to remember if you can see the patterns, both down the columns and across the rows. Adjacent Locative/Allative and Ablative/from pronouns only vary in the final letter, (*a/i*) and they mostly 'include' the possessive/Dative pronoun form (e.g. *nginu* in **nginu**nda). Remember that the names (Locative, Ablative/from, etc.) are, to a fair extent, labels – they distinguish the particular set of pronouns but do not describe the range of uses of those sets. The same is true of the 'translation' such as 'to, at, on her/him'. The 'translation' indicates some major uses but does not by any means fully describe the use of the pronoun. In some cases, English 'to, at, on her/him' will be translated by other forms, and *ngurungunda* will have translations apart from those listed. Read Giacon (2017) and the *Dictionary*, pp. 286ff, for more information. You may find the pronoun section in the *Gaay Garay Dhadhin: Gamilaraay & Yuwaalaraay Picture Dictionary* (Yuwaalaraay and Gamilaraay Language Program, 2006) helpful (see Appendix 5).

Note that there has been revision of many areas of third person pronouns. The Nominative case singular third person is not *nguru* as in the original *Picture Dictionary* chart. There has also been extensive revision of the third person dual pronouns.

## Locative/Allative

See Lesson 7 for uses of the Locative case and Lesson 5 for use of Allative case.

 **Audio:** GGU 20.2.mp3 is available in the electronic edition

From earlier lessons you know:

*Warranhi Kim **buruma-ga.***
Kim stood on/near the dog.

*Buruma-ga* has the **Locative** suffix. The Locative pronouns are used the same way as *buruma-ga*. Nominative/Ergative pronouns are generally second.

*Warranhi **ngalingunda** Kim.*
Kim stood near(on) us(2).

*Warranhi **ngiyaningunda** Kim.*
Kim stood near(on) us(>2).

*Warranhi **nginaayngunda** Kim.*
Kim stood near(on) you(>2).

***Ngaanngunda** warranhi Kim?*
Who did Kim stand near(on)?

*Warranhi **ngurungunda** Kim.*
Kim stood near(on) her/him.

***Ngaandi nginunda** warranhi?*
Who stood near you(1)?

I have recently realised that Locative case is also used to translate 'with' when it could also be translated 'near', as in the sentences above. Seeing this used of Locative in Pitjantjatjara helped to see this.

 **Audio:** GGU 20.3.mp3 is available in the electronic edition

Remember, **Locative** is used for 'talking to'.

*Garay Chrisgu guwaay **buruma-ga**.*
Chris talked to the dog.

Locative pronouns are also used with 'talk to'.

*Giirr **nganunda** Chrisgu garay guwaay.*
Chris talked to me.

*Giirr **ngurungunda** garay guwaay Chrisgu.*
Chris talked to him/her.

*Giirr **nginaalingunda** Chrisgu garay guwaay.*
Chris talked to you(2).

***Ngaanngunda** garay Chrisgu guwaay?*
Who did Chris talk to?

*Yaama Chrisgu garay guwaay **nginunda**?*
Did Chris talk to you(1)?

*Gamil garay **nganunda** Chrisgu guwaay.*
Chris didn't talk to me.

The Locative and Allative pronouns have the same form, so the pronouns just used are also used for 'movement to'.

*Dhaay yananga, **nganunda**.*
Come here, to me.

***Ngaanngunda**nda yanawaanha?*
Who(m) are you going to?

*Yananhi **ngurungunda** Kim.*
Kim went to her/him.

## Ablative/Source

See Lesson 9.

 **Audio:** GGU 20.4.mp3 is available in the electronic edition

*Banaganhi Kim **buruma-dhi**.*
Kim ran away from the dog.

*Buruma-dhi* has the **Ablative** suffix. The Ablative pronouns are used the same way as *buruma-dhi*.

*Banaganhi **nganundi** Kim.*
Kim ran away from me.

*Banaganhi Kim **ngiyaningundi**.*
Kim ran away from us(>2).

*Banaganhi **nginaayngundi** Kim.*
Kim ran away from you(>2).

*Banaganhi **ngurungundi** Kim.*
Kim ran away from her/him.

***Ngaanngundi** banaganhi Chris?*
Who did Chris run away from?

*Banaganhi **nganundi** Kim?*
Did Kim run away from me?

*Gamilbala **nganundi** banaganhi Kim.*
Kim did not run away from me.

 **Audio:** GGU 20.5.mp3 is available in the electronic edition

Ablative nouns and pronouns are also used with *giyal* 'afraid'.

*Giyal Kim dhurudhi.*
Kim is afraid of the snake.

*Giyal **nganundi** Kim.*
Kim is afraid of me.

*Gamil Kim **nganundi** giyal.*
Kim is not afraid of me.

*Yaama **nginundi** giyal Kim?*
Is Kim is afraid of you(1)?

***Ngaanngundi** giyal Kim?*
Who is Kim afraid of?

## Practice

 **Audio:** GGU 20.6.mp3 is available in the electronic edition

To use these pronouns work in two groups.

---

A: *Dhaay banagaya, ngalingunda. // ngiyaningunda.*
Run (here) to us(2) // us(>2)

B: *Banagay ngaya nginaalingunda, yilaa ngaya nginaalingunda warray, yilaa ngaya banagay nginaalingundi.*
I will run to you(2), then I will stand near/with you(2), then I will run (away) from you(2).

C: *Ngamila, B banaganhi ganungunda, yilaa warranhi ganungunda, yilaa banaganhi ganungundi.*
Look, B ran to them, then stood with them, then ran away from them.

A: *Ngaandi gindamanhi ngalingundi?*
Who laughed at us(2)?

B: *Gamilbala ngaya gindamanhi nginaayngundi.*
I did not laugh at you(2).

C: *Giirrbala nginda gindamanhi ngurugaalingundi.*
You **did** laugh at them(2).

---

## *Winangala, garay guwaala, yawala.*
## Listen, say and read.

 **Audio:** GGU 20.7.mp3 is available in the electronic edition

*Giirr burruluubidi nginunda.*
There is a big fly on you(1).

*Gamilbala, marayrr nganunda burruluu.*
Nope, no flies on me.

*Garay ngiyaningunda guwaala.*
Talk to us(>2).

## LESSON 20. PRONOUNS: LOCATIVE/ALLATIVE AND ABLATIVE

*Nginaalingundi yarraaman banaganhi?*
Did the horse run away from you(2)?

*Yawu, yilaabala ngalingunda yarraaman banaganhi.*
Yes, and then the horse ran to us(2).

*Ngaanngunda nhama burruluu?*
Who are the flies on?

*Giirr ngaya giyal nginaayngundi.*
I am afraid of you lot.

# LESSON 21
# Other Third Person Pronouns

This lesson introduces a range of third person plural pronouns ('they, them, their', etc.). Some third person dual pronouns are listed, but the information about them is uncertain and they are rarely used, so do not worry too much about them.

## Vocabulary

Some pronouns from previous lessons are repeated, so that the patterns are easier to see.

 **Audio:** GGU 21.1.mp3 is available in the electronic edition

| *Garay* | Words |
|---|---|
| *nhamagaalay*\* | they(2) (Nominative) |
| *ngurugaalay*\* | they/them(2) (Ergative) |
| *nhamagaalaynya*\* | they(2) (Accusative) |
| *ngurugaalayngu*\* | their(s)(2) (Dative) |
| *ngurugaalayngunda*\* | to/at/on them(2) (Locative) |
| *ngurugaalayngundi*\* | from them(2) (Ablative) |
| | |
| *ganunga* | they/them(>2) (doer/Nominative, done.to/Accusative) |
| *ganugu* | they(>2) (doer.to/Ergative) |
| *ganungu* | their(s)(>2) (possessive/Dative) |
| *ganungunda* | to/at/on them(>2) (Locative, Allative) |
| *ganungundi* | from them(>2) (Ablative ) |
| | |
| *wiya-gi* | cook **tr** |

237

*The traditional sources all have the same forms for all Gamilaraay Yuwaalaraay pronouns except the third person dual pronouns. That is, all sources have *ngaya, ngindaay, ganunga*, etc. – with the exception of third person singular *nguru* GR/*nguu* GY. In contrast, there are multiple sets of third person dual pronouns. It may be that they had slightly different meanings. The set given here has the most reliable Gamilaraay forms. It is unique in having three different forms for Nominative, Accusative and Ergative. For all other pronouns two of the cases have the same form.

## Grammar

The most important part of this section is the plural pronouns, and the change in the pattern of use between the third person pronouns and first and second person pronouns. For first person and second person pronouns the **doer** and **doer.to** (Nominative and Ergative) are the same (e.g. *ngaya* 'I', *ngindaay* 'you(>2)') and the **done.to** (Accusative) is different (*nganha* 'me', *nginaaynya* 'you(>2)'). But third person plural pronouns follow the same pattern as third person singular pronouns, nouns and adjectives – the **doer** and **done.to** are the same, *ganunga* – and the **doer.to** is different *ganugu*. The third person dual pronouns are different from all others, they have three forms, *nhamagaalay, ngurugaalay* and *nhamagaalaynya*. However, the historical evidence for these is not strong. Question pronouns and adjectives use the same pattern as nouns and third person pronouns.

Study the following examples carefully, looking at which pronouns and nouns are the **same**.

 **Audio:** GGU 21.2.mp3 is available in the electronic edition

### First person pronoun

*Yananhi **ngaya**.*
I walked. (doer/Nominative)

*Ngamiy **ngaya** bandaarr.*
I saw a kangaroo. (doer.to/Ergative)

*Bandaarru **nganha** ngamiy.*
The kangaroo saw me. (done.to/Accusative)

## Third person pronoun

*Yananhi **ganunga**.*
They(>2) walked. (doer/Nominative)

*Ngamiy **ganugu** bandaarr.*
They(>2) saw a kangaroo. (doer.to/Ergative)

*Bandaarru **ganunga** ngamiy.*
The kangaroo saw them. (done.to/Accusative)

*Yananhi **yinarr**.*
The woman walked. (doer/Nominative)

*Ngamiy **yinarru** bandaarr.*
The woman saw a kangaroo. (doer.to/Ergative)

*Bandaarru **yinarr** ngamiy.*
The kangaroo saw the woman. (done.to/Accusative)

Again, the rule is:

For first person and second person pronouns the **doer** and **doer.to** (Nominative and Ergative) are the same.

For **other pronouns and all nouns** the **doer** and **done.to** (Nominative and Accusative) are the same (except for third person dual pronouns).

Below are some examples of the dual and plural(>2) pronouns.

 **Audio:** GGU 21.3.mp3 is available in the electronic edition

*Dhalaa ganunga?*
Where are they?

*Garrawalgu ganunga yananhi.*
They went to the shop.

*Dhalaagu ganunga yananhi?*
Where did they go?

There are many possible answers, such as:

*Garrawalgu ganunga yananhi.*
They went to the shop.

# WIIDHAA

or

*Garrawalgu yananhi.*
They went to the shop.

or

*Garrawalgu.*
To the shop.

*Dhalaagu nhamagaalay yanay?*
Where will they(2) go?

*Minya ngurugaalay dhali?*
What will they(2) eat?

*Gali ngaya ngurugaalayngu wuunhi.*
I gave them(2) some water.

*Ngamila, bubaa ngurugaalayngunda banagawaanha.*
Look, dad is running to them(2).

*Minya ganugu dhiyamay?*
What did they pick up/get?

*Giirr ganugu dhuwarr dhiyamay.*
They got some bread.

*Yaama ganugu bubaa ngamiy?*
Did they see dad?

*Gamilbala. Bubaagubala ganunga ngamiy.*
No, but dad saw them.

*Giirr gaba ganunga.*
They are good.

As with the third person singular pronouns, you need to signal change in the transitivity of the verb.

*Giirr ganunga dhaay yananhi, bamba ganugu dhinggaa dhay.*
They came here and had a good feed of meat.

The use of the possessive/Dative, Locative and Ablative pronouns is like other pronouns.

LESSON 21. OTHER THIRD PERSON PRONOUNS

🔊 **Audio:** GGU 21.4.mp3 is available in the electronic edition

*Ngamila, wilbaarr ganungu nhama.*
Look, that is their car.

*Dhalaa wilbaarr ganungu?*
Where is their(>2) car?

*Biibabiiba nhalay ganungu wuuna.*
Give them this book.

*Ganungunda warraya.*
Stand near them.

*Garay ganungunda guwaala.*
Talk to them.

*Garriya ganungunda garay guwaala.*
Don't talk to them.

*Giirr ngaya giyal ganungundi.*
I am afraid of them.

*Gindamaya ganungundi.*
Laugh at them.

*Gindamaya ganungundi, yilaa ganungundi banagaya, bamba.*
Laugh at them, then run away from them, fast.

# Practice

 **Audio:** GGU 21.5.mp3 is available in the electronic edition

Use exercises like those in other pronoun lessons.

You can use a picture of two people, and one of more than two people.

Point to them and say the appropriate pronoun: *nhamagaalay/ganunga.*

Touch the people and say the appropriate pronoun: *nhamagaalaynya/ganunga.*

WIIDHAA

Give them something and say the appropriate pronoun: *ngurugaalayngu/ganungu*.

Take the object from them: *ngurugaalayngundi/ganungundi*.

## Sentences

 **Audio:** GGU 21.6.mp3 is available in the electronic edition

*Gaba nhamagaalay. Gaba ganunga.*
They(2) are good. They(>2) are good.

*Ngamildanha ngurugaalay nganha. Ngamildanha ganugu nganha.*
They(2) are looking at me. They(>2) are looking at me.

*Ngamildanha ngaya nhamagaalaynya/ganunga.*
I am looking at them(2)/them(>2).

*Yanay ngaya ngurugaalayngunda/ganungunda.*
I will walk towards them(2)/them(>2).

*Yanawaanha ngaya ngurugaalayngunda/ganungunda.*
I am walking towards them(2)/them(>2).

*Banagawaanha ngaya ngurugaalayngundi/ganungundi.*
I am running from them(2)/them(>2).

## *Winangala, garay guwaala, yawala.*
## Listen, say and read.

You can read further examples for Lesson 21 and listen to them as the sound files are made.

 **Audio:** GGU 21.7.mp3 is available in the electronic edition

*Ngaandi yanay?*
Who will go?

*Ngaandi mirridhu yiiy?*
Who(m) did the dog bite?

## LESSON 21. OTHER THIRD PERSON PRONOUNS

*Ngaandu mirri ngamiy?*
Who saw the dog?

*Dhurugu ganunga yiiy.*
The snake(s) bit them.

*Gamil ganunga bandaarrgu yanay.*
They won't walk to the kangaroos.

*Giirr ganugu bamba dhinggaa dhay.*
(*bamba dhali* = have a good feed)
They had a good feed of meat.

*Giirr ganunga banaganhi garrawalgu.*
They(>2) ran to the shop.

*Dhinggaa bulaarru wiyanhi.*
The two of them cooked meat.
(*Bulaarr* 'two' is regularly used as in the previous sentence, almost like a pronoun.)

🔊 **Audio:** GGU 21.8.mp3 is available in the electronic edition

*Ngamiy ganugu nginaaynya, gamilbala ngindaay ganunga ngamiy.*
They(>2) saw you(>2), but you did not see them.

*Ngaandu ganungunda yarral gaanhi?*
Who took the money to them?

*Garriya ganungunda garay guwaala, birraydha ngarragaaga.*
Don't talk to them, to those hopeless boys.

*Yaama ngali yanay ganungundi, miyaydhi?*
Will we(2) walk away from them, from the girls?

*Giirr giyal nhama mirri bulaarri.*
The dog is frightened of those two.

*Gindamanhi ngindaali ganungundi, giwiirri.*
You(2) laughed at them, at the men.

*Garriya nganundi gindamaya.*
Don't laugh at me.

WIIDHAA

That is it for *Garay Guwaala 1*.

*Giirr maaru.*
*Giirr maaru=nda gimubiy.*

Well done.
*Garay Guwaala 2* is in the pipeline.

# APPENDIX 1
# Resources

**Printed materials** are available from fivesenseseducation.com.au (search for Gamilaraay). Most resources are also available online at yuwaalaraay.com.

**Dictionary:** The *Gamilaraay, Yuwaalaraay & Yuwaalayaay Dictionary* (Ash, Lissarrague & Giacon, 2003) is available as a book and online.

Giacon (2017) refers to the published versions of his 2014 thesis, 'Yaluu: A recovery grammar of Yuwaalaraay and Gamilaraay based on 160 years of records'. The book is available as a free pdf download, an ebook or in printed form.

**Website:** At yuwaalaraay.com there is a blog, information about courses and links to many resources, including *Gayarragi, Winangali*, a computer program with a comprehensive dictionary, as well as sound files, many sentences, songs, games and more.

Sound files associated with *Wiidhaa* are also on yuwaalaraay.com.

**Tapes:** Reference is sometimes made to the Yuwaalaraay tapes of Arthur Dodd and Fred Reece, which are held at AIATSIS (Australian Institute of Aboriginal and Torres Strait Islander Studies), Canberra. The reference has the tape number and the number of seconds into the tape. For instance, tape 3219B 544 indicates 544 seconds from the beginning of tape 3219B.

# APPENDIX 2
# Pronunciation Guide

This pronunciation guide has a general guide to Gamilaraay Yuwaalaraay pronunciation, and then a longer, more detailed discussion of the topic. The guide owes a lot to the material in Peter Austin's *A Reference Dictionary of Gamilaraay, Northern New South Wales* (1993) and in particular to comments from John Hobson, but they are not responsible for any errors in the final product.

## *Dhaalan* Pronunciation

The following is a **brief introduction** to pronunciation rules in Gamilaraay Yuwaalaraay (GY). These languages are being relearnt and rebuilt, and it will not be possible to get exactly the sounds that traditional Gamilaraay Yuwaalaraay people made. We do not have those people to listen to us, model pronunciation and correct us. However, with effort and care we will get closer to those sounds, and our Gamilaraay Yuwaalaraay will sound less like English and more like it should.

Note that in the Gamilaraay Yuwaalaraay writing system two letters (such as *dh*, *ng* and *dj*) can be used to represent one sound. Also, many people used to speaking English have trouble saying the *ng* sound at the start of a word and *rr*. But, with practise, you will master them.

In March 2009 *Gayarragi, Winangali* was released. This multimedia resource based on the *Gamilaraay, Yuwaalaraay & Yuwaalayaay Dictionary* (Ash, Lissarrague & Giacon, 2003) contains a lot of sound. It is a very useful resource, particularly for improving pronunciation, and you can download it from the link at yuwaalaraay.com.

In the following vowel and consonant description the format is:

GY spelling      Similar English sound

## Vowels

There is a more detailed discussion of vowels later.

| | |
|---|---|
| *a* | short vowel, as in 'cut', but sounds like 'o' in 'cot' after w |
| *aa* | long vowel, as in 'card' |
| *i* | short vowel, as in 'fit/feet' |
| *ii* | long vowel, as in 'feed' |
| *u* | short vowel, as in 'soot/suit' |
| *uu* | long vowel, as in 'sued' |
| *ay* | as in 'bay' or 'hay' |
| *aay* | as in 'buy' (but sometimes like 'oy', as in 'boy') |

## Consonants

| | |
|---|---|
| *b* | like 'b' in 'bin' or 'p' in 'spin' but never like 'p' in 'pin' |
| *d* | like 'd' in 'duck' or 't' in 'tuck' but never like 't' in 'stuck' |
| *g* | like 'g' in 'git' or 'k' in 'kit' but never like 'k' in 'skit' [That is, there is no significant puff of air with any of b, d or g.] |
| *nh* | like English 'n' but with the tip of your tongue between your teeth |
| *dh* | like English 'd' and 't', but with the tip of your tongue between your teeth |
| *ny* | like 'n' in 'onion', but with the tip of your tongue against your bottom teeth, and the top of your tongue pressed against the roof of your mouth |
| *dj* | like 'judge' or 'church' and even like the 'ch' in 'catcher', but the tongue position is the same as for *ny*. |
| *ng* | a single sound, as in 'sing', not two sounds, as in 'finger' |
| *rr* | a rolled 'r', as some Scottish or German people say it. Often, at the end of a word, it can sound like the 'd' in 'bed' |

The following are pronounced much the same as in English:
m, n, l, r

| | |
|---|---|
| *w* | though *wu* at the start of a word is mostly pronounced like *u* |
| *y* | though *yi* at the start of a word is mostly pronounced like *i* |

The above guide will get you started on correct Gamilaraay Yuwaalaraay pronunciation, but it is only an introduction, and there is a lot more to learn, including the variations in some sounds, and stress patterns. Some of that is covered in the material below.

APPENDIX 2. PRONUNCIATION GUIDE

# More detailed information

## The sounds of Gamilaraay Yuwaalaraay

You can read more about the Gamilaraay Yuwaalaraay pronunciation system on pp. 6–8 of the *Gamilaraay, Yuwaalaraay & Yuwaalayaay Dictionary*. Chapter 2 of *Yaluu* (Giacon, 2017) has a more complete and up-to-date, but more technical, description. It is important to realise that any written description of sound is limited. So take what is written below as a general guide, not as a precise description. The only way to really learn about the sounds is to listen to them, so to learn good Gamilaraay Yuwaalaraay pronunciation you need to use material from the archival tapes, and listen to it carefully. Even that material is limited because the speakers had sometimes lost their teeth, or were remembering a language that they had not used for many years. And to get the sound really accurately you would need a fluent speaker commenting on your pronunciation.

Gamilaraay Yuwaalaraay uses many sounds that are also used in English, and others that are not. Our mouths and ears are trained to the language(s) we know, so you may have to get used to making new sounds and noticing differences that you did not notice before.

Because the spelling system for Gamilaraay Yuwaalaraay is fairly new it is a lot more consistent and so a lot easier to read than English. Generally, there is only one letter or pair of letters for each sound. In English the pronunciation of many words has changed over the centuries but the spelling has not, and so the spelling system is inconsistent and quite difficult to learn. (Think of the different sounds represented by 'ough' in 'plough', 'through', 'cough', 'rough' and 'bought'.) In Gamilaraay Yuwaalaraay the pronunciation of words has not changed recently, so the spelling system is very friendly, and does not take long to get used to.

The Gamilaraay Yuwaalaraay sounds that are similar to English include the three vowels *a*, *i* and *u*, and the consonants *l*, *m*, *n*, *r*, *w* and *y*. In Gamilaraay Yuwaalaraay (and in most Aboriginal languages) there is little or no distinction between the sounds made by English 'b' or 'p'. You can use either, but we have chosen to use the letter *b* in Gamilaraay Yuwaalaraay spelling. Similarly there is no distinction between 'd' and 't' (we have used *d*) or between 'g' and 'k' (we have used *g*).

**249**

## Variation in pronunciation

In any language there will be variation in pronunciation. Sometimes this variation is dialectal – people in one place or family might pronounce things differently from others. Sometimes it depends on whether the person is speaking casually or formally, slowly or quickly. Listen to the many different ways people say 'going to' in English (e.g. 'They're gunna do it.'). So it is perfectly normal to have variations in pronunciation within a language. But, to begin with, it is better to try to develop standard Gamilaraay Yuwaalaraay pronunciation, because if you try to talk it casually, you will probably introduce patterns of casual English rather than casual Gamilaraay Yuwaalaraay.

### Vowels

Vowels are sounds that can be made continuously with the mouth fairly open. There are three short vowels in Gamilaraay Yuwaalaraay, and they are written *a*, *i* and *u*. When the sound is made for a longer period it is called a long vowel, and these are written *aa*, *ii* and *uu*. Since vowels are particularly influenced by the sounds immediately before or after them, there is some variation in the way vowels are pronounced. While *a* is often like the 'u' in the English word 'cut', it is different after *w*, when it often sounds like 'o' in 'cot'. This also often happens after b, so the *a* in *bawi-li* sing can be like 'o' in 'lot'. After *y* (*yanay* 'walk') *a* can be a bit like 'e' in 'bet'.

There seems to be less variation in the vowels *i* and *u*.

The sequence *guw* at the start of a word is often pronounced *gw*. In *guwaali* 'tell' *waal* sounds like English 'wall', so the first part of the word is said *gwaal*.

The difference between long and short vowels is important. It can be the only difference between two similar words, as in:

| | |
|---|---|
| *milan* | one |
| *milaan* | a type of yam |
| *dhurri* | will spear |
| *dhuurri* | will crawl |
| *yili* | lip |
| *yiili* | savage |

APPENDIX 2. PRONUNCIATION GUIDE

The Gamilaraay Yuwaalaraay word *gabaa* is used by some old people for 'white person', and they use *gaba* for 'good'. Some young people do not know the 'good' meaning of *gaba* and use *gaba* to mean 'white person'. This is an example of a language changing so that you no longer need to make a sound distinction. At times, vowel length does not seem to make a difference to the meaning. In some of the recordings the word for rock is pronounced as both *maayama* and *mayama*.

## Non-English sounds and spellings

There are some sounds that people who only speak English have difficulty learning to distinguish and find hard to make. These include *dh*, *nh*, *dj*, *ny*, *rr* and also *ng* at the start of a word. As well, the way unstressed vowels are pronounced in Gamilaraay Yuwaalaraay is very different to the English pattern.

Remember that *ng* is always one soft sound, as in 'sing'. If you see *ngg* then this is two sounds together (ng and g) and so has a hard pronunciation, more like English 'finger'. A full stop between the letters *n* and *g* (*n.g*) means that there are two distinct sounds (*n* and *g*, as in 'turnkey' or 'sunglasses'), not one sound, as in *ng*.

It is a good idea to practise these by yourself somewhere – in the shower or when driving or walking. You can practise *ng* by saying 'singingingingingin...', and then gradually dropping the 'si' at the start. For *nga* say 'singanganga...' and once again try to drop the 'si'. For *rr* try to make machine gun or engine noises.

The Gamilaraay Yuwaalaraay sounds *nh* and *dh* are similar to English 'n' and 'd' but are both made with your tongue tip on your bottom teeth or between your teeth. The sound *dh* has a similar tongue position to English 'th', but *dh* is a stop – the air is released quickly – whereas in 'th' there is ongoing air vibration, and you can continue the 'th' sound for a long time.

The Gamilaraay Yuwaalaraay sounds *ny* and *dj* are both made with the tip of your tongue against your bottom teeth, and the flat part of your tongue pressed against the roof of your mouth. You can practise *ny* by acting like a cheeky child and saying 'nya-nya-nya-nya-nya'. Previous descriptions had *ny* as similar to the sound in 'onion', but that sound is made with the tongue tip touching the top of the mouth.

When a *nh* is followed by a *dh* the *nhdh* that would result is simplified and written *ndh*. Similarly *nydj* is written *ndj*.

Gamilaraay Yuwaalaraay words can begin with *b, m, dh, nh, g, ng, w* and *y* and a small number of words may begin with *dj* and *ny*. Gamilaraay Yuwaalaraay words can end with *a, aa, i, ii, u, uu, n, l, rr* and *y*. One exception recorded is *maang*, meaning 'message stick'. This could well be a borrowed word, possibly from Wiradjuri, since that language uses a final *ng*.

## Stress patterns

Gamilaraay Yuwaalaraay has patterns for stressing or emphasising parts of a word. The stressed part of the word is emphasised or said a bit louder, and maybe for a bit longer. In English the first syllable of '**ha**ppy' is stressed, but in 'be**side**' it is the second syllable that is stressed.

A syllable is a part of a word that contains a vowel, such as ri-ver, ju-ve-nile, al-pha-be-ti-cal. In Gamilaraay Yuwaalaraay each syllable begins with a consonant and contains one vowel, such as: *ga-ba, mi-laan*.

For the great majority of words in Gamilaraay Yuwaalaraay, the rules are as follows. First, you need to work out where the main emphasis goes. When there are single vowels only in the word, the emphasis falls on the first syllable. Thus, ***ga**ba*, ***gu**ni* and ***wam**banhiya*. However, when there are double vowels in the word they are emphasised. Thus, *bu**baa**, dhaa**dhaa**, birra**lii*** and *y**aa**ma*. But remember, unstressed vowels always remain recognisable, unlike many unstressed English vowels, as discussed below.

The second step is to work out the lesser emphasis. This occurs on the syllables two to the left or right of the main emphasis. The underlining shows the lesser emphasis:

***wam**banhiya*         *<u>bi</u>rra**lii***         *<u>bu</u>rru**laa***

### Unstressed vowels

In English, unstressed vowels tend to be said in a way that loses a lot of the distinction between the vowels. For instance, when most people say 'principal', the second 'i' and the 'a' do not sound much like 'i' or 'a', but more like the 'er' in 'butter'. However, in Gamilaraay, Yuwaalaraay, and in many Aboriginal languages, the vowels retain their basic sound much more strongly. When you say *bigibila* each of the 'i' sounds and the 'a' needs to be pronounced clearly. Most people need lots of practice to use the Gamilaraay Yuwaalaraay pattern rather than the English pattern for pronouncing vowels.

APPENDIX 2. PRONUNCIATION GUIDE

To recap, here are a few examples of Gamilaraay Yuwaalaraay pronunciation:

| GY word | Meaning | 'English' spelling |
|---|---|---|
| *gagil* | bad | guggil [but with an 'i' sound in the second syllable] |
| *walaay* | camp | wol-eye [emphasis on 'eye'] |
| *wamba* | mad | womba [keep the 'a' sound in the second syllable] |
| *yinarr* | woman | inarr or inud |
| *wuulaa* | bearded dragon | oohlaa [both syllables long and stressed] |

## Sentences and phrases

This is a preliminary discussion of the sound patterns of GY phrases and sentences. The area needs more research.

As a very general observation, much GY talk consists of short phrases, whereas English talk tends to have longer sections of continuous sound, and more variation in volume. The following two diagrams are of Arthur Dodd speaking in Yuwaalaraay and then in English.

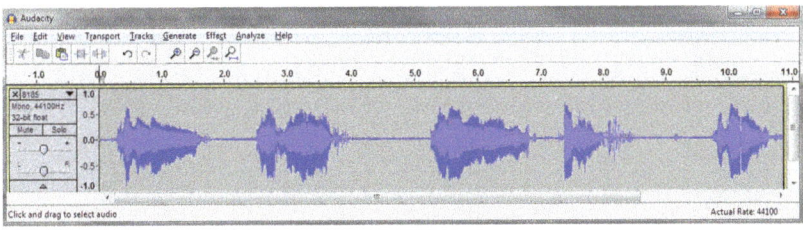

Figure 1: Arthur Dodd speaking in Yuwaalaraay.
Source: Giacon, 2017, p. 349. It shows the volume as Arthur Dodd speaks Yuwaalaraay (tape 8185, 2211 seconds into the tape).

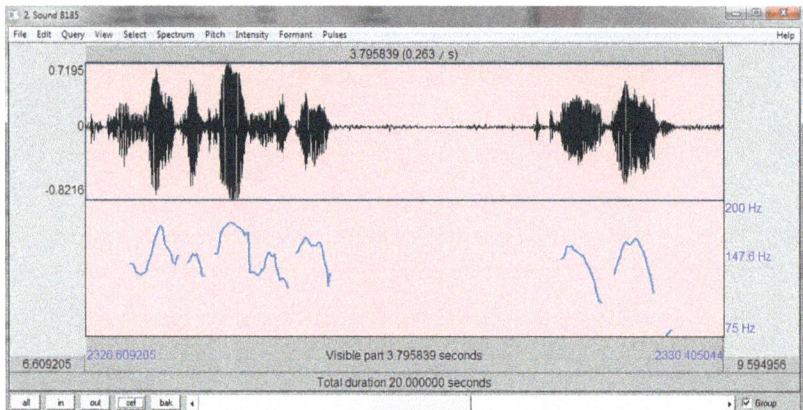

Figure 2: Arthur Dodd speaking in English.
Source: Giacon, 2017, p. 349. It shows the volume and pitch (frequency) as Arthur Dodd says, in English, 'He brought the crawfish back, to his wife' (tape 8185, 2326 seconds in).

In Figure 1 there are short bursts of sound, starting loudly and mostly decreasing in volume. There are pauses between the phrases. In Figure 2, an English sentence, the continuous sound is longer and there is much more variation in volume. As a starting hypothesis, it may be that GY emphasises words by putting them at the start of a phrase, whereas in English the word order is much more fixed, and so words are stressed wherever they occur in the sentence.

# APPENDIX 3
# Case Summary

This document has a summary of case form and case uses. Case is a linguistic term, used to refer to the way nominals (nouns, pronouns, adjective, demonstratives, etc.) are modified to show their function in a clause (this is a quick description of *case*). One case can have a number of functions.

Most of the material here is relevant to Gamilaraay 1, but some is for more advanced Gamilaraay.

**Note:** Case suffixes are not found on pronouns. There are special pronouns forms.

## Main cases

The table below summarises the form of the main cases for pronouns, other nominals and some irregular forms. It is followed by examples using these cases.

| Case | Examples of case forms | | | | |
|---|---|---|---|---|---|
| | 1st and 2nd person pronouns follow the pattern of *ngaya* | 3rd person pronoun pattern | Other nominals | | Special (only some given here) |
| | | | marking | example | |
| Nominative/doer | *ngaya (nginda)* | *=nha, nhama+* | Ø | *yinarr* | *minya* |
| Ergative/doer.to | *ngaya (nginda)* | *nguru* | -Gu | *yinarr-u* | *minya-dhu* |
| Accusative/done.to | *nganha (nginunha)* | *=nha, nhama+* | Ø | *yinarr* | *minya* |

|  | Examples of case forms | | | | |
|---|---|---|---|---|---|
| Case | 1st and 2nd person pronouns follow the pattern of *ngaya* | 3rd person pronoun pattern | Other nominals | | Special (only some given here) |
|  |  |  | marking | example |  |
| Dative/given.to/owner | *ngay (nginu)* | *ngurungu* | -gu | *yinarr-gu* |  |
| Locative/at.on.in.near | *nganunda (nginunda)* | *ngurungunda* | -Ga | *yinarr-a* |  |
| Allative/move.to |  |  | -gu | *yinarr-gu* |  |
| Ablative/from | *nganundi (nginundi)* | *ngurungundi* | -DHi | *yinarr-i* |  |

## Main functions of cases

### Nominative

| Verbless clause | *Yinggil ngaya. / Yinggil yinarr.* | I am tired. / The woman is tired. |
|---|---|---|
| Subject of **intransitive** verb | *Yanay ngaya. / Yinarr yanay.* | I will go. / The woman will go. |

### Ergative

| Subject of **transitive** verb | *Dhali ngaya nhama. / Dhali nhama yinarru.* | I will eat it. / The woman will eat it. |
|---|---|---|
| Instrument | *Dhali=nha yinarru, gula-gu.* | The woman will eat it with a fork. |

### Accusative

| Object of transitive verb. | *Ngamili ngaya yinarr.* | I will look at the woman. / I will see the woman. |
|---|---|---|

APPENDIX 3. CASE SUMMARY

## Locative

| | | |
|---|---|---|
| Place | *Burruluu* **nganunda.** | There are flies on me. |
| Person spoken to | *Garay ngaya* **guwaay yinarra.** | I talked to the woman. |

## Allative

| | | |
|---|---|---|
| movement to | *Yanay ngaya* **yinarrgu.** | I will walk to the woman. |

## Dative

| | | |
|---|---|---|
| Possession | *Buruma* **yinarrgu.** | The woman's dog. |
| Recipient with *wuurri*. | *Yinarrgu giwiirr-u buruma* **wuurri.** | The man will give the dog to the woman. |
| Purpose | *Dhaay yinarr* **yananhi, galigu.** | The woman came here for water. |
| | Note that verbs can have *-gu* 'purpose' (future + *-gu*) | |
| Purpose | *Dhaay yinarr* **yananhi, dhaligu.** | The woman came here to eat. |

## Ablative (main uses below; there are others)

| | | |
|---|---|---|
| Movement from | *Yinarr-i ngaya* **banaganhi.** | I ran from the woman. |
| Fear of | *Yinarr-i ngaya* **giyal.** | I am afraid of the woman. |
| Laugh 'at' | *Yinarr-i ngaya* **gindama-nhi.** | I laughed at the woman. |
| With *wuru-gi* 'go in' | *Gundhi-dhi ngaya* **wuru-nhi.** | I went into the house. |
| With *galiya-y* 'climb' | *Gundhi-dhi ngaya* **galiya-nhi.** | I climbed on the house. |

WIIDHAA

## Be careful with these verbs

### guwaa-li '~tell'

Garay *guwaa-li* is 'talk' (*garay* 'word'). The 'spoken to' is in Locative case.

| | |
|---|---|
| Garay ngaya *guwaay yinarra.* | I talked to the woman. |

But *garay* can be replaced:

| | |
|---|---|
| Gamilaraay giwiirr-u *guwaay yinarra.* | The man talked Gamilaraay to the woman. |
| 'Yaama' ngaya *guwaay yinarra.* | I said 'hello' to the woman. |

*Guwaali* can also be translated **'tell'** (something like 'ordered to do something'), and then the one spoken to is in Accusative case.

| | |
|---|---|
| Yinarr-u nganha *guwaay yana-y-gu.* | The woman told me to go. |
| Yinarr-u giwiirr *guwaay yana-y-gu.* | The woman told the man to go. |

### Wuurri 'give'

The thing given is Accusative, the recipient Dative.

| | |
|---|---|
| Yinarr-u wiyayl *wuunhi giwiirr-gu.* | The woman gave the pen to the man/gave the man the pen. |
| Wiyayl ngaya *nginu wuu-nhi.* | I gave you the pen. |

### Winanga-li 'listen, hear'

| | |
|---|---|
| *Winanga-y* ngaya dhigaraa. | I heard/listened.to the bird. |

**N.B.** Do not translate 'listen to' with Locative or Allative. The thing heard/listened to is **Accusative**.

### Ngami-li 'see, look at'

As with *winanga-li*, the thing perceived is **Accusative** case.

| | |
|---|---|
| *Ngami-y* birralii-dhu dhigaraa. | The child saw/looked.at the bird. |

# Other cases

The following suffixes are not categorised as cases in some descriptions. They are similar in some ways to the cases above, but are also different in some respects.

| Gamilaraay | English | Notes |
|---|---|---|
| *-Baraay* | having | *-araay* after *l, rr* |
| *-DHalibaa* | without | can be *dalibaa* after *n, l, rr* |
| *-nginda* | wanting | |
| *-guwaay* | like | pronounced gwoi |

## Pronouns

These suffixes, like other case suffixes, are not found on pronouns. To translate 'with', as in 'go with you, her', use the Locative pronoun.

We do not know how to say: 'without you/him' and 'want you/her'.

My instinct is that *-guwaay* could follow a pronoun, but it would be good to see if this happens in other languages.

There are dual and plural forms of pronouns, so no suffixes are needed.

## For investigation

*Dhayali* 'ask' is a three place verb. **I ask you something**. The case structure is clear when the something is an action:

*Dhayay ngaya nginunha yanaygu.* 'I asked you to go.' (*nginunha* Accusative)

The case structure is not clear when something is a noun.

'I asked you the name of the town.'

Perhaps town Accusative you Locative, as happens with 'talk'.

# APPENDIX 4
# Verb Summary

As with other summaries, this one assumes you understand the basic concepts and need to check on details. It summarises material used in *Wiidhaa*, but also has considerable other information on GY verbs.

The example verbs are Gamilaraay. Some Yuwaalaraay verbs are different, for example *yanay* GR/ *yanaay* YR 'go'; however, it is only the stem that is different, except for *yanay*, whose command form is irregular: *yananga*. The YR command is *yanaaya*.

## Gamilaraay verbs – simple forms

| Command | Future | Past | |
|---|---|---|---|
| **Y Class** | | | |
| *yana**nga*** (was *yanaya*) | *yanay* | *yana**nhi*** | walk/come/go |
| *banaga**ya*** | *banagay* | *banaga**nhi*** | run |
| *gubi**ya*** | *gubiy* | *gubi**nyi*** | swim |
| **L Class** | | | |
| *buma**la*** | *buma**li*** | *bumay* | hit/beat |
| **NG Class** | | | |
| *yulu**nga*** | *yulugi* | *yulu**nhi*** | dance |
| *gi**nga*** | *gigi* | *gi**nyi*** | become/get |
| **RR Class** | | | |
| *wuu**na*** | *wuu**rri*** | *wuu**nhi*** | give |

WIIDHAA

# Gamilaraay verbs – continuous forms

## Non-moving continuous verbs

| Command | Future | Present | Past |
|---|---|---|---|
| **Y Class** | | | |
| *warra-y-la-ya* | *warra-y-la-y* | *warra-y-la-nha* | *warra-y-la-nhi* |
| keep standing | will be standing | is/am/are standing | was standing |
| **L Class** | | | |
| *dha-lda-ya* | *dha-lda-y* | *dha-lda-nha* | *dha-lda-nhi* |
| keep eating | will be eating | is eating | was eating |
| **NG Class** | | | |
| *ngaru-gi-la-ya* | *ngaru-gi-la-y* | *ngaru-gi-la-nha* | *ngaru-gi-la-nhi* |
| keep drinking | will be drinking | is drinking | was drinking |
| **RR Class** | | | |
| *wuu-dha-ya* | *wuu-dha-y* | *wuu-dha-nha* | *wuu-dha-nhi* |
| keep giving | will be giving | is giving | was giving |

## Moving continuous verbs

| Command | Future | Present | Past |
|---|---|---|---|
| **Y Class** | | | |
| *yana-waa-ya* | *yana-waa-y* | *yana-waa-nha* | *yana-waa-nhi* |
| keep walking | will be walking | is/am/are walking | was walking |
| *gubi-yaa-ya* | *gubi-yaa-y* | *gubi-yaa-nha* | *gubi-yaa-nhi* |
| keep swimming | will be swimming | is swimming | was swimming |
| **L Class** | | | |
| *dhurra-laa-ya* | *dhurra-laa-y* | *dhurra-laa-nha* | *dhurra-laa-nhi* |
| keep coming | will be coming | is coming | was coming |
| **NG Class** | | | |
| *gaa-waa-ya* | *gaa-waa-y* | *gaa-waa-nha* | *gaa-waa-nhi* |
| keep bringing | will be bringing | is bringing | was bringing |

| Command | Future | Present | Past |
|---|---|---|---|
| *gi-yaa-ya* | *gi-yaa-y* | *gi-yaa-nha* | *gi-yaa-nhi* |
| keep getting | will be getting | is getting | was getting |

**RR Class**

| | | | |
|---|---|---|---|
| *dhuu-rraa-ya* | *dhuu-rraa-y* | *dhuu-rraa-nha* | *dhuu-rraa-nhi* |
| keep crawling | will be crawling | is crawling | was crawling |

The continuous suffixes are summarised in the following table.

## YG continuous suffixes

| Inflection | Verb class | | | |
|---|---|---|---|---|
| | L | Y | NG | RR |
| Moving | *-l.aa-y* | *-W.aa-y* | *-W.aa-y* | *-rr.aa-y* |
| Non-moving | *-lda-y* | *-y.la-y* | *-gi.la-y* | *-dha-y* |

The following table sets out the continuous suffixes in another arrangement, showing that the *Y* class and *NG* class suffixes are similar.

| Inflection | Verb class | | | | Gloss |
|---|---|---|---|---|---|
| | L | Y | NG | RR | (Example) |
| **Non-moving** continuous | | | | | |
| Future | *dha-li* 'eat' | *yana-y* 'go' | *gaa-gi* 'take' | *wuu-rri* 'give' | |
| CTS+**FUT** | *dha-lda-y* | *yana-y. la-y* | *gaa-gi. la-y* | *wuu-dha-y* | will be (eat)ing |
| CTS+**PRS** | *dha-lda-nha* | *yana-y. la-nha* | *gaa-gi. la-nha* | *wuu-dha-nha* | is (eat)ing |
| CTS+**PAST** | *dha-lda-nhi* | *yana-y. la-nhi* | *gaa-gi. la-nhi* | *wuu-dha-nhi* | was (eat)ing |
| CTS+**IMP** | *dha-lda-ya* | *yana-y. la-ya* | *gaa-gi. la-ya* | *wuu-dha-ya* | keep (eat)ing |
| CTS+**SUB** | *dha-lda-ndaay* | *yana-y.la-ndaay* | *gaa-gi. la-ndaay* | *wuu-dha-ndaay* | when+(eat)ing |

| Inflection | Verb class | | | | Gloss (Example) |
|---|---|---|---|---|---|
| | L | Y | NG | RR | |
| **Moving** continuous | | | | | |
| MOV+**FUT** | dha-***laa**-y* | *yana-**waa**-y#* | *gaa-**waa**-y#* | *wuu-**rraa**-y* | will be (eat)ing |
| MOV+**PRS** | dha-***laa**-nha* | *yana-**waa**-nha* | *gaa-**waa**-nha* | *wuu-**rraa**-nha* | is (eat)ing |
| MOV+**PAST** | dha-***laa**-nhi* | *yana-**waa**-nhi* | *gaa-**waa**-nhi* | *wuu-**rraa**-nhi* | was (eat)ing |
| MOV+**IMP** | dha-***laa**-ya* | *yana-**waa**-ya* | *gaa-**waa**-ya#* | *wuu-**rraa**-ya* | keep (eat)ing |
| MOV+**SUB** | dha-***laa**-ndaay* | *yana-**waa**-ndaay* | *gaa-**waa**-ndaay* | *wuu-**rraa**-ndaay* | when+ (eat)ing |

# indicates a hypothesised form.

## The functions of continuous suffixes

The **non-moving continuous** form is used:

- when the action or situation does not involve linear motion
- when the action or situation is habitual/regular/steady.state
- to show the ability to do something.

The **moving continuous** form is used:

- when the action involves linear motion
- when there is a change of state/situation
- inchoatively – to show something is beginning to happen.

# Verb suffixes: Summary tables

Most of the following material is adapted from *Yaluu* (Giacon, 2017). It includes information about verb forms that are not covered in Gamilaraay 1.

The next table shows the subordinate and purposive forms of actual non-continuous verbs, as well as the simple forms already given.

## Paradigm of simple YG verbs (root + one morpheme)

| Verb class | L | Y | NG | RR |
|---|---|---|---|---|
| **Gloss** | eat | run | bring | give |
| **Inflection** | | | | |
| FUTure | dha-**li** | banaga-**y** | gaa-**gi** | wuu-**rri** |
| PAST | dha-**y** | banaga-**nhi** | gaa-**nhi** | wuu-**nhi** |
| IMPerative | dha-**la** | banaga-**ya** | gaa-**nga** | wuu-**na** |
| SUBordinate | dha-**ldaay** | banaga-**ngindaay** | gaa-**ngindaay** | wuu-**dhaay** |
| SUB Cts | Continuous form+*ndaay*, e.g. dha-**lda-ndaay** | | | |
| PURPosive | dha-**li.gu** | banaga-**y.gu** | gaa-**gi.gu** | wuu-**rri.gu** |

Remember the irregular imperative, *yananga*.

The next table is similar to the previous one, but just has the suffixes, not the verb roots.

## YG verbs: Final inflections, including continuous subordinate

| Inflection | Verb class | | | |
|---|---|---|---|---|
| | L | Y | NG | RR |
| FUTure | -li | -y | -gi | -rri |
| PRESent (only after continuous) | | -nha | | |
| PAST | -y | -NHi | -NHi | -NHi |
| IMPerative | -la | -ya/(-nga) | -nga | -na |
| SUBordinate | -ldaay | -ngindaay | -ngindaay | -dhaay |
| SUBordinate (continuous) | -ndaay | | | |
| PURPosive | -li-gu | -y-gu | -gi-gu | -rri-gu |

Upper case NH indicates that there are allomorphs: *-nhi* and *-nyi*.

The next table shows that suffixes sometimes vary, depending on the class of the stem they are attached to. The variation below is just in the first element of the suffix, a consonant. This element is called the Class Marker (or sometimes conjugation marker in other texts), CM.

## Verb Class Marker examples

| Verb | Gloss | Class Marker | Verb class |
|---|---|---|---|
| buma-**l**.uwi-y | will hit back | l | L |
| banaga-**w**.uwi-y | will run back | w | Y |
| gubi-**y**.uwi-y | will swim back | y | Y |
| gaa-**g**.uwi-y | will tack back | g | NG |
| wuu-**rr**.uwi-y | will give back | rr | RR |

If a non-final suffix is added to a verb stem, the resulting verb is Y class, with one exception, -aaba-li 'ALL': for instance, all the verb stems created by -CM-uwi- in this table are Y class, irrespective of the class of the root.

## Properties of YG verb classes

| Properties | Verb class | | | |
|---|---|---|---|---|
| | L | Y | NG | RR |
| size | large: ca 200 | large: ca 100 | 23 | 9 |
| transitivity | mostly transitive | mostly intransitive | mixed transitivity | mixed transitivity |
| syllables | mostly polysyllabic | mostly polysyllabic | high proportion monosyllabic | high proportion monosyllabic |
| root | a or i-final | a or i-final | a, i or u-final | a, i or u-final some y-final |

# Other verb suffixes

Some of these are fairly well understood, but for some suffixes all we have is the form and a one-word gloss. In these instances we may learn more by looking at the use of similar suffixes, particularly in Wangaaybuwan. Some of the better understood suffixes are discussed in Gamilaraay 2.

## Valency reducing verb suffixes

The reciprocal and reflexive suffixes derive an intransitive verb from a transitive verb.

### Reciprocal and Reflexive suffixes and Class Markers

| Suffix | | Verb class Class Marker | | | |
|---|---|---|---|---|---|
| Form | Gloss | L | Y | NG | RR |
| *-ngiili-y* | REFlexive | Ø | y | Ø | rr |
| *-ngii-li* | REFlexive (before continuous suffix) | Ø | y | Ø | rr |
| *-la-y* | RECiprocal | Ø | Ø# | Ø# | rri# |

\# indicates a hypothesised form.

## Valency increasing verb suffixes

These suffixes increase the number of arguments, things obligatorily involved. So an intransitive verb becomes transitive, a transitive verb becomes a three-place verb.

| Suffix | | Verb class Class Marker | | | |
|---|---|---|---|---|---|
| Form | Gloss | L | Y | NG | RR |
| *-:li-y\** | Additional argument | Yes | ? | Not used | |
| *-n.giili-y* | Additional argument | Not used | | Ø | rr |

*':' means lengthen the preceding vowel: *buma-li* > *buma-ali-y*. *ngami-li* > *ngami-i-li-y*

A number of other valency increasing suffixes found in Chapter 8 of Giacon (2014) and in *Yaluu* are not listed here.

## Suffixes with no effect on valency

(See Giacon, 2017)

As with other suffixes, some of these are well understood with many examples in the sources, while there is little information about others.

### 'Time' suffixes – current paradigm

| Suffix | | Verb class Class Marker | | | |
|---|---|---|---|---|---|
| Form | Typical meaning | L | Y | NG | RR |
| **Time of day (TOD)** | | | | | |
| *-ngayi-y* | morning | *l* | Ø | Ø | *rr* |
| *-nga-y* | day/afternoon | *l#* | *y* | Ø | *rr* |
| *-(y)-aa-y* | night | *l#* | *W#* | *g (y)* | *rr* |
| *-ngabi-y* | night | *l* | Ø | Ø | *rr* |
| **Distance in Time (DIT)** | | | | | |
| *-mayaa-y* | ~one day distant | *l* | *y* | Ø | *rr* |
| *-ayi-y* | < ~1 week | *l* | *W* | *ng, b* | *rr* |
| *-awayi-y* | > ~1 week | *l* | *W* | *g# (y)* | *rr#* |
| **Other** (see section 7.5.4 in Giacon, 2014; or *Yaluu*) | | | | | |
| *-dhii-y* | for a long time, long time ago | *l*, Ø | *W#* | Ø# | Ø# |

# indicates a hypothesised form.

### Derivational suffixes with no syntactic effect

| Suffix | | Verb class Class Marker | | | |
|---|---|---|---|---|---|
| Form | Gloss | L | Y | NG | RR |
| *-uwi-y* | BACK | *l* | *W\** | *g/b* | *rr* |
| *-aaba-li* | TOTal | *l* | *W* | *w/b; ?y* | *rr* |
| *-DHa-y* | EAT | Ø | Ø | Ø | Ø |

The suffixes below are not well understood. There is generally limited evidence for the suffix.

APPENDIX 4. VERB SUMMARY

| Suffix | | Verb class Class Marker | | | |
|---|---|---|---|---|---|
| Form | Gloss | L | Y | NG | RR |
| -ngila-y | TOGether | Ø | Ø | Ø | rr |
| -mayi-y | UP | l | y | Ø | rr |
| -Nami-y | WANT | Ø | Ø | Ø | Ø |
| -mi-y | DARE | l | W | Ø | rr |
| -NHumi-y | BEFORE | l | Ø | Ø | rr |
| -dhiya-li | AFTER | Ø | Ø | Ø | Ø |

*Upper-case *W* indicates that the CM is *w* after *a* and *u*, and *y* after *i*.

No syntactic effect means that the transitivity of the verb is not changed, nor the number of things necessarily involved with the verb (the argument structure, to use a linguistic term).

# APPENDIX 5
# Pronoun Summary

This document has summarised information on Gamilaraay and Yuwaalaraay pronouns. For more on this, see Chapter 4 of *Yaluu* (Giacon, 2017). There is much more information here than is covered in Gamilaraay 1.

The first table has the main pronoun forms, but does not include exclusive pronouns – i.e. forms of 'we' used when the person(s) spoken to are not included in 'we'. This topic is covered in more detail later. The rules for use of pronouns in sentences follows.

## Pronouns in sentences

Nominative and Ergative pronouns are predominantly in second position in the sentence. If they are the focus, the main information, they can be first.

The position of other pronouns is more flexible. They, and demonstratives, are often in second position, or third position if there is a Nominative or Ergative pronoun in second position.

## Gamilaraay personal pronouns

| Simpler name | Doer/ Doer.to | Done to | Owner/ given to | Place at; Movement to | Source |
|---|---|---|---|---|---|
| Case | Nominative, Ergative | Accusative | Dative | Locative, Allative | Ablative |
| **Speaker(s) [first person]** | | | | | |
| Singular | *ngaya* | *nganha* | *ngay* | *nganunda* | *nganundi* |
|  | I | me | my/mine | to, at, on me | from me |
| Dual | *ngali* | *ngalinya* | *ngalingu* | *ngalingunda* | *ngalingundi* |
|  | we(2) | us(2) | our(s)(2) | to, at, on us(2) | from us(2) |

| Simpler name | Doer/ Doer.to | Done to | Owner/ given to | Place at; Movement to | Source |
|---|---|---|---|---|---|
| Case | Nominative, Ergative | Accusative | Dative | Locative, Allative | Ablative |
| Plural | *ngiyani* | *ngiyaninya* | *ngiyaningu* | *ngiyaningunda* | *ngiyaningundi* |
| | we(>2) | us(>2) | our(s)(>2) | to, at, on us(>2) | from us(>2) |
| **Spoken to [second person]** | | | | | |
| Singular | *nginda* | *nginunha* | *nginu* | *nginunda* | *nginundi* |
| | you(1) | you(1) | your(s)(1) | to, at, on you(1) | from you(1) |
| Dual | *ngindaali* | *nginaalinya* | *nginaalingu* | *nginaalingunda* | *nginaalingundi* |
| | you(2) | you(2) | your(s)(2) | to, at, on you(2) | from you(2) |
| Plural | *ngindaay* | *nginaaynya* | *nginaayngu* | *nginaayngunda* | *nginaayngundi* |
| | you(>2) | you(>2) | your(s)(>2) | to, at, on you(>2) | from you(>2) |
| **Spoken about [third person]** | | | | | |
| Singular | *nguru* | **See below*** | *ngurungu* | *ngurungunda* | *ngurungundi* |
| | s/he, it | her/him/it | his/her(s)/its | to, at, her/him/it | from him/her/it |
| Dual | **See below** | | | | |
| Plural | *ganugu* | *ganunga* | *ganungu* | *ganungunda* | *ganungundi* |
| | they(>2) | they/them(>2) | their(s)(>2) | to, at them(>2) | from them(>2) |

*Gamilaraay and Yuwaalaraay do not have pronouns that directly correspond to he/she/it her/him/it. We do not have a full description of what to translate these with, but the most common form is =*NHa* (=*nha*, =*nya* or =*na*) on the first word of the clause. Also common is Ø, i.e. nothing; *Nhama* is sometimes used but is more like 'that one'.

The pronoun pages from *Gaay Garay Dhadhin* (Yuwaalaraay and Gamilaraay Language Program, 2006) – a GY picture dictionary – may help you to understand the **main** functions of these pronouns. Note that there is an error in the first row of the third person singular – see above for the correct form.

## Yuwaalaraay pronouns

The pronouns in the table above are also found in Yuwaalaraay, **except** that YR uses *nguu* where GR has *nguru*; e.g. *ngurungu* GR/ *nguungu* YR 'her/his/its'.

## Changes in description of pronouns

The analysis of some pronouns has changed, with the most recent description in *Yaluu* (Giacon, 2017). The table above differs from previous descriptions in Williams (1980) and Yuwaalaraay and Gamilaraay Language Program (2006), which have *nguru* GR/ *nguu* YR as the Nominative singular third person pronoun. Closer examination of the sources shows that *nguu* is not used in those circumstances.

## Third person dual pronouns

While most pronouns have a consistent form across the range of sources, the **third person duals** are rare and a range of forms are recorded, given below. These are unique in having quite different forms in GR and YR. They are also unique in having three different forms for the Ergative, Nominative and Accusative.

(Different texts will have different information for these pronouns, depending on when they were written/updated.)

## Yuwaalaraay and Gamilaraay third person pronoun dual pronouns

| Ergative | Nominative | Accusative | Dative | Locative/ Allative | Ablative |
|---|---|---|---|---|---|
| **Yuwaalaraay dual** | | | | | |
| *gaaladhu* | *gaalanha* | | *gaalayngu* | *gaalayngunda* | *gaalayngundi* |
| *bulaayu* | *bulaarrnga* | | *bulaarrngu* | *bulaarrngunda* | *bulaarrngundi* |
| **Gamilaraay dual** | | | | | |
| *nguru-gaalay* | *nhama-gaalay* | *nhama-gaalaynya* | *nguru-gaalayngu* | *nguru-gaalayngunda* | *nguru-gaalayngundi* |

There are relatively few examples of these pronouns in the sources, so it is not clear how they were used. It may be that different forms had different meanings. It is also quite likely that not all forms were recorded.

## Suffixed pronouns

Suffixed pronouns are common in Aboriginal languages. In many, including Gamilaraay Yuwaalaraay, they are suffixed on the first word of the clause. The highlighted suffixed pronouns in the table are commonly found, the others rare or likely, based on what usually happens, and forms in related languages.

### Reconstructed GY clitic Nominative/Ergative pronoun paradigm

|  | Clitic forms | | Full forms | |
| --- | --- | --- | --- | --- |
|  | Nominative | Ergative | Nominative | Ergative |
| **First person** | | | | |
| Singular | =DHu | | ngaya | |
| Dual Incl. | =li | | ngali | |
| Dual Excl. | =li-nya | =li-lu | ngali-nya | ngali-lu/yu |
|  |  | =li-nguru GR |  | ngali-nguru GR |
| Plural Incl. | =ni | | ngiyani | |
| Plural Excl. | =ni-nya | =ni-lu | ngiyani-nya | ngiyani-lu/yu |
| **Second person** | | | | |
| Singular | =nda | | nginda | |
| Dual | =ndaali | | ngindaali | |
| Plural | =ndaay | | ngindaay | |
| **Third person** | | | | |
| Singular | =NHa | | | |
| Plural |  | =nugu | | ganugu |

## Inclusive and exclusive pronouns

(See Giacon, 2017, p. 377)

The inclusive/exclusive distinction applies to dual and plural first person pronouns, i.e. 'we'. Inclusive means that both the speaker(s) and listener(s) are part of 'we', exclusive means that the listener(s) are not part of 'we'.

# APPENDIX 5. PRONOUN SUMMARY

If A is talking to B and says: 'We (A+B) will go now', 'we' is inclusive. If A is talking to B and says: 'We (A+C) will go now', 'we' is exclusive. Many languages have different inclusive and exclusive pronouns. In GY the inclusive/exclusive distinction is found only in Nominative and Ergative pronouns.

## Gamilaraay Yuwaalaraay inclusive/exclusive pronouns (we)

|         | Inclusive | Exclusive        |                |
|---------|-----------|------------------|----------------|
|         |           | Nominative       | Ergative       |
| Dual    | *ngali*   | *ngali-nya*      | *ngali-lu*     |
| Plural  | *ngiyani* | *ngiyani-nha?nya*| *ngiyani-lu(u)*|

## Inclusory constructions

This will be touched on very briefly here. (See Giacon, 2017, p. 377)

In GY if you want to say 'Kim and I' you say *ngali Kim* 'we(2) Kim'. 'Jack and Jill and Kim' is *Kim ganunga Jack, Jill* (*ganunga* 'they>2'). The inclusory construction consists of the pronoun that includes everyone then lists the people who are not speakers – i.e. 'I' is not mentioned. GY exclusive pronouns are actually inclusory constructions.

## Other pronoun suffixes

Another suffix found on pronouns has the forms *-yuu/-uu/-wu*. Examples and meaning are seen below.

| *ngali*     | we(2)   | *ngali-yuu*     | both of us      |
| *ngiyani*   | we(>2)  | *ngiyani-yuu*   | all of us       |
| *ngindaali* | you(2)  | *ngindaali-yuu* | both of you     |
| *ngindaay*  | you(>2) | *ngindaay-uu*   | all of you      |
| *bulaarr*   | two     | *bulaarr-uu*    | both of (them)  |
| *ganunga*   | they    | *ganunga-wu*    | all of them     |

The particle *yiyal* 'just, only' is also found immediately after pronouns. It is not clear if it is a suffix or a separate word that immediately follows the pronoun.

WIIDHAA

# Visual guide to pronouns talking about people[1]

## First person pronouns

---

1   Reproduced from Yuwaalaraay and Gamilaraay Language Program, 2006.

APPENDIX 5. PRONOUN SUMMARY

# Second person pronouns

277

WIIDHAA

## Third person pronouns

### Singular

**often clitic =NHa, or Ø, sometimes nhama.**
he, she (doer)

was **nguru/nguu**

**nguru** GR / **nguu** YR
he, she (doer to)

**often clitic =NHa, or Ø, sometimes nhama.**
her, him (done to)

**ngurungu** GR / **nguungu** YR
her(s), his, to her, him

**ngurungunda** GR / **nguungunda** YR
to / at / on him / her

**ngurungundi** GR / **nguungundi** YR
from him / her

### Dual

**nhamagaalay** GR / **gaalanha** YR / **bulaarrnga** YR
they two people (doers)

was **gaali**

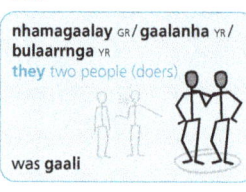

ngurugaalay  GR
gaaladhu  YR
bulaayu  YR

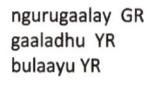

nhamagaalaynya   GR
gaalanha  YR
bulaarrnga

ngurugaalayngu GR
galaayngu YR
bulaarrngu YR

ngurugaalayngunda GR
gaalayngunda YR
bulaarrngunda YR

ngurugaalayngundi  GR
gaalayngundi  YR
bulaarrngundi  YR

### Plural

**ganunga**
they more than two people (doers)

**ganugu**
they more than two people (doers to)

**ganunga**
them more than two people (done to)

**ganungu**
their, to them more than two people

**ganungunda**
to/at/on them more than two people

**ganungundi**
from them more than two people

APPENDIX 5. PRONOUN SUMMARY

## Question pronouns

**ngaandi**
who? (doer)

**ngaandu**
who? (doer to)
Who is throwing the boomerang?

**ngaandi**
who? (done to)
Who is being bitten by the dog?

**ngaanngu**
whose?
Whose ball is this?

**ngaanngunda**
to who?
Who are you talking to on the phone?

**ngaanngundi**
from who?
Who is the letter from?

## About pronouns

The GY pronoun system has much in common with the English system; both have first, second and third person pronouns, and some distinctions between singular (I, he, she) and plural (we, they). It also distinguishes the role that the pronoun plays in the sentence.

(doer) **I** saw the dog.
(done to) The dog saw **me**.
(owner) **My** dog.

The significant differences are that GY pronouns have dual forms (i.e. referring to two people) and they do not have a gender distinction – there are no separate words for 'he' and 'she'. Also, many English phrases which consist of a pronoun and preposition ('to me', 'from you', 'on them') have one-word equivalents in GY.

There are other more complicated aspects of pronoun use which are not covered here. For more information about pronouns see Chapter 3 of the *Gamilaraay Yuwaalaraay Yuwaalayaay Dictionary*, and the entries for individual pronouns in the body of the dictionary.

In general, when using pronouns you need to work out:

1. Who the pronoun is **about**:

   The person/people **speaking** (I, we, us, our, etc.)    **First** person (p. 276)
   The person/people **spoken to** (you, your, yours etc.)    **Second** person (p. 277)
   The person/people **spoken about** (she, them, etc.)    **Third** person (p. 278)

2. **How many people** are involved:

   If it is **one** person: use the singular form (the left-hand column on pp. 276–8)
   If it is **two** people: use the dual form (the middle column on pp. 276–8)
   If it is **more than two** people: use the plural form (the right-hand column on pp. 276–8)

3. What do you **want to say about** the person/people?

   To translate '**She** ate the meat' go to third person (p. 278) singular (left-hand column) 'doer to' (row 2). The word you need is *nguru* (in Gamilaraay) or *nguu* (in Yuwaalaraay).

   If you want to say to two people 'your house' (house is *gundhi*), then you go to second person (p. 277), dual (middle column), owner (row 4). The word you find is *nginaalingu* and so you get: gundhi nginaalingu 'your house'.

Some second person pronouns have an abbreviated form: =*nda*, =*ndaali*, =*ndaay* (see rows 1 and 2, p. 277). These are called clitics because they are usually attached to the first word in the sentence or clause, whereas unabbreviated pronouns are found in different positions in the sentence.

So, to say to one person 'What will you eat?', you can say:

*Minya nginda dhali?* or
*Minya=nda dhali?*

These abbreviated pronouns are generally found with *garriya* (don't) and with question words such as *minya* (what) and *yaama* (hello).

# APPENDIX 6
# Wordlist

The words from all the vocabularies are given below, in Gamilaraay alphabetical order.

| *Gamilaraay* | English | Lesson |
|---|---|---|
| *baabila!* | sleep/lie **int** | 11 |
| *baadhal* | bottle | 1 |
| *baawaa* | sister | 1 |
| *baawul* | chicken | 9 |
| *baayandhu* | goodbye, see ya | 1 |
| *badjigal* | bicycle | 3 |
| *=bala* | contrast clitic | 3 |
| *balu-gi* | die **int** | 17 |
| *bamba* | with energy | 15 |
| *banagaya!* | run! **int** | 5 |
| *bandaarr* | kangaroo (grey) | 3 |
| *banggabaa* | white | 10 |
| *-Baraay* | having | 18 |
| *baraya!* | hop! **int** | 5 |
| *barran* | boomerang | 3 |
| *barraya!* | fly! **int** | 5 |
| *barriyay* | window | 6 |
| *bawila!* | sing! **tr** | 2 |
| *-bidi* | big | 10 |
| *biiba* | paper | 1 |
| *bina* | ear | 1 |
| *birralii* | child | 7 |
| *birray* | boy | 4 |
| *bubaa* | dad (father) | 5 |

| *Gamilaraay* | English | Lesson |
|---|---|---|
| *budjigarr* | cat | 3 |
| *bulaarr* | two | 10 |
| *buluuy* | black | 10 |
| *bumala!* | hit! **tr** | 11 |
| *bundaanga!* | fall! **int** | 13 |
| *bundi* | club | 2 |
| *burrul* | big | 4 |
| *burrulaa* | many | 10 |
| *burrulbidi* | great big | 10 |
| *burruluu* | fly | 9 |
| *buruma* | dog | 2 |
| *dhaay* | to here, to the place being talked about | 9 |
| *dhagaan* | brother | 1 |
| *dhala!* | eat! **tr** | 11 |
| *dhalaa dhaay* | where from? | 9 |
| *dhalaa?* | where? | 6 |
| *dhalaa=nda?* | where are you? | 7 |
| *dhalaadhi* | where from? | 9 |
| *dhalaagu?* | where to? | 6 |
| *-DHalibaa* | without | 18 |
| *dhamala!* | touch! **tr** | 14 |
| *dhawun* | ground | 7 |
| *dhayn* | person | 5 |
| *-DHi* | from suffix (Ablative) | 9 |
| *dhigaraa* | bird | 2 |
| *dhina* | foot | 1 |
| *dhinggaa* | meat | 4 |
| *dhiyamala!* | pick up! **tr** | 3 |
| *dhiyarral* | spoon | 12 |
| *dhuliya!* | bend/ stoop! **int** | 6 |
| *dhulu* | tree, stick | 6 |
| *dhuna!* | poke! **tr** | 13 |
| *dhurrala!* | come, appear! **int** | 11 |
| *dhurra-li* | come **int** | 17 |

APPENDIX 6. WORDLIST

| *Gamilaraay* | English | Lesson |
|---|---|---|
| *dhuru* | snake | 2 |
| *-DHuul* | small, one | 10 |
| *dhuuna!* | crawl! **int** | 13 |
| *dhuwadi* | shirt | 8 |
| *dhuwarr* | bread | 7 |
| *-Ga* | place suffix (Locative) | 7 |
| *gaabu!* | hush! | 2 |
| *gaala* | mug | 2 |
| *-gaali* | dual | 18 |
| *gaanga!* | bring/take! **tr** | 9 |
| *gaay* | small | 4 |
| *gaba* | good | 1 |
| *gagil* | bad | 4 |
| *-gal* | plural on *birralii, gaayli* | 18 |
| *-galgaa* | plural | 18 |
| *gali* | water | 2 |
| *galiyaya!* | climb! **int** | 8 |
| *gambaay* | sweetheart | 17 |
| *gamil* | no/not | 1 |
| *ganugu* | they(>2) (doer.to/Ergative) | 21 |
| *ganunga* | they/them(>2) (doer/Nominative, done.to/Accusative) | 21 |
| *ganungu* | their(s)(>2) (possessive/Dative) | 21 |
| *ganungunda* | to/at/on them(>2) (Locative, Allative) | 21 |
| *ganungundi* | from them(>2) (Ablative) | 21 |
| *garay guwaala!* | speak! **tr** | 1 |
| *garay guwaaldaya!* | speak! **tr** | 1 |
| *garrala!* | cut! **tr** | 11 |
| *garrangay* | duck | 4 |
| *garrawal* | shop | 9 |
| *garriya!* | don't! | 3 |
| *garruu* | uncle | 17 |
| *gayrr* | name | 8 |
| *giidjaa* | ant (small, black) | 3 |

| Gamilaraay | English | Lesson |
|---|---|---|
| *giiri-gi* | itch **int** | 17 |
| *giirr* | truly | 4 |
| *gilay* | moon | 17 |
| *gimubila!* | do/make! **tr** | 12 |
| *gindama-y* | laugh **int** | 9 |
| *ginga!* | become! **int** | 13 |
| *ginyi* | happened | 6 |
| *girrinil* | door | 3 |
| *giwiirr* | man | 5 |
| *giyal* | afraid | 9 |
| *-gu* | to (movement to) | 5 |
| *-gu* | purpose (Dative) | 14 |
| *-gu* | possessive/owning suffix (Dative) | 8 |
| *gubiya!* | swim! **int** | 5 |
| *gula* | fork | 12 |
| *gulaban* | chair | 8 |
| *gulibaa* | three | 10 |
| *gundhi* | house | 9 |
| *gundhilgaa* | town | 7 |
| *gunhugunhu* | cough (noun) | 16 |
| *gunhugunhu dhu-rri* | cough (verb phrase) **tr** | 16 |
| *gunii* | mum (mother) | 5 |
| *-guwaay (and -giirr)* | like | 18 |
| *guwaymbarra* | red | 10 |
| *maal* | one | 10 |
| *magal* | knife | 12 |
| *malawil* | shadow | 8 |
| *maliyaa* | friend | 1 |
| *man.ga* | table | 4 |
| *man.garr* | bag | 4 |
| *mara* | hand | 1 |
| *marayrr* | none | 10 |
| *Mari* | (Aboriginal) person | 5 |
| *mil* | eye | 1 |

## APPENDIX 6. WORDLIST

| *Gamilaraay* | English | Lesson |
|---|---|---|
| *milimili* | mud | 7 |
| *minya ginyi?* | what happened? | 5 |
| *minya?* | what? | 2 |
| *minyadhu?* | what with? | 12 |
| *minyagu?* | what for? | 14 |
| *minya-gu-waayaa* | I don't know what for | 14 |
| *minyangay?* | how many? | 10 |
| *miyay* | girl | 4 |
| *mungin* | mosquito | 12 |
| *murru* | bum | 3 |
| *muru* | nose | 3 |
| *=nga* | then | 14 |
| *ngaandi?* | who? | 4 |
| *ngaandi?* | who?/whom? | 20 |
| *ngaandu?* | who did it? (Ergative) | 12 |
| *ngaanngu?* | whose? for who(m)? | 14 |
| *ngaanngu?* | whose? (give) to who? | 20 |
| *ngaanngunda?* | to, at, on who(m)? | 20 |
| *ngaanngundi?* | from who(m)? | 20 |
| *ngali* | we two | 19 |
| *ngalingu* | our(s) two | 19 |
| *ngalingunda* | to, at, on us(2) | 20 |
| *ngalingundi* | from us(2) | 20 |
| *ngalinya* | us two | 19 |
| *ngamila!* | look! **tr** | 1 |
| *ngamildaya!* | look! **tr** | 1 |
| *nganha* | me (done.to) (Accusative) | 15 |
| *nganunda* | to, at, on me | 15 |
| *nganundi* | from me (Ablative) | 15 |
| *ngarragaa* | hopeless, sad | 15 |
| *ngarriya!* | sit! **int** | 6 |
| *ngarunga!* | drink! **tr** | 13 |
| *ngay* | my/mine (Dative) | 8 |

WIIDHAA

| *Gamilaraay* | English | Lesson |
|---|---|---|
| *ngaya* | I | 4 |
| *nginaalingu* | your(s)(2) | 19 |
| *nginaalingunda* | to, at, on you(2) | 20 |
| *nginaalingundi* | from you(2) | 20 |
| *nginaalinya* | you(2) (done.to) | 19 |
| *nginaayngu* | your(s) mob(>2) | 19 |
| *nginaayngunda* | to, at, on you mob(>2) | 20 |
| *nginaayngundi* | from you(>2) | 20 |
| *nginaaynya* | you mob(>2) (done.to) | 19 |
| *nginda* | you(1 person) | 4 |
| *-nginda* | wanting | 18 |
| *ngindaali* | you(2) (doer) | 19 |
| *ngindaay* | you mob(>2) (doer) | 19 |
| *nginu* | your(s)(1) | 8 |
| *nginunda* | to/at/on/near you(1) (Locative and Allative) | 15 |
| *nginundi* | from you(1) (Ablative) | 15 |
| *nginunha* | you(1) (done.to) (Accusative) | 15 |
| *ngirilay/ngiilay* | from here | 9 |
| *ngirima/ngiima* | from there | 9 |
| *ngiyani* | we mob(>2) | 19 |
| *ngiyaningu* | our(s) mob(>2) | 19 |
| *ngiyaningunda* | to, at, on us mob(>2) | 20 |
| *ngiyaningundi* | from us(>2) | 20 |
| *ngiyaninya* | us mob(>2) | 19 |
| *nguru* | she, he, it (Ergative) | 12 |
| *ngurugaalay* | they/them(2) (Ergative) | 21 |
| *ngurugaalayngu* | their(s)(2) (Dative) | 21 |
| *ngurugaalayngunda* | to/at/on them(2) (Locative) | 21 |
| *ngurugaalayngundi* | from them(2) (Ablative) | 21 |
| *ngurungu* | his/her(s)/its | 8 |
| *ngurungunda* | to/at/on/near her/him/it (Locative and Allative) | 15 |
| *ngurungundi* | from her/him/it (Ablative) | 15 |

## APPENDIX 6. WORDLIST

| *Gamilaraay* | English | Lesson |
|---|---|---|
| *nguu,biibabiiba* | book | 1 |
| *nguwalay* | here | 9 |
| *nguwama* | there | 9 |
| *=nha, Ø, nhama, +* | she/he/her/him/it (Nominative and Accusative case) | 4 |
| *nhaayba* | knife | 12 |
| *nhalay* | this, here, that | 2 |
| *nhama* | that, this, the, there | 2 |
| *nhamagaalay* | they(2) (Nominative) | 21 |
| *nhamagaalaynya* | they(2) (Accusative) | 21 |
| *nhamalay* | that | 2 |
| *wadjiin* | white woman | 5 |
| *walgan* | aunt | 17 |
| *wamba* | mad, silly | 15 |
| *wanagidjay!* | leave it! | 2 |
| *wanda* | white man | 5 |
| *warraya!* | stand! **int** | 6 |
| *wiibi-li* | be sick **int** | 17 |
| *wiimala!* | put down! **tr** | 3 |
| *wilbaarr* | car | 6 |
| *winangala!* | listen! **tr** | 1 |
| *winangaldaya!* | listen! **tr** | 1 |
| *wirri* | plate | 7 |
| *wiya-gi* | cook **tr** | 21 |
| *wiyayl* | pen | 2 |
| *wuru-gi* | go in; set (sun/moon) **int**; + Ablative | 17 |
| *wurunga!* | go.in! **int** | 13 |
| *wuuna!* | give! **tr** | 13 |
| *yaama* | hello | 1 |
| *yaama* | question word | 1 |
| *yaamanda?* | *yaama nginda* | 8 |
| *yaliwunga* | always | 16 |
| *yaluu* | goodbye, see ya | 1 |
| *yananga!* | walk/go! **int** | 5 |

| *Gamilaraay* | English | Lesson |
|---|---|---|
| yanawaanha | am/is/are walking | 6 |
| yaraay | sun | 17 |
| yarraaman | horse | 9 |
| yarral | stone/coin | 3 |
| yawu | yes | 1 |
| yiila! | bite! **tr** | 11 |
| yilaa | then, short time | 14 |
| yilaadhu | now | 16 |
| yinarr | woman | 5 |
| yinggil | tired, lazy | 4 |
| yira | teeth | 8 |
| yulunga! | dance! play! **int** | 2 |
| yuruun | road | 9 |
| yuulngin | hungry | 4 |

# References

The references below include works referred to in this book and also a few other major historical sources. A fuller list of historical materials can be found in Giacon (2017, p. 4).

Materials originally published by IAD Press and Coolabah Press are now available from fivesenseseducation.com.au. There are also online versions of many materials: see yuwaalaraay.com.

Ash, A., Lissarrague, A. & Giacon, J. (2003). *Gamilaraay, Yuwaalaraay & Yuwaalayaay dictionary*. Alice Springs, NT: IAD Press.

Austin, P. (1993). *A reference dictionary of Gamilaraay, northern New South Wales*. Bundoora, Vic.: Department of Linguistics, La Trobe University.

Austin, P., Williams, C. & Wurm, S.A. (1980). The linguistic situation in north central New South Wales. In B. Rigsby & P. Sutton (eds), *Papers in Australian Linguistics No. 13: Contributions of Australian Linguistics* (pp. 167–180). Canberra: Pacific Linguistics.

Eckert, P. & J. Hudson (1988). *Wangka wiru: A handbook for the Pitjantjatjara language learner*. Underdale, SA: South Australian College of Advanced Education.

Giacon, J. (1997). *Yuwaalaraay transcripts*. Transcript. Australian Institute of Aboriginal and Torres Strait Islanders, Canberra.

Giacon, J. (2002). *Yugal: Gamilaraay & Yuwaalaraay songs* [CD]. New South Wales: Coolabah Publishing.

Giacon, J. (2008). Associated eating and movement: Further examination of Yuwaalaraay Gamilaraay verb suffixes. In C. Bowern, B. Evans & L. Miceli (eds), *Morphology and language history: In honour of Harold Koch* (pp. 107–14). Amsterdam: John Benjamins Publishing Company.

Giacon, J. (2014). Yaluu: A recovery grammar of Yuwaalaraay and Gamilaraay: A description of two New South Wales languages based on 160 years of records (Doctoral dissertation, The Australian National University, Canberra). Retrieved from hdl.handle.net/1885/12377.

Giacon, J. (2017). *Yaluu: A recovery grammar of Yuwaalaraay and Gamilaraay: A description of two New South Wales languages based on 160 years of records.* (ebook) Canberra: Asia-Pacific Linguistics, College of Asia and the Pacific, The Australian Natonal University; (print edition) Sydney: Five Senses Education.

Mathews, R. H. (1902). Languages of some Native tribes of Queensland, New South Wales and Victoria. *Journal of the Royal Society of New South Wales, 36,* 135–90.

Mathews, R. H. (1903). Languages of the Kamilaroi and other Aboriginal tribes of New South Wales. *Journal of the Royal Anthropological Institute of Great Britain and Ireland, 33,* 259–83.

Nathan, D., Giacon, J. & Gamilaraay Yuwaalaraay Language Program. (c. 2009). *Gayarragi, Winangali = Find and hear* (Downloadable and CD-ROM). Armidale, NSW: Catholic Schools Office.

Ridley, W. (1856). *Gurre Kamilaroi, or, Kamilaroi sayings.* Sydney: Printed at the Empire General Steam Printing Office.

Ridley, R. W. (1875). *Kamilaroi and other Australian languages.* Sydney: Government Printer.

Williams, C. (1980). *A grammar of Yuwaalaraay.* Canberra: Pacific Linguistics.

Yuwaalaraay and Gamilaraay Language Program. (2006). *Gaay Garay Dhadhin: Gamilaraay & Yuwaalaraay picture dictionary.* Alice Springs, NT: IAD Press.

www.ingramcontent.com/pod-product-compliance
Lightning Source LLC
Chambersburg PA
CBHW041924220426
43670CB00032B/2953